THE
READER'S
DIGEST
BIBLE

LARGE-TYPE EDITION

THE READER'S DIGEST BIBLE

CONDENSED FROM
THE REVISED STANDARD VERSION
OLD AND NEW TESTAMENTS

LARGE-TYPE EDITION
VOLUME II

General Editor
BRUCE M. METZGER
Ph.D., D.D., L.H.D., D.Theol.
Princeton Theological Seminary

Published by
Reader's Digest Fund for the Blind, Inc.
with permission of
THE READER'S DIGEST ASSOCIATION
PLEASANTVILLE, NEW YORK
LONDON, MONTREAL, SYDNEY, CAPE TOWN, HONG KONG

Note:
The full-length text of
the Revised Standard Version
is available from the following:

Holman Bible Publishers
Thomas Nelson Publishers
Oxford University Press Inc.
World Bible Publishers Inc.
The Zondervan Corporation

First Edition

Library of Congress Catalog Card Number: 86-060255
ISBN 0-89577-235-3 (Volume Two)
ISBN 0-89577-237-X (Set)
Printed in the United States of America

The Reader's Digest Bible, Large-Type Edition,
is published in 1986.

CONTENTS

CONTENTS

THE
OLD TESTAMENT

PSALMS – MALACHI

PSALMS

Since a time well before Christ, the Book of Psalms has been the great hymnal of the Jews, and subsequently of Christendom. Its spiritual depth and beauty make it an unparalleled treasury of resources for public and private devotion. The original Hebrew title means "Praises," and praise is certainly one of the book's themes. But there is far more than this, for the poems vary widely in tone and subject. Some express contrition or call down curses. Others are meant to teach, and still others seem to have been adapted for use on special occasions, such as a coronation or a royal wedding. Some are regarded as messianic, being quoted in this light by New Testament writers.

Divided into five books, the individual Psalms are of differing date and authorship, with many attributed to King David. Most took their present form during the time of the second temple, somewhere between 537 B.C. and 100 B.C. Standard numbers for the Psalms in this selection may be found by a glance at the Index, under *Psalms,* where opening phrases are listed.

———

BOOK I

Blessed is the man
who walks not in the counsel
    of the wicked,
nor stands in the way of sinners,
    nor sits in the seat of scoffers;
but his delight is in the law of the LORD,
    and on his law he meditates
        day and night.
He is like a tree
    planted by streams of water,
that yields its fruit in its season,
    and its leaf does not wither.
In all that he does, he prospers.

The wicked are not so,
    but are like chaff which the wind
        drives away.
Therefore the wicked will not stand
        in the judgment,
    nor sinners in the congregation
        of the righteous;
for the LORD knows the way
        of the righteous,
    but the way of the wicked will perish.

Why do the nations conspire,
    and the peoples plot in vain?
The kings of the earth set themselves,
    and the rulers take counsel together,
    against the LORD and his anointed,
        saying,
"Let us burst their bonds asunder,
    and cast their cords from us."
He who sits in the heavens laughs;
    the LORD has them in derision.
Then he will speak to them in his wrath,
    and terrify them in his fury, saying,
"I have set my king
    on Zion, my holy hill."
I will tell of the decree of the LORD:

He said to me, "You are my son,
  today I have begotten you.
Ask of me, and I will make the nations
    your heritage,
    and the ends of the earth
    your possession.
You shall break them with a rod of iron,
  and dash them in pieces
    like a potter's vessel."
Now therefore, O kings, be wise;
  be warned, O rulers of the earth.
Serve the LORD with fear,
  with trembling kiss his feet,
lest he be angry, and you perish in the way;
  for his wrath is quickly kindled.
Blessed are all who take refuge in him.

Give ear to my words, O LORD;
  give heed to my groaning.
Hearken to the sound of my cry,
  my King and my God,
  for to thee do I pray.
O LORD, in the morning thou dost
    hear my voice;
  in the morning I prepare a sacrifice
    for thee, and watch.

For thou art not a God who delights
    in wickedness;
  evil may not sojourn with thee.
But I through the abundance
    of thy steadfast love
  will enter thy house.

Lead me, O LORD, in thy righteousness
  because of my enemies;
  make thy way straight before me.
For there is no truth in their mouth;
  their heart is destruction,
their throat is an open sepulcher,
  they flatter with their tongue.
Make them bear their guilt, O God;
  let them fall by their own counsels;
because of their many transgressions
    cast them out,
  for they have rebelled against thee.
But let all who take refuge in thee rejoice,
  let them ever sing for joy.
For thou dost bless the righteous, O LORD;
  thou dost cover him with favor
    as with a shield.

O LORD, rebuke me not in thy anger,
  nor chasten me in thy wrath.

Be gracious to me, O Lord,
　　for I am languishing;
　　O Lord, heal me, for my bones
　　　　are troubled.
My soul also is sorely troubled.
　　But thou, O Lord—how long?

Turn, O Lord, save my life;
　　deliver me for the sake
　　　　of thy steadfast love.
For in death there is no remembrance
　　　　of thee;
　　in Sheol who can give thee praise?
I am weary with my moaning;
　　every night I flood my bed
　　　　with tears;
　　I drench my couch with my weeping.
My eye wastes away because of grief,
　　it grows weak because of all my foes.

Depart from me, all you workers of evil;
　　for the Lord has heard the sound
　　　　of my weeping.
The Lord has heard my supplication;
　　the Lord accepts my prayer.
All my enemies shall be ashamed and
　　　　sorely troubled;

they shall turn back, and be put to
    shame in a moment.

O LORD, our Lord,
  how majestic is thy name
    in all the earth!
Thou whose glory above the heavens
    is chanted
  by the mouth of babes and infants,
thou hast founded a bulwark
    because of thy foes,
  to still the enemy and the avenger.
When I look at thy heavens, the work
    of thy fingers,
  the moon and the stars which thou
    hast established;
what is man that thou art mindful of him,
  and the son of man that thou dost
    care for him?
Yet thou hast made him little less
    than God,
  and dost crown him with glory
    and honor.
Thou hast given him dominion over the
    works of thy hands;
  thou hast put all things under his feet,

all sheep and oxen,
  and also the beasts of the field,
the birds of the air, and the fish of the sea,
  whatever passes along the paths
    of the sea.
O Lord, our Lord,
  how majestic is thy name
    in all the earth!

How long, O Lord? Wilt thou forget me
    for ever?
  How long wilt thou hide thy face
    from me?
How long must I bear pain in my soul,
  and have sorrow in my heart all the day?
How long shall my enemy be exalted
    over me?
Consider and answer me,
    O Lord my God;
  lighten my eyes, lest I sleep the sleep
    of death;
lest my enemy say, "I have prevailed
    over him";
  lest my foes rejoice because
    I am shaken.
But I have trusted in thy steadfast love;

my heart shall rejoice in thy salvation.
I will sing to the LORD,
   because he has dealt bountifully with me.

The fool says in his heart,
   "There is no God."
They are corrupt, they do
     abominable deeds,
   there is none that does good.
The LORD looks down from heaven
     upon the children of men,
   to see if there are any that act wisely,
   that seek after God.
They have all gone astray, they are all
     alike corrupt;
   there is none that does good,
   no, not one.

Have they no knowledge, all the evildoers
   who eat up my people as they eat bread,
   and do not call upon the LORD?
There they shall be in great terror,
   for God is with the generation
   of the righteous.
You would confound the plans of the poor,
   but the LORD is his refuge.

O that deliverance for Israel would come
   out of Zion!
   When the LORD restores the fortunes
   of his people,
   Jacob shall rejoice, Israel shall be glad.

O LORD, who shall sojourn in thy tent?
   Who shall dwell on thy holy hill?
He who walks blamelessly, and does
      what is right,
   and speaks truth from his heart;
who does not slander with his tongue,
   and does no evil to his friend,
      nor takes up a reproach
      against his neighbor;
in whose eyes a reprobate is despised,
   but who honors those who fear
      the LORD;
who swears to his own hurt and
      does not change;
who does not put out his money
      at interest,
   and does not take a bribe against
      the innocent.
He who does these things shall never
      be moved.

Preserve me, O God, for in thee
  I take refuge.
I say to the LORD, "Thou art my Lord;
  I have no good apart from thee."
As for the saints in the land,
  they are the noble,
  in whom is all my delight.
Those who choose another god
  multiply their sorrows;
  their libations of blood I will not
    pour out
  or take their names upon my lips.
The LORD is my chosen portion
  and my cup;
  thou holdest my lot.
The lines have fallen for me
  in pleasant places;
  yea, I have a goodly heritage.
I bless the LORD who gives me counsel;
  in the night also my heart instructs me.
I keep the LORD always before me;
  because he is at my right hand,
  I shall not be moved.
Therefore my heart is glad,
  and my soul rejoices;
  my body also dwells secure.
For thou dost not give me up to Sheol,

or let thy godly one see the Pit.
Thou dost show me the path of life;
in thy presence there is fulness of joy,
in thy right hand are pleasures
for evermore.

I love thee, O LORD, my strength.
The LORD is my rock, and my fortress,
and my deliverer,
my God, my rock, in whom
I take refuge,
my shield, and the horn of my salvation,
my stronghold.
In my distress I called upon the LORD;
to my God I cried for help.
From his temple he heard my voice,
and my cry to him reached his ears.
Then the earth reeled and rocked;
the foundations of the mountains
trembled
and quaked, because he was angry.
Smoke went up from his nostrils,
and devouring fire from his mouth;
glowing coals flamed forth from him.
He bowed the heavens, and came down;
thick darkness was under his feet.

He rode on a cherub, and flew;
   he came swiftly upon the wings
     of the wind.
He made darkness his covering around him,
   his canopy thick clouds dark with water.
Out of the brightness before him
   there broke through his clouds
   hailstones and coals of fire.
The Lord also thundered in the heavens,
   and the Most High uttered his voice.
And he sent out his arrows,
    and scattered them;
   he flashed forth lightnings,
    and routed them.
Then the channels of the sea were seen,
   and the foundations of the world
    were laid bare,
at thy rebuke, O Lord,
   at the blast of the breath of thy nostrils.
He reached from on high, he took me,
   he drew me out of many waters.
The Lord rewarded me according
    to my righteousness;
   according to the cleanness of my hands
    he recompensed me.
For I have kept the ways of the Lord,
   and have not wickedly departed
    from my God.

With the loyal thou dost
   show thyself loyal;
   with the blameless man thou dost
   show thyself blameless;
with the pure thou dost show thyself pure;
   and with the crooked thou dost
   show thyself perverse.
For thou dost deliver a humble people;
   but the haughty eyes thou dost
      bring down.
Yea, thou dost light my lamp;
   the LORD my God lightens my darkness.
Yea, by thee I can crush a troop;
   and by my God I can leap over a wall.
This God—his way is perfect;
   he is a shield for all those
      who take refuge in him.
He made my feet like hinds' feet,
   and set me secure on the heights.
He trains my hands for war,
   so that my arms can bend a bow
      of bronze.
I pursued my enemies and overtook them;
   and did not turn back till they
      were consumed.
I thrust them through, so that they
      were not able to rise;

they fell under my feet.
For thou didst gird me with strength
  for the battle;
thou didst make my assailants sink
  under me.
Thou didst make my enemies turn their
  backs to me,
and those who hated me I destroyed.
They cried for help, but there was none
  to save,
they cried to the LORD, but he did not
  answer them.
I beat them fine as dust before the wind;
I cast them out like the mire
  of the streets.
Thou didst deliver me from strife
  with the peoples;
thou didst make me the head
  of the nations;
people whom I had not known
  served me.

For this I will extol thee, O LORD,
  among the nations,
and sing praises to thy name.
Great triumphs he gives to his king,
  and shows steadfast love to his anointed,
  to David and his descendants for ever.

The heavens are telling the glory of God;
    and the firmament proclaims
       his handiwork.
Day to day pours forth speech,
    and night to night declares knowledge.
There is no speech, nor are there words;
    their voice is not heard;
yet their voice goes out
       through all the earth,
    and their words to the end of the world.
In them he has set a tent for the sun,
which comes forth like a bridegroom
       leaving his chamber,
    and like a strong man runs its course
       with joy.
Its rising is from the end of the heavens,
    and its circuit to the end of them;
    and there is nothing hid from its heat.

The law of the LORD is perfect,
    reviving the soul;
the testimony of the LORD is sure,
    making wise the simple;
the precepts of the LORD are right,
    rejoicing the heart;
the commandment of the LORD is pure,
    enlightening the eyes;

the fear of the LORD is clean,
  enduring for ever;
the ordinances of the LORD are true,
  and righteous altogether.
More to be desired are they than gold,
  even much fine gold;
sweeter also than honey
  and drippings of the honeycomb.
Moreover by them is thy servant warned;
  in keeping them there is great reward.
But who can discern his errors?
  Clear thou me from hidden faults.
Keep back thy servant also
    from presumptuous sins;
  let them not have dominion over me!
Then I shall be blameless,
  and innocent of great transgression.

Let the words of my mouth and
    the meditation of my heart
  be acceptable in thy sight,
  O LORD, my rock and my redeemer.

My God, my God, why hast thou
    forsaken me?
  Why art thou so far from helping me,
    from the words of my groaning?

O my God, I cry by day, but thou
    dost not answer;
  and by night, but find no rest.
Yet thou art holy,
  enthroned on the praises of Israel.
In thee our fathers trusted;
  they trusted, and thou didst deliver them.
To thee they cried, and were saved;
  in thee they trusted,
    and were not disappointed.

But I am a worm, and no man;
  scorned by men, and despised
    by the people.
All who see me mock at me,
  they make mouths at me, they wag
    their heads;
"He committed his cause to the LORD;
    let him deliver him,
  let him rescue him, for he delights
    in him!"
Yet thou art he who took me
    from the womb;
  thou didst keep me safe upon my
    mother's breasts.
Upon thee was I cast from my birth,
  and since my mother bore me

    thou hast been my God.
Be not far from me,
  for trouble is near
  and there is none to help.
Many bulls encompass me,
  strong bulls of Bashan surround me;
they open wide their mouths at me,
  like a ravening and roaring lion.
I am poured out like water,
  and all my bones are out of joint;
my heart is like wax,
  it is melted within my breast;
my strength is dried up like a potsherd,
  and my tongue cleaves to my jaws;
  thou dost lay me in the dust of death.
Yea, dogs are round about me;
  a company of evildoers encircle me;
  they have pierced my hands and feet—
I can count all my bones—
  they stare and gloat over me;
they divide my garments among them,
  and for my raiment they cast lots.
But thou, O LORD, be not far off!
  O thou my help, hasten to my aid!
Deliver my soul from the sword,
  my life from the power of the dog!
Save me from the mouth of the lion,

my afflicted soul from the horns
  of the wild oxen!

I will tell of thy name to my brethren;
  in the midst of the congregation
    I will praise thee:
You who fear the LORD, praise him!
  all you sons of Jacob, glorify him,
  and stand in awe of him, all you sons
    of Israel!
For he has not despised or abhorred
  the affliction of the afflicted;
and he has not hid his face from him,
  but has heard, when he cried to him.
From thee comes my praise in the
    great congregation;
  my vows I will pay before those
    who fear him.
The afflicted shall eat and be satisfied;
  those who seek him shall praise
    the LORD!
  May your hearts live for ever!
All the ends of the earth shall remember
  and turn to the LORD;
and all the families of the nations
  shall worship before him.
For dominion belongs to the LORD,

and he rules over the nations.
Yea, to him shall all the proud of the earth
    bow down;
  before him shall bow all who go down
    to the dust,
  and he who cannot keep himself alive.
Posterity shall serve him;
  men shall tell of the Lord to the
    coming generation,
and proclaim his deliverance to a people
    yet unborn,
  that he has wrought it.

The LORD is my shepherd,
    I shall not want;
  he makes me lie down in green pastures.
He leads me beside still waters;
  he restores my soul.
He leads me in paths of righteousness
  for his name's sake.
Even though I walk through the valley
    of the shadow of death,
  I fear no evil;
for thou art with me;
  thy rod and thy staff,
  they comfort me.

Thou preparest a table before me
  in the presence of my enemies;
thou anointest my head with oil,
  my cup overflows.
Surely goodness and mercy shall follow me
  all the days of my life;
and I shall dwell in the house of the LORD
  for ever.

The earth is the LORD's and
    the fulness thereof,
    the world and those who dwell therein;
for he has founded it upon the seas,
    and established it upon the rivers.
Who shall ascend the hill of the LORD?
    And who shall stand in his holy place?
He who has clean hands and a pure heart,
    who does not lift up his soul
      to what is false,
    and does not swear deceitfully.
He will receive blessing from the LORD,
    and vindication from the God
      of his salvation.
Such is the generation of those
    who seek him,
    who seek the face of the God of Jacob.

Lift up your heads, O gates!
  and be lifted up, O ancient doors!
  that the King of glory may come in.
Who is the King of glory?
  The LORD, strong and mighty,
  the LORD, mighty in battle!
Lift up your heads, O gates!
  and be lifted up, O ancient doors!
  that the King of glory may come in.
Who is this King of glory?
  The LORD of hosts,
  he is the King of glory!

The LORD is my light and my salvation;
  whom shall I fear?
The LORD is the stronghold of my life;
  of whom shall I be afraid?
When evildoers assail me,
  uttering slanders against me,
my adversaries and foes,
  they shall stumble and fall.
Though a host encamp against me,
  my heart shall not fear;
though war arise against me,
  yet I will be confident.
One thing have I asked of the LORD,

that will I seek after;
that I may dwell in the house of the LORD
  all the days of my life,
to behold the beauty of the LORD,
  and to inquire in his temple.

For he will hide me in his shelter
  in the day of trouble;
he will conceal me under the cover
    of his tent,
  he will set me high upon a rock.
And now my head shall be lifted up
  above my enemies round about me;
and I will offer in his tent
  sacrifices with shouts of joy;
I will sing and make melody to the LORD.

Hear, O LORD, when I cry aloud,
  be gracious to me and answer me!
Thou hast said, "Seek ye my face."
  My heart says to thee,
"Thy face, LORD, do I seek."
  Hide not thy face from me.
Turn not thy servant away in anger,
  thou who hast been my help.
Cast me not off, forsake me not,
  O God of my salvation!

For my father and my mother
    have forsaken me,
  but the LORD will take me up.
Teach me thy way, O LORD;
  and lead me on a level path
  because of my enemies.
Give me not up to the will
    of my adversaries;
  for false witnesses have risen against me,
  and they breathe out violence.
I believe that I shall see the goodness
    of the LORD
  in the land of the living!
Wait for the LORD;
  be strong, and let your heart
    take courage;
  yea, wait for the LORD!

Ascribe to the LORD, O heavenly beings,
  ascribe to the LORD glory and strength.
Ascribe to the LORD the glory of his name;
  worship the LORD in holy array.
The voice of the LORD is upon the waters;
  the God of glory thunders,
  the LORD, upon many waters.
The voice of the LORD is powerful,

the voice of the LORD is full of majesty.
The voice of the LORD breaks the cedars,
    the LORD breaks the cedars of Lebanon.
He makes Lebanon to skip like a calf,
    and Mount Hermon like a young wild ox.
The voice of the LORD flashes forth
        flames of fire.
The voice of the LORD shakes
        the wilderness,
    the LORD shakes the wilderness
        of Kadesh.
The voice of the LORD makes the oaks
        to whirl,
    and strips the forests bare;
    and in his temple all cry, "Glory!"
The LORD sits enthroned over the flood;
    the LORD sits enthroned as king for ever.
May the LORD give strength to his people!
    May the LORD bless his people
        with peace!

I will extol thee, O LORD, for thou
        hast drawn me up,
    and hast not let my foes rejoice over me.
O LORD my God, I cried to thee for help,
    and thou hast healed me.

O LORD, thou hast brought up my soul
    from Sheol,
  restored me to life from among those
    gone down to the Pit.
Sing praises to the LORD, O you his saints,
  and give thanks to his holy name.
For his anger is but for a moment,
  and his favor is for a lifetime.
Weeping may tarry for the night,
  but joy comes with the morning.
As for me, I said in my prosperity,
  "I shall never be moved."
By thy favor, O LORD,
  thou hadst established me
    as a strong mountain;
thou didst hide thy face,
  I was dismayed.
To thee, O LORD, I cried;
  and to the LORD I made supplication:
"What profit is there in my death,
  if I go down to the Pit?
Will the dust praise thee?
  Will it tell of thy faithfulness?
Hear, O LORD, and be gracious to me!
  O LORD, be thou my helper!"
Thou hast turned for me my mourning
    into dancing;

thou hast loosed my sackcloth
and girded me with gladness,
that my soul may praise thee
and not be silent.
O LORD my God, I will give thanks
to thee for ever.

Blessed is he whose transgression
is forgiven,
whose sin is covered.
Blessed is the man to whom the LORD
imputes no iniquity,
and in whose spirit there is no deceit.
When I declared not my sin, my body
wasted away
through my groaning all day long.
For day and night thy hand was heavy
upon me;
my strength was dried up as by the heat
of summer.
I acknowledged my sin to thee,
and I did not hide my iniquity;
I said, "I will confess my transgressions
to the LORD";
then thou didst forgive the guilt
of my sin.

Therefore let every one who is godly offer
 prayer to thee;
at a time of distress, in the rush
 of great waters,
 they shall not reach him.
Thou art a hiding place for me,
 thou preservest me
  from trouble;
 thou dost encompass me
  with deliverance.

I will instruct you and teach you
 the way you should go;
 I will counsel you with my eye
  upon you.
Be not like a horse or a mule,
 without understanding,
 which must be curbed with bit
  and bridle,
 else it will not keep with you.
Many are the pangs of the wicked;
 but steadfast love surrounds him
  who trusts in the LORD.
Be glad in the LORD, and rejoice,
 O righteous,
 and shout for joy, all you upright
  in heart!

Rejoice in the LORD, O you righteous!
    Praise befits the upright.
Praise the LORD with the lyre,
    make melody to him with the harp
        of ten strings!
Sing to him a new song,
    play skilfully on the strings,
        with loud shouts.
For the word of the LORD is upright;
    and all his work is done in faithfulness.
He loves righteousness and justice;
    the earth is full of the steadfast love
        of the LORD.
By the word of the LORD the heavens
        were made,
    and all their host by the breath
        of his mouth.
He gathered the waters of the sea
        as in a bottle;
    he put the deeps in storehouses.
Let all the earth fear the LORD,
    let all the inhabitants of the world stand
        in awe of him!
For he spoke, and it came to be;
    he commanded, and it stood forth.
The LORD brings the counsel of the nations
        to nought;

    he frustrates the plans of the peoples.
The counsel of the LORD stands for ever,
    the thoughts of his heart
        to all generations.
Blessed is the nation whose God
        is the LORD,
    the people whom he has chosen
        as his heritage!
The LORD looks down from heaven,
    he sees all the sons of men;
from where he sits enthroned
        he looks forth
    on all the inhabitants of the earth,
he who fashions the hearts of them all,
    and observes all their deeds.
A king is not saved by his great army;
    a warrior is not delivered by his
        great strength.
The war horse is a vain hope for victory,
    and by its great might it cannot save.
Behold, the eye of the LORD is on those
        who fear him,
    on those who hope in his steadfast love,
that he may deliver their soul from death,
    and keep them alive in famine.
Our soul waits for the LORD;
    he is our help and shield.

Yea, our heart is glad in him,
   because we trust in his holy name.
Let thy steadfast love, O LORD, be upon us,
   even as we hope in thee.

Fret not yourself because of the wicked,
   be not envious of wrongdoers!
For they will soon fade like the grass,
   and wither like the green herb.
Trust in the LORD, and do good;
   so you will dwell in the land,
      and enjoy security.
Take delight in the LORD,
   and he will give you the desires
      of your heart.
Commit your way to the LORD;
   trust in him, and he will act.
He will bring forth your vindication
      as the light,
   and your right as the noonday.
Be still before the LORD, and wait patiently
      for him;
   fret not yourself over him who prospers
      in his way,
   over the man who carries out
      evil devices!

Refrain from anger, and forsake wrath!
　　Fret not yourself; it tends only to evil.
For the wicked shall be cut off;
　　but those who wait for the LORD
　　　shall possess the land.
Yet a little while, and the wicked
　　will be no more;
　　though you look well at his place,
　　　he will not be there.
But the meek shall possess the land,
　　and delight themselves
　　　in abundant prosperity.
The wicked plots against the righteous,
　　and gnashes his teeth at him;
but the LORD laughs at the wicked,
　　for he sees that his day is coming.
The wicked draw the sword
　　and bend their bows,
　　to bring down the poor and needy,
　　to slay those who walk uprightly;
their sword shall enter their own heart,
　　and their bows shall be broken.
Better is a little that the righteous has
　　than the abundance of many wicked.
For the arms of the wicked shall be broken;
　　but the LORD upholds the righteous.
The LORD knows the days of the blameless,

and their heritage will abide for ever;
they are not put to shame in evil times,
   in the days of famine they
      have abundance.
But the wicked perish;
   the enemies of the LORD are like
      the glory of the pastures,
   they vanish—like smoke they
      vanish away.
The wicked borrows, and cannot pay back,
   but the righteous is generous and gives;
for those blessed by the LORD
      shall possess the land,
   but those cursed by him shall be cut off.
The steps of a man are from the LORD,
   and he establishes him in whose way
      he delights;
though he fall, he shall not
      be cast headlong,
   for the LORD is the stay of his hand.
I have been young, and now am old;
   yet I have not seen the
      righteous forsaken
   or his children begging bread.
He is ever giving liberally and lending,
   and his children become a blessing.
Depart from evil, and do good;

so shall you abide for ever.
For the LORD loves justice;
  he will not forsake his saints.
The righteous shall be preserved for ever,
  but the children of the wicked
    shall be cut off.
The righteous shall possess the land,
  and dwell upon it for ever.
The mouth of the righteous utters wisdom,
  and his tongue speaks justice.
The law of his God is in his heart;
  his steps do not slip.
The wicked watches the righteous,
  and seeks to slay him.
The LORD will not abandon him
    to his power,
  or let him be condemned when he
    is brought to trial.
Wait for the LORD, and keep to his way,
  and he will exalt you to possess the land;
  you will look on the destruction
    of the wicked.
I have seen a wicked man overbearing,
  and towering like a cedar of Lebanon.
Again I passed by, and, lo, he was no more;
  though I sought him, he could not
    be found.

Mark the blameless man, and
    behold the upright,
  for there is posterity for the man
    of peace.
But transgressors shall be
    altogether destroyed;
  the posterity of the wicked shall
    be cut off.
The salvation of the righteous is
    from the LORD;
  he is their refuge in the time of trouble.
The LORD helps them and delivers them;
  he delivers them from the wicked,
    and saves them,
  because they take refuge in him.

I said, "I will guard my ways,
  that I may not sin with my tongue;
I will bridle my mouth,
  so long as the wicked are
    in my presence."
I was dumb and silent,
  I held my peace to no avail;
my distress grew worse,
  my heart became hot within me.
As I mused, the fire burned;

then I spoke with my tongue:
"LORD, let me know my end,
   and what is the measure of my days;
   let me know how fleeting my life is!
Behold, thou hast made my days
    a few handbreadths,
   and my lifetime is as nothing in thy sight.
   Surely every man stands
    as a mere breath!
   Surely man goes about as a shadow!
Surely for nought are they in turmoil;
   man heaps up, and knows not
    who will gather!
And now, Lord, for what do I wait?
   My hope is in thee.
Deliver me from all my transgressions.
   Make me not the scorn of the fool!
I am dumb, I do not open my mouth;
   for it is thou who hast done it.
Remove thy stroke from me;
   I am spent by the blows of thy hand.
When thou dost chasten man
   with rebukes for sin,
thou dost consume like a moth
    what is dear to him;
   surely every man is a mere breath!
Hear my prayer, O LORD,

and give ear to my cry;
    hold not thy peace at my tears!
For I am thy passing guest,
    a sojourner, like all my fathers.
Look away from me, that I may
      know gladness,
    before I depart and be no more!"

I waited patiently for the LORD;
    he inclined to me and heard my cry.
He drew me up from the desolate pit,
    out of the miry bog,
and set my feet upon a rock,
    making my steps secure.
He put a new song in my mouth,
    a song of praise to our God.
Many will see and fear,
    and put their trust in the LORD.
Blessed is the man who makes the LORD
      his trust,
who does not turn to the proud,
    to those who go astray after false gods!
Thou hast multiplied, O LORD my God,
    thy wondrous deeds and thy thoughts
      toward us;
    none can compare with thee!

Sacrifice and offering thou dost not desire;
    but thou hast given me an open ear.
Burnt offering and sin offering
    thou hast not required.
Then I said, "I delight to do thy will,
        O my God;
    thy law is within my heart."
I have told the glad news of deliverance
    in the great congregation;
lo, I have not restrained my lips,
    as thou knowest, O LORD.
I have not hid thy saving help
        within my heart,
    I have spoken of thy faithfulness
        and thy salvation.

Do not thou, O LORD, withhold
    thy mercy from me,
let thy steadfast love and thy faithfulness
    ever preserve me!
For evils have encompassed me
    without number;
my iniquities have overtaken me,
    till I cannot see.
Be pleased, O LORD, to deliver me!
    O LORD, make haste to help me!
Let them be put to shame and
        confusion altogether

who seek to snatch away my life!
Let them be appalled because of
    their shame
who say to me, "Aha, Aha!"
But may all who seek thee
    rejoice and be glad in thee;
may those who love thy salvation
    say continually, "Great is the LORD!"
As for me, I am poor and needy;
    but the Lord takes thought for me.
Thou art my help and my deliverer;
    do not tarry, O my God!

Blessed is he who considers the poor!
    The LORD delivers him in the day
        of trouble;
the LORD protects him and keeps him alive;
    he is called blessed in the land;
    thou dost not give him up to the will
        of his enemies.
The LORD sustains him on his sickbed;
    in his illness thou healest
        all his infirmities.

As for me, I said, "O LORD,
    be gracious to me;

heal me, for I have sinned against thee!"
My enemies say of me in malice:
    "When will he die, and
        his name perish?"
And when one comes to see me, he utters
        empty words,
    while his heart gathers mischief;
    when he goes out, he tells it abroad.
All who hate me whisper together
        about me;
    they imagine the worst for me.
They say, "A deadly thing has fastened
        upon him;
    he will not rise again from where
        he lies."
Even my bosom friend in whom I trusted,
    who ate of my bread, has lifted his heel
        against me.
But do thou, O LORD, be gracious to me,
    and raise me up, that I may
        requite them!
By this I know that thou art pleased
        with me,
    in that my enemy has not triumphed
        over me.
But thou hast upheld me because of
        my integrity,

and set me in thy presence for ever.
Blessed be the LORD, the God of Israel,
  from everlasting to everlasting!
  Amen and Amen.

BOOK II

As a hart longs
  for flowing streams,
so longs my soul
  for thee, O God.
My soul thirsts for God,
  for the living God.
When shall I come and behold
  the face of God?
My tears have been my food
  day and night,
while men say to me continually,
  "Where is your God?"
These things I remember,
  as I pour out my soul:
how I went with the throng,
  and led them in procession
    to the house of God,
with glad shouts and songs of thanksgiving,
  a multitude keeping festival.

Why are you cast down, O my soul,
  and why are you disquieted within me?
Hope in God; for I shall again praise him,
  my help and my God.

My soul is cast down within me,
  therefore I remember thee
from the land of Jordan and of Hermon,
  from Mount Mizar.
Deep calls to deep
  at the thunder of thy cataracts;
all thy waves and thy billows
  have gone over me.
By day the LORD commands
    his steadfast love;
  and at night his song is with me,
  a prayer to the God of my life.
I say to God, my rock:
  "Why hast thou forgotten me?
Why go I mourning
  because of the oppression
    of the enemy?"
As with a deadly wound in my body,
  my adversaries taunt me,
while they say to me continually,
  "Where is your God?"
Why are you cast down, O my soul,

and why are you disquieted within me?
Hope in God; for I shall again praise him,
my help and my God.

Vindicate me, O God, and defend
my cause
against an ungodly people;
from deceitful and unjust men
deliver me!
For thou art the God in whom
I take refuge;
why hast thou cast me off?
Why go I mourning
because of the oppression of the enemy?

Oh send out thy light and thy truth;
let them lead me,
let them bring me to thy holy hill
and to thy dwelling!
Then I will go to the altar of God,
to God my exceeding joy;
and I will praise thee with the lyre,
O God, my God.
Why are you cast down, O my soul,
and why are you disquieted within me?
Hope in God; for I shall again praise him,
my help and my God.

My heart overflows with a goodly theme;
   I address my verses to the king;
   my tongue is like the pen
     of a ready scribe.

You are the fairest of the sons of men;
   grace is poured upon your lips;
   therefore God has blessed you for ever.
Gird your sword upon your thigh,
     O mighty one,
   in your glory and majesty!
In your majesty ride forth victoriously
   for the cause of truth and
     to defend the right;
   let your right hand teach you
     dread deeds!
Your arrows are sharp
   in the heart of the king's enemies;
   the peoples fall under you.

Your divine throne endures for ever
     and ever.
   Your royal scepter is a scepter of equity;
   you love righteousness
     and hate wickedness.
Therefore God, your God,
     has anointed you

with the oil of gladness
    above your fellows;
your robes are all fragrant
with myrrh and aloes and cassia.
From ivory palaces stringed instruments
    make you glad;
    daughters of kings are among
        your ladies of honor;
    at your right hand stands the queen
        in gold of Ophir.

Hear, O daughter, consider, and
    incline your ear;
    forget your people and
        your father's house;
    and the king will desire your beauty.
Since he is your lord, bow to him;
    the people of Tyre will sue your favor
        with gifts,
    the richest of the people with all
        kinds of wealth.

The princess is decked in her
    chamber with gold-woven robes,
    in many-colored robes she is led
        to the king,
    with her virgin companions, her escort,

in her train.
With joy and gladness they are led along
  as they enter the palace of the king.

Instead of your fathers shall be your sons;
  you will make them princes
    in all the earth.
I will cause your name to be celebrated
    in all generations;
  therefore the peoples will praise you
    for ever and ever.

God is our refuge and strength,
  a very present help in trouble.
Therefore we will not fear, though
    the earth should change,
  though the mountains shake
    in the heart of the sea;
though its waters roar and foam,
  though the mountains tremble
    with its tumult.
There is a river whose streams make glad
    the city of God,
  the holy habitation of the Most High.
God is in the midst of her, she shall
    not be moved;

God will help her right early.
The nations rage, the kingdoms totter;
  he utters his voice, the earth melts.
The LORD of hosts is with us;
  the God of Jacob is our refuge.

Come, behold the works of the LORD,
  how he has wrought desolations
    in the earth.
He makes wars cease to the end
    of the earth;
  he breaks the bow, and shatters
    the spear,
  he burns the chariots with fire!
"Be still, and know that I am God.
  I am exalted among the nations,
  I am exalted in the earth!"
The LORD of hosts is with us;
  the God of Jacob is our refuge.

Hear this, all peoples!
  Give ear, all inhabitants
    of the world,
both low and high,
  rich and poor together!
My mouth shall speak wisdom;

the meditation of my heart
    shall be understanding.
I will incline my ear to a proverb;
    I will solve my riddle to the music
       of the lyre.

Why should I fear in times of trouble,
    when the iniquity of my persecutors
       surrounds me,
men who trust in their wealth
    and boast of the abundance
       of their riches?
Truly no man can ransom himself,
    or give to God the price of his life,
for the ransom of his life is costly,
    and can never suffice,
that he should continue to live on for ever,
    and never see the Pit.
Yea, he shall see that even the wise die,
    the fool and the stupid alike
       must perish
    and leave their wealth to others.
Their graves are their homes for ever,
    their dwelling places to all generations,
    though they named lands their own.
Man cannot abide in his pomp,
    he is like the beasts that perish.

This is the fate of those who have
    foolish confidence,
  the end of those who are pleased
    with their portion.
Like sheep they are appointed
    for Sheol;
  Death shall be their shepherd;
straight to the grave they descend,
    and their form shall waste away;
  Sheol shall be their home.
But God will ransom my soul
    from the power of Sheol,
  for he will receive me.
Be not afraid when one becomes rich,
  when the glory of his house increases.
For when he dies he will carry
    nothing away;
  his glory will not go down after him.
Though, while he lives, he counts
    himself happy,
  and though a man gets praise when he
    does well,
he will go to the generation
    of his fathers,
  who will never more see the light.
Man cannot abide in his pomp,
  he is like the beasts that perish.

Have mercy on me, O God,
 according to thy steadfast love;
 according to thy abundant mercy
 blot out my transgressions.
Wash me thoroughly from my iniquity,
 and cleanse me from my sin!
For I know my transgressions,
 and my sin is ever before me.
Against thee, thee only, have I sinned,
 and done that which is evil in thy sight,
so that thou art justified in thy sentence
 and blameless in thy judgment.
Behold, I was brought forth in iniquity,
 and in sin did my mother conceive me.

Behold, thou desirest truth
 in the inward being;
 therefore teach me wisdom
 in my secret heart.
Purge me with hyssop, and I shall
 be clean;
 wash me, and I shall be whiter
 than snow.
Fill me with joy and gladness;
 let the bones which thou hast
 broken rejoice.
Hide thy face from my sins,

and blot out all my iniquities.
Create in me a clean heart, O God,
 and put a new and right spirit
  within me.
Cast me not away from thy presence,
 and take not thy holy Spirit from me.
Restore to me the joy of thy salvation,
 and uphold me with a willing spirit.

Then I will teach transgressors thy ways,
 and sinners will return to thee.
Deliver me from bloodguiltiness, O God,
 thou God of my salvation,
 and my tongue will sing aloud
  of thy deliverance.
O Lord, open thou my lips,
 and my mouth shall show forth
  thy praise.
For thou hast no delight in sacrifice;
 were I to give a burnt offering,
 thou wouldst not be pleased.
The sacrifice acceptable to God
  is a broken spirit;
 a broken and contrite heart, O God,
  thou wilt not despise.

Do good to Zion in thy good pleasure;

rebuild the walls of Jerusalem,
then wilt thou delight in right sacrifices,
  in burnt offerings and
    whole burnt offerings;
  then bulls will be offered on thy altar.

Give ear to my prayer, O God;
  and hide not thyself from
    my supplication!
Attend to me, and answer me;
  I am overcome by my trouble.
I am distraught by the noise of the enemy,
  because of the oppression of the wicked.
Fear and trembling come upon me,
  and horror overwhelms me.
And I say, "O that I had wings like a dove!
  I would fly away and be at rest;
yea, I would wander afar,
  I would lodge in the wilderness,
I would haste to find me a shelter
  from the raging wind and tempest."
It is not an enemy who taunts me—
  then I could bear it;
it is not an adversary who deals
    insolently with me—
  then I could hide from him.

But it is you, my equal,
  my companion, my familiar friend.
We used to hold sweet converse together;
  within God's house we walked
    in fellowship.
Let death come upon them;
  let them go down to Sheol alive;
  let them go away in terror
    into their graves.
My companion stretched out his hand
    against his friends,
  he violated his covenant.
His speech was smoother than butter,
  yet war was in his heart;
his words were softer than oil,
  yet they were drawn swords.

Cast your burden on the LORD,
  and he will sustain you;
he will never permit
  the righteous to be moved.

But thou, O God, wilt cast them down
  into the lowest pit;
men of blood and treachery
  shall not live out half their days.
But I will trust in thee.

Hear my cry, O God,
  listen to my prayer;
from the end of the earth
    I call to thee,
  when my heart is faint.

Lead thou me
  to the rock that is higher than I;
for thou art my refuge,
  a strong tower against the enemy.

Let me dwell in thy tent for ever!
  Oh to be safe under the shelter
    of thy wings!
For thou, O God, hast heard my vows,
  thou hast given me the heritage
    of those who fear thy name.

Prolong the life of the king;
  may his years endure to all generations!
May he be enthroned for ever before God;
  bid steadfast love and faithfulness
    watch over him!

So will I ever sing praises to thy name,
  as I pay my vows day after day.

For God alone my soul waits in silence;
  from him comes my salvation.

He only is my rock and my salvation,
   my fortress; I shall not be greatly moved.
How long will you set upon a man
   to shatter him, all of you,
     like a leaning wall, a tottering fence?
They only plan to thrust him down
    from his eminence.
   They take pleasure in falsehood.
They bless with their mouths,
   but inwardly they curse.
For God alone my soul waits in silence,
   for my hope is from him.
He only is my rock and my salvation,
   my fortress; I shall not be shaken.
On God rests my deliverance
    and my honor;
   my mighty rock, my refuge is God.

Trust in him at all times, O people;
   pour out your heart before him;
   God is a refuge for us.
Men of low estate are but a breath,
   men of high estate are a delusion;
in the balances they go up;
   they are together lighter than a breath.
Put no confidence in extortion,
   set no vain hopes on robbery;

if riches increase, set not your heart
  on them.

Once God has spoken;
  twice have I heard this:
that power belongs to God;
  and that to thee, O Lord, belongs
    steadfast love.
For thou dost requite a man
  according to his work.

O God, thou art my God, I seek thee,
  my soul thirsts for thee;
my flesh faints for thee,
  as in a dry and weary land
    where no water is.
So I have looked upon thee
    in the sanctuary,
  beholding thy power and glory.
Because thy steadfast love is better
    than life,
  my lips will praise thee.
So I will bless thee as long as I live;
  I will lift up my hands and call
    on thy name.
My soul is feasted as with marrow and fat,

and my mouth praises thee
    with joyful lips,
when I think of thee upon my bed,
    and meditate on thee in the watches
        of the night;
for thou hast been my help,
    and in the shadow of thy wings
        I sing for joy.
My soul clings to thee;
    thy right hand upholds me.

But those who seek to destroy my life
    shall go down into the depths
        of the earth;
they shall be given over to the power
        of the sword,
    they shall be prey for jackals.
But the king shall rejoice in God;
    all who swear by him shall glory;
    for the mouths of liars will be stopped.

Praise is due to thee,
    O God, in Zion;
and to thee shall vows be performed,
    O thou who hearest prayer!
To thee shall all flesh come

on account of sins.
When our transgressions prevail over us,
    thou dost forgive them.
Blessed is he whom thou dost choose
        and bring near,
    to dwell in thy courts!
We shall be satisfied with the goodness
        of thy house,
    thy holy temple!
By dread deeds thou dost answer us
        with deliverance,
    O God of our salvation,
who art the hope of all the ends
        of the earth,
    and of the farthest seas;
who by thy strength hast established
        the mountains,
    being girded with might;
who dost still the roaring of the seas,
    the roaring of their waves,
    the tumult of the peoples;
so that those who dwell at earth's
        farthest bounds
    are afraid at thy signs;
thou makest the outgoings of the morning
        and the evening
    to shout for joy.

Thou visitest the earth and waterest it,
  thou greatly enrichest it;
the river of God is full of water;
  thou providest their grain,
  for so thou hast prepared it.
Thou waterest its furrows abundantly,
  settling its ridges,
softening it with showers,
  and blessing its growth.
Thou crownest the year with thy bounty;
  the tracks of thy chariot drip
    with fatness.
The pastures of the wilderness drip,
  the hills gird themselves with joy,
the meadows clothe themselves
    with flocks,
  the valleys deck themselves with grain,
  they shout and sing together for joy.

May God be gracious to us and bless us
  and make his face to shine upon us,
that thy way may be known upon earth,
  thy saving power among all nations.
Let the peoples praise thee, O God;
  let all the peoples praise thee!
Let the nations be glad and sing for joy,

for thou dost judge the peoples
with equity
and guide the nations upon earth.
Let the peoples praise thee, O God;
let all the peoples praise thee!
The earth has yielded its increase;
God, our God, has blessed us.
God has blessed us;
let all the ends of the earth fear him!

Save me, O God!
For the waters have come up to my neck.
I sink in deep mire,
where there is no foothold;
I have come into deep waters,
and the flood sweeps over me.
I am weary with my crying;
my throat is parched.
My eyes grow dim
with waiting for my God.
More in number than the hairs of my head
are those who hate me without cause;
mighty are those who would destroy me,
those who attack me with lies.
What I did not steal
must I now restore?

O God, thou knowest my folly;
  the wrongs I have done are not hidden
    from thee.

Let not those who hope in thee be
      put to shame through me,
  O Lord GOD of hosts.
For it is for thy sake that I have
      borne reproach,
  that shame has covered my face.
For zeal for thy house has consumed me,
    and the insults of those who insult thee
      have fallen on me.

But as for me, my prayer is to thee,
      O LORD.
  At an acceptable time, O God,
  in the abundance of thy steadfast love
      answer me.
With thy faithful help rescue me
    from sinking in the mire;
let me be delivered from my enemies
    and from the deep waters.
Thou knowest my reproach,
    and my shame and my dishonor;
    my foes are all known to thee.
They gave me poison for food,

and for my thirst they gave me
    vinegar to drink.
Let their own table before them
    become a snare;
  let their sacrificial feasts be a trap.
Let their eyes be darkened, so that
    they cannot see;
  and make their loins tremble continually.
May their camp be a desolation,
  let no one dwell in their tents.
For they persecute him whom thou
    hast smitten,
  and him whom thou hast wounded,
    they afflict still more.
Let them be blotted out of the book
    of the living;
  let them not be enrolled
    among the righteous.

But I am afflicted and in pain;
  let thy salvation, O God, set me on high!

I will praise the name of God with a song;
  I will magnify him with thanksgiving.
Let the oppressed see it and be glad.
For the LORD hears the needy,
  and does not despise his own
    that are in bonds.

Let heaven and earth praise him,
  the seas and everything
    that moves therein.
For God will save Zion
  and rebuild the cities of Judah;
and his servants shall dwell there
    and possess it;
  the children of his servants
    shall inherit it,
  and those who love his name
    shall dwell in it.

Give the king thy justice, O God,
  and thy righteousness to the royal son!
May he judge thy people
    with righteousness,
  and thy poor with justice!
Let the mountains bear prosperity
    for the people,
  and the hills, in righteousness!
May he defend the cause of the poor
    of the people,
  give deliverance to the needy,
  and crush the oppressor!
May he live while the sun endures,
  and as long as the moon,

throughout all generations!
May he be like rain that falls
   on the mown grass,
 like showers that water the earth!
In his days may righteousness flourish,
  and peace abound, till the moon
    be no more!
May he have dominion from sea to sea,
  and from the river Euphrates
    to the ends of the earth!
May his foes bow down before him,
  and his enemies lick the dust!
May the kings of Tarshish and of the isles
  render him tribute,
may the kings of Sheba and Seba
    bring gifts!
May all kings fall down before him,
  all nations serve him!
For he delivers the needy when he calls,
  the poor and him who has no helper.
He has pity on the weak and the needy,
  and saves the lives of the needy.
From oppression and violence
   he redeems their life;
  and precious is their blood in his sight.

Long may he live,
  may gold of Sheba be given to him!

May prayer be made for him continually,
  and blessings invoked for him
    all the day!
May there be abundance of grain
    in the land;
  on the tops of the mountains
    may it wave;
  may its fruit be like Lebanon;
and may men blossom forth from the cities
  like the grass of the field!
May his name endure for ever,
  his fame continue as long as the sun!
May men bless themselves by him,
  all nations call him blessed!

Blessed be the LORD, the God of Israel,
  who alone does wondrous things.
Blessed be his glorious name for ever;
  may his glory fill the whole earth!
  Amen and Amen!

BOOK III

Truly God is good to the upright,
  to those who are pure in heart.

But as for me, my feet had
    almost stumbled,
  my steps had well nigh slipped.
For I was envious of the arrogant,
  when I saw the prosperity of the wicked.
For they have no pangs;
  their bodies are sound and sleek.
They are not in trouble as other men are;
  they are not stricken like other men.
Therefore pride is their necklace;
  violence covers them as a garment.
Their eyes swell out with fatness,
  their hearts overflow with follies.
They scoff and speak with malice;
  loftily they threaten oppression.
They set their mouths against the heavens,
  and their tongue struts
    through the earth.
Therefore the people turn and praise them;
  and find no fault in them.
And they say, "How can God know?
  Is there knowledge in the Most High?"
Behold, these are the wicked;
  always at ease, they increase
    in riches.
All in vain have I kept my heart clean
  and washed my hands in innocence.

For all the day long I have been stricken,
  and chastened every morning.

If I had said, "I will speak thus,"
  I would have been untrue to the
    generation of thy children.
But when I thought how
  to understand this,
  it seemed to me a wearisome task,
until I went into the sanctuary of God;
  then I perceived their end.
Truly thou dost set them in slippery places;
  thou dost make them fall to ruin.
How they are destroyed in a moment,
  swept away utterly by terrors!
They are like a dream when one awakes,
  on awaking you despise their phantoms.
When my soul was embittered,
  when I was pricked in heart,
I was stupid and ignorant,
  I was like a beast toward thee.
Nevertheless, I am continually with thee;
  thou dost hold my right hand.
Thou dost guide me with thy counsel,
  and afterward thou wilt receive me
    to glory.
Whom have I in heaven but thee?

And there is nothing upon earth
   that I desire besides thee.
My flesh and my heart may fail,
   but God is the strength of my heart
     for ever.
For, lo, those who are far from thee
   shall perish;
   thou dost put an end to those who are
     false to thee.
But for me it is good to be near God;
   I have made the Lord GOD my refuge,
   that I may tell of all thy works.

Give ear, O my people, to my teaching;
   incline your ears to the words
     of my mouth!
I will open my mouth in a parable;
   I will utter dark sayings from of old,
things that we have heard and known,
   that our fathers have told us.
We will not hide them from their children,
   but tell to the coming generation
the glorious deeds of the LORD,
     and his might,
     and the wonders which he has wrought.
He established a testimony in Jacob,

and appointed a law in Israel,
which he commanded our fathers
  to teach to their children;
that the next generation might know them,
  the children yet unborn,
and arise and tell them to their children,
  so that they should set their hope
    in God,
and not forget the works of God,
  but keep his commandments;
and that they should not be
    like their fathers,
  a stubborn and rebellious generation,
a generation whose heart
    was not steadfast,
  whose spirit was not faithful to God.

In the sight of their fathers
    he wrought marvels
  in the land of Egypt, in the fields
    of Zoan.
He divided the sea and let them pass
    through it,
  and made the waters stand like a heap.
In the daytime he led them with a cloud,
  and all the night with a fiery light.
He cleft rocks in the wilderness,

and gave them drink abundantly
    as from the deep.
Yet they sinned still more against him,
   rebelling against the Most High
    in the desert.
They tested God in their heart
   by demanding the food they craved.
They spoke against God, saying,
   "Can God spread a table
    in the wilderness?
He smote the rock so that water gushed out
   and streams overflowed.
Can he also give bread,
   or provide meat for his people?"

Therefore, when the LORD heard,
    he was full of wrath;
   his anger mounted against Israel;
because they had no faith in God,
   and did not trust his saving power.
Yet he commanded the skies above,
   and opened the doors of heaven;
and he rained down upon them
    manna to eat,
   and gave them the grain of heaven.
He rained flesh upon them like dust,
   winged birds like the sand of the seas;

he let them fall in the midst of their camp,
    all around their habitations.
And they ate and were well filled,
    for he gave them what they craved.
But before they had sated their craving,
    while the food was still in their mouths,
the anger of God rose against them
    and he slew the strongest of them,
    and laid low the picked men of Israel.

In spite of all this they still sinned;
    despite his wonders they did not believe.
Their heart was not steadfast toward him;
    they were not true to his covenant.
Yet he, being compassionate,
    forgave their iniquity,
    and did not destroy them;
he restrained his anger often,
    and did not stir up all his wrath.
He remembered that they were but flesh,
    a wind that passes and comes not again.
He led them in safety, so that they
        were not afraid.
And he brought them to his holy land,
    to the mountain which his right hand
        had won.
He drove out nations before them;

he apportioned them for a possession
and settled the tribes of Israel
   in their tents.
Yet they tested and rebelled against
   the Most High God,
and did not observe his testimonies,
but turned away and acted treacherously
   like their fathers;
they twisted like a deceitful bow.
For they provoked him to anger
   with their high places;
they moved him to jealousy
   with their graven images.
When God heard, he was full of wrath,
   and he utterly rejected Israel.
He forsook his dwelling at Shiloh,
   the tent where he dwelt among men,
and delivered his power to captivity,
   his glory to the hand of the foe.
He gave his people over to the sword,
   and vented his wrath on his heritage.
Fire devoured their young men,
   and their maidens had
      no marriage song.
Their priests fell by the sword,
   and their widows made
      no lamentation.

Then the Lord awoke as from sleep,
   like a strong man shouting
      because of wine.
And he put his adversaries to rout;
   he put them to everlasting shame.
He rejected the tent of Joseph,
   he did not choose the tribe of Ephraim;
but he chose the tribe of Judah,
   Mount Zion, which he loves.
He built his sanctuary like the
      high heavens,
   like the earth, which he has founded
      for ever.
He chose David his servant,
   and took him from the sheepfolds;
from tending the ewes that had young
      he brought him
      to be the shepherd of Jacob his people.
With upright heart he tended them,
   and guided them with skilful hand.

God has taken his place in the
      divine council;
   in the midst of the gods
      he holds judgment:
"How long will you judge unjustly

and show partiality to the wicked?
Give justice to the weak and the fatherless;
  maintain the right of the afflicted
    and the destitute.
Rescue the weak and the needy;
  deliver them from the hand
    of the wicked."
They have neither knowledge
    nor understanding,
  they walk about in darkness;
  all the foundations of the earth
    are shaken.
I say, "You are gods,
  sons of the Most High, all of you;
nevertheless, you shall die like men,
  and fall like any prince."

Arise, O God, judge the earth;
  for to thee belong all the nations!

How lovely is thy dwelling place,
  O LORD of hosts!
My soul longs, yea, faints
  for the courts of the LORD;
my heart and flesh sing for joy
  to the living God.

Even the sparrow finds a home,
　　and the swallow a nest for herself,
　　where she may lay her young,
at thy altars, O Lord of hosts,
　　my King and my God.
Blessed are those who dwell in thy house,
　　ever singing thy praise!
Blessed are the men whose strength
　　　is in thee,
　　in whose heart are the highways
　　　to Zion.
As they go through the valley of Baca
　　they make it a place of springs;
　　the early rain also covers it with pools.
They go from strength to strength;
　　the God of gods will be seen in Zion.

O Lord God of hosts, hear my prayer;
　　give ear, O God of Jacob!
Behold our shield, O God;
　　look upon the face of thine anointed!

For a day in thy courts is better
　　than a thousand elsewhere.
I would rather be a doorkeeper
　　　in the house of my God
　　than dwell in the tents of wickedness.

For the LORD God is a sun and shield;
  he bestows favor and honor.
No good thing does the LORD withhold
  from those who walk uprightly.
O LORD of hosts,
  blessed is the man who trusts
    in thee!

On the holy mount stands the city
    he founded;
  the LORD loves the gates of Zion
  more than all the dwelling places
    of Jacob.
Glorious things are spoken of you,
  O city of God.

Among those who know me I mention
    Rahab and Babylon;
  behold, Philistia and Tyre,
    with Ethiopia—
"This one was born there," they say.
And of Zion it shall be said,
  "This one and that one were born
    in her";
  for the Most High himself
    will establish her.

The LORD records as he registers
    the peoples,
  "This one was born there."
Singers and dancers alike say,
  "All my springs are in you."

O LORD, my God, I call for help by day;
  I cry out in the night before thee.
Let my prayer come before thee,
  incline thy ear to my cry!
For my soul is full of troubles,
  and my life draws near to Sheol.
I am reckoned among those who go down
    to the Pit;
  I am a man who has no strength,
like one forsaken among the dead,
  like the slain that lie in the grave,
like those whom thou dost remember
    no more,
  for they are cut off from thy hand.
Thou hast put me in the depths
    of the Pit,
  in the regions dark and deep.
Thy wrath lies heavy upon me,
  and thou dost overwhelm me
    with all thy waves.

Thou hast caused my companions
    to shun me;
  thou hast made me a thing of horror
    to them.
I am shut in, so that I cannot escape;
  my eye grows dim through sorrow.
Every day I call upon thee, O LORD;
  I spread out my hands to thee.
Dost thou work wonders for the dead?
  Do the shades rise up to praise thee?
Is thy steadfast love declared in the grave,
  or thy faithfulness in Abaddon?
Are thy wonders known in the darkness,
  or thy saving help in the land
    of forgetfulness?

But I, O LORD, cry to thee;
  in the morning my prayer comes
    before thee.
O LORD, why dost thou cast me off?
  Why dost thou hide thy face from me?
Afflicted and close to death
    from my youth up,
  I suffer thy terrors; I am helpless.
Thy wrath has swept over me;
  thy dread assaults destroy me.
They surround me like a flood all day long;

they close in upon me together.
Thou hast caused lover and friend
 to shun me;
 my companions are in darkness.

I will sing of thy steadfast love, O LORD,
 for ever;
 I will proclaim thy faithfulness
 to all generations.
For thy steadfast love was established
 for ever,
 thy faithfulness is firm as the heavens.
Thou hast said, "I have made a covenant
 with my chosen one,
 I have sworn to David my servant:
'I will establish your descendants for ever,
 and build your throne for all
 generations.' "
Let the heavens praise thy wonders,
 O LORD,
 thy faithfulness in the assembly
 of the holy ones!
O LORD God of hosts,
 who is mighty as thou art?
The heavens are thine, the earth also
 is thine;

the world and all that is in it,
    thou hast founded them.
Righteousness and justice are the
    foundation of thy throne;
steadfast love and faithfulness go
    before thee.

Blessed are the people who know
    the festal shout,
    who walk, O LORD, in the light
    of thy countenance,
who exult in thy name all the day,
    and extol thy righteousness.
For thou art the glory of their strength;
    by thy favor our horn is exalted.
For our shield belongs to the LORD,
    our king to the Holy One of Israel.

Of old thou didst speak in a vision
    to thy faithful one, and say:
"I have set the crown upon one
    who is mighty,
    I have exalted one chosen
    from the people.
I have found David, my servant;
    with my holy oil I have anointed him;
so that my hand shall ever abide with him,

my arm also shall strengthen him.
The enemy shall not outwit him,
  the wicked shall not humble him.
I will crush his foes before him
  and strike down those who hate him.
And I will make him the first-born,
  the highest of the kings of the earth.
My steadfast love I will keep for him
    for ever,
  and my covenant will stand firm for him.
I will establish his line for ever
  and his throne as the days
    of the heavens.
If his children forsake my law
  and do not walk according
    to my ordinances,
if they violate my statutes
  and do not keep my commandments,
then I will punish their transgression
    with the rod
  and their iniquity with scourges;
but I will not remove from him
    my steadfast love,
  or be false to my faithfulness."

But now thou hast cast off
  and rejected,

thou art full of wrath against thy
    anointed.
Thou hast renounced the covenant
    with thy servant;
  thou hast defiled his crown in the dust.
Thou hast breached all his walls;
  thou hast laid his strongholds in ruins.
All that pass by despoil him;
  he has become the scorn
    of his neighbors.
Thou hast exalted the right hand
    of his foes;
  thou hast made all his enemies rejoice.
Yea, thou hast turned back the edge
    of his sword,
  and thou hast not made him
    stand in battle.
Thou hast removed the scepter
    from his hand,
  and cast his throne to the ground.
Thou hast cut short the days of his youth;
  thou hast covered him with shame.

How long, O LORD? Wilt thou hide thyself
    for ever?
  How long will thy wrath burn like fire?
Remember, O Lord, what the measure
    of life is,

for what vanity thou hast created
   all the sons of men!
What man can live and never see death?
   Who can deliver his soul from the
     power of Sheol?
Lord, where is thy steadfast love of old,
   which by thy faithfulness thou
     didst swear to David?
Remember, O Lord, how thy servant
   is scorned;
   how I bear in my bosom the insults
     of the peoples,
with which thy enemies taunt, O LORD,
   with which they mock the footsteps
     of thy anointed.

Blessed be the LORD for ever!
Amen and Amen.

BOOK IV

Lord, thou hast been our dwelling place
   in all generations.
Before the mountains were brought forth,
   or ever thou hadst formed the earth
     and the world,

from everlasting to everlasting
   thou art God.
Thou turnest man back to the dust,
  and sayest, "Turn back, O children
   of men!"
For a thousand years in thy sight
  are but as yesterday when it is past,
  or as a watch in the night.
Thou dost sweep men away; they are
   like a dream,
  like grass which is renewed
   in the morning:
in the morning it flourishes
   and is renewed;
  in the evening it fades and withers.

For we are consumed by thy anger;
  by thy wrath we are overwhelmed.
Thou hast set our iniquities before thee,
  our secret sins in the light
   of thy countenance.
For all our days pass away
   under thy wrath,
  our years come to an end like a sigh.
The years of our life are threescore
   and ten,
  or even by reason of strength fourscore;

yet their span is but toil and trouble;
    they are soon gone, and we fly away.
Who considers the power of thy anger,
    and thy wrath according to the fear
      of thee?
So teach us to number our days
    that we may get a heart of wisdom.

Return, O LORD! How long?
    Have pity on thy servants!
Satisfy us in the morning with thy
      steadfast love,
    that we may rejoice and be glad
      all our days.
Make us glad as many days as thou
      hast afflicted us,
    and as many years as we have seen evil.
Let thy work be manifest to thy servants,
    and thy glorious power to their children.
Let the favor of the LORD our God
      be upon us,
    and establish thou the work
      of our hands upon us,
yea, the work of our hands establish thou it.

He who dwells in the shelter
      of the Most High,

who abides in the shadow
  of the Almighty,
will say to the LORD, "My refuge
  and my fortress;
  my God, in whom I trust."
For he will deliver you from the snare
  of the fowler
  and from the deadly pestilence;
he will cover you with his pinions,
  and under his wings you will find refuge;
  his faithfulness is a shield and buckler.
You will not fear the terror of the night,
  nor the arrow that flies by day,
nor the pestilence that stalks in darkness,
  nor the destruction that wastes
  at noonday.
A thousand may fall at your side,
  ten thousand at your right hand;
  but it will not come near you.
You will only look with your eyes
  and see the recompense of the wicked.
Because you have made the LORD
  your refuge,
  the Most High your habitation,
no evil shall befall you,
  no scourge come near your tent.
For he will give his angels charge of you

to guard you in all your ways.
On their hands they will bear you up,
  lest you dash your foot against a stone.
You will tread on the lion and the adder,
  the young lion and the serpent
    you will trample under foot.

Because he cleaves to me in love,
    I will deliver him;
  I will protect him, because he knows
    my name.
When he calls to me, I will answer him;
  I will be with him in trouble,
  I will rescue him and honor him.
With long life I will satisfy him,
  and show him my salvation.

It is good to give thanks to the LORD,
  to sing praises to thy name,
    O Most High;
to declare thy steadfast love
    in the morning,
  and thy faithfulness by night,
to the music of the lute and the harp,
  to the melody of the lyre.
For thou, O LORD, hast made me glad

by thy work;
at the works of thy hands I sing for joy.

How great are thy works, O LORD!
Thy thoughts are very deep!
The dull man cannot know,
the stupid cannot understand this:
that, though the wicked sprout like grass
and all evildoers flourish,
they are doomed to destruction for ever,
but thou, O LORD, art on high for ever.
For, lo, thy enemies, O LORD, shall perish;
all evildoers shall be scattered.

But thou hast exalted my horn like that
of the wild ox;
thou hast poured over me fresh oil.
My eyes have seen the downfall
of my enemies,
my ears have heard the doom
of my evil assailants.
The righteous flourish like the palm tree,
and grow like a cedar in Lebanon.
They are planted in the house of the LORD,
they flourish in the courts of our God.
They still bring forth fruit in old age,
they are ever full of sap and green,

to show that the LORD is upright;
  he is my rock, and there is no
    unrighteousness in him.

O come, let us sing to the LORD;
  let us make a joyful noise to the rock
    of our salvation!
Let us come into his presence
    with thanksgiving;
  let us make a joyful noise to him
    with songs of praise!
For the LORD is a great God,
    and a great King above all gods.
In his hand are the depths of the earth;
    the heights of the mountains
      are his also.
The sea is his, for he made it;
  for his hands formed the dry land.
O come, let us worship and bow down,
    let us kneel before the LORD, our Maker!
For he is our God,
    and we are the people of his pasture,
    and the sheep of his hand.

O that today you would hearken
    to his voice!

Harden not your hearts, as at Meribah,
as on the day at Massah
in the wilderness,
when your fathers tested me,
and put me to the proof, though
they had seen my work.
For forty years I loathed that generation
and said, "They are a people
who err in heart,
and they do not regard my ways."
Therefore I swore in my anger
that they should not enter my rest.

O sing to the LORD a new song;
sing to the LORD, all the earth!
Sing to the LORD, bless his name;
tell of his salvation from day to day.
Declare his glory among the nations,
his marvelous works among
all the peoples!
For great is the LORD, and greatly
to be praised;
he is to be feared above all gods.
For all the gods of the peoples are idols;
but the LORD made the heavens.
Honor and majesty are before him;

strength and beauty are in his sanctuary.
Ascribe to the LORD, O families
    of the peoples,
  ascribe to the LORD glory and strength!
Ascribe to the LORD the glory
    due his name;
  bring an offering, and come
    into his courts!
Worship the LORD in holy array;
  tremble before him, all the earth!
Say among the nations, "The LORD reigns!
    Yea, the world is established,
      it shall never be moved;
  he will judge the peoples with equity."
Let the heavens be glad, and let
    the earth rejoice;
  let the sea roar, and all that fills it;
  let the field exult, and everything in it!
Then shall all the trees of the wood
    sing for joy
  before the LORD, for he comes,
  for he comes to judge the earth.
He will judge the world with righteousness,
  and the peoples with his truth.

The LORD reigns; let the earth rejoice;
  let the many coastlands be glad!

Clouds and thick darkness are round
    about him;
  righteousness and justice are the
    foundation of his throne.
Fire goes before him,
  and burns up his adversaries
    round about.
His lightnings lighten the world;
  the earth sees and trembles.
The mountains melt like wax before
    the LORD,
  before the Lord of all the earth.
The heavens proclaim his righteousness;
  and all the peoples behold his glory.
All worshipers of images are put to shame,
  who make their boast in worthless idols;
  all gods bow down before him.
Zion hears and is glad,
  and the daughters of Judah rejoice,
  because of thy judgments, O God.
For thou, O LORD, art most high
    over all the earth;
  thou art exalted far above all gods.
The LORD loves those who hate evil;
  he preserves the lives of his saints;
  he delivers them from the hand
    of the wicked.

Light dawns for the righteous,
     and joy for the upright in heart.
Rejoice in the LORD, O you righteous,
     and give thanks to his holy name!

O sing to the LORD a new song,
     for he has done marvelous things!
His right hand and his holy arm
          have gotten him victory.
The LORD has made known his victory,
     he has revealed his vindication
          in the sight of the nations.
He has remembered his steadfast love
          and faithfulness
     to the house of Israel.
All the ends of the earth have seen
     the victory of our God.

Make a joyful noise to the LORD,
          all the earth;
     break forth into joyous song
          and sing praises!
Sing praises to the LORD with the lyre,
     with the lyre and the sound
          of melody!
With trumpets and the sound of the horn

make a joyful noise before the King,
   the LORD!
Let the sea roar, and all that fills it;
   the world and those who dwell in it!
Let the floods clap their hands;
   let the hills sing for joy together
before the LORD, for he comes
   to judge the earth.
He will judge the world
    with righteousness,
   and the peoples with equity.

Make a joyful noise to the LORD,
    all the lands!
  Serve the LORD with gladness!
  Come into his presence with singing!
Know that the LORD is God!
  It is he that made us, and we are his;
  we are his people, and the sheep
   of his pasture.
Enter his gates with thanksgiving,
  and his courts with praise!
  Give thanks to him, bless his name!
For the LORD is good;
  his steadfast love endures for ever,
  and his faithfulness to all generations.

Hear my prayer, O Lord;
   let my cry come to thee!
Do not hide thy face from me
   in the day of my distress!
Incline thy ear to me;
      answer me speedily in the day
         when I call!

For I eat ashes like bread,
   and mingle tears with my drink,
because of thy indignation and anger;
   for thou hast taken me up
      and thrown me away.
My days are like an evening shadow;
   I wither away like grass.

But thou, O Lord, art enthroned for ever;
   thy name endures to all generations.
Thou wilt arise and have pity on Zion;
   it is the time to favor her;
   the appointed time has come.

Let this be recorded for a generation
      to come,
   so that a people yet unborn
      may praise the Lord:
that he looked down from his holy height,

from heaven the LORD looked
    at the earth,
to hear the groans of the prisoners,
    to set free those who were doomed
      to die;
that men may declare in Zion the name
      of the LORD,
    and in Jerusalem his praise,
when peoples gather together,
    and kingdoms, to worship the LORD.

He has broken my strength in mid-course;
    he has shortened my days.
"O my God," I say, "take me not hence
    in the midst of my days,
thou whose years endure
    throughout all generations!"
Of old thou didst lay the foundation
      of the earth,
    and the heavens are the work
      of thy hands.
They will perish, but thou dost endure;
    they will all wear out like a garment.
Thou changest them like raiment,
      and they pass away;
    but thou art the same, and thy years
      have no end.

The children of thy servants
 shall dwell secure;
  their posterity shall be established
  before thee.

Bless the LORD, O my soul;
 and all that is within me,
  bless his holy name!
Bless the LORD, O my soul,
 and forget not all his benefits,
who forgives all your iniquity,
 who heals all your diseases,
who redeems your life from the Pit,
 who crowns you with steadfast love
  and mercy,
who satisfies you with good
  as long as you live,
 so that your youth is renewed
  like the eagle's.

The LORD works vindication
 and justice for all who are oppressed.
He made known his ways to Moses,
 his acts to the people of Israel.
The LORD is merciful and gracious,
 slow to anger and abounding

in steadfast love.
He will not always chide,
  nor will he keep his anger for ever.
He does not deal with us according
    to our sins,
  nor requite us according
    to our iniquities.
For as the heavens are high
    above the earth,
  so great is his steadfast love
    toward those who fear him;
as far as the east is from the west,
  so far does he remove our transgressions
    from us.
As a father pities his children,
  so the LORD pities those who fear him.
For he knows our frame;
  he remembers that we are dust.

As for man, his days are like grass;
  he flourishes like a flower
    of the field;
for the wind passes over it, and it is gone,
  and its place knows it no more.
But the steadfast love of the LORD
    is from everlasting to everlasting
  upon those who fear him,

and his righteousness to children's
    children,
to those who keep his covenant
    and remember to do his commandments.

The LORD has established his throne
    in the heavens,
    and his kingdom rules over all.
Bless the LORD, O you his angels,
    you mighty ones who do his word,
    hearkening to the voice of his word!
Bless the LORD, all his hosts,
    his ministers that do his will!
Bless the LORD, all his works,
    in all places of his dominion.
Bless the LORD, O my soul!

Bless the LORD, O my soul!
    O LORD my God, thou art very great!
Thou art clothed with honor and majesty,
    who coverest thyself with light
        as with a garment,
who hast stretched out the heavens
    like a tent,
    who hast laid the beams of thy
        chambers on the waters,

who makest the clouds thy chariot,
  who ridest on the wings of the wind,
who makest the winds thy messengers,
  fire and flame thy ministers.

Thou didst set the earth on its foundations,
  so that it should never be shaken.
Thou didst cover it with the deep
    as with a garment;
  the waters stood above the mountains.
At thy rebuke they fled;
  at the sound of thy thunder
    they took to flight.
The mountains rose, the valleys sank down
  to the place which thou didst
    appoint for them.
Thou didst set a bound which they
    should not pass,
  so that they might not again
    cover the earth.
Thou makest springs gush forth
    in the valleys;
  they flow between the hills.
Thou dost cause the grass to grow
    for the cattle,
  and plants for man to cultivate,
that he may bring forth food
    from the earth,

and wine to gladden the heart of man,
oil to make his face shine,
   and bread to strengthen man's heart.
The trees of the LORD
      are watered abundantly,
   the cedars of Lebanon which he planted.
In them the birds build their nests;
   the stork has her home
      in the fir trees.
The high mountains are
      for the wild goats;
   the rocks are a refuge for the badgers.
Thou hast made the moon to mark
      the seasons;
   the sun knows its time for setting.
Thou makest darkness, and it is night,
   when all the beasts of the forest
      creep forth.
The young lions roar for their prey,
   seeking their food from God.
When the sun rises, they get them away
   and lie down in their dens.
Man goes forth to his work
   and to his labor until the evening.
O LORD, how manifold are thy works!
   In wisdom hast thou made them all;
   the earth is full of thy creatures.

Yonder is the sea, great and wide,
  which teems with things innumerable,
  living things both small and great.
There go the ships,
  and Leviathan which thou didst form
    to sport in it.

May the glory of the LORD endure
    for ever,
  may the LORD rejoice in his works,
who looks on the earth and it trembles,
  who touches the mountains
    and they smoke!
I will sing to the LORD as long as I live;
  I will sing praise to my God
    while I have being.
May my meditation be pleasing to him,
  for I rejoice in the LORD.
Let sinners be consumed from the earth,
  and let the wicked be no more!
Bless the LORD, O my soul!
Praise the LORD!

Blessed be the LORD, the God of Israel,
  from everlasting to everlasting!
And let all the people say, "Amen!"

BOOK V

O give thanks to the LORD,
    for he is good;
for his steadfast love endures for ever!
Let the redeemed of the LORD say so,
    whom he has redeemed from trouble
and gathered in from the lands,
    from the east and from the west,
    from the north and from the south.

Some wandered in desert wastes,
    finding no way to a city to dwell in;
hungry and thirsty,
    their soul fainted within them.
Then they cried to the LORD
        in their trouble,
    and he delivered them
        from their distress;
he led them by a straight way,
    till they reached a city to dwell in.
Let them thank the LORD
        for his steadfast love,
    for his wonderful works
        to the sons of men!

For he satisfies him who is thirsty,
  and the hungry he fills with good things.

Some sat in darkness and in gloom,
  prisoners in affliction and in irons,
for they had rebelled against the words
    of God,
  and spurned the counsel
    of the Most High.
Their hearts were bowed down
    with hard labor;
  they fell down, with none to help.
Then they cried to the LORD
    in their trouble,
  and he delivered them
    from their distress;
he brought them out of darkness
    and gloom,
  and broke their bonds asunder.
Let them thank the LORD
    for his steadfast love,
  for his wonderful works
    to the sons of men!
For he shatters the doors of bronze,
  and cuts in two the bars of iron.

Some were sick through their sinful ways,

and because of their iniquities
suffered affliction;
they loathed any kind of food,
and they drew near to the gates
of death.
Then they cried to the LORD
in their trouble,
and he delivered them
from their distress;
he sent forth his word, and healed them,
and delivered them from destruction.
Let them thank the LORD
for his steadfast love,
for his wonderful works
to the sons of men!
And let them offer sacrifices
of thanksgiving,
and tell of his deeds in songs of joy!

Some went down to the sea in ships,
doing business on the great waters;
they saw the deeds of the LORD,
his wondrous works in the deep.
For he commanded, and raised
the stormy wind,
which lifted up the waves of the sea.
They mounted up to heaven, they went

down to the depths;
  their courage melted away
  in their evil plight;
they reeled and staggered
  like drunken men,
  and were at their wits' end.
Then they cried to the LORD
  in their trouble,
and he delivered them
  from their distress;
he made the storm be still,
  and the waves of the sea were hushed.
Then they were glad because
  they had quiet,
and he brought them
  to their desired haven.
Let them thank the LORD
  for his steadfast love,
  for his wonderful works
  to the sons of men!
Let them extol him in the congregation
  of the people,
and praise him in the assembly
  of the elders.

He turns rivers into a desert,
  springs of water into thirsty ground,

a fruitful land into a salty waste,
　　because of the wickedness
　　　　of its inhabitants.
He turns a desert into pools of water,
　　a parched land into springs of water.
And there he lets the hungry dwell,
　　and they establish a city to live in;
they sow fields and plant vineyards,
　　and get a fruitful yield.
By his blessing they multiply greatly;
　　and he does not let their cattle decrease.
When they are diminished and brought low
　　through oppression, trouble, and sorrow,
he pours contempt upon princes
　　and makes them wander
　　　　in trackless wastes;
but he raises up the needy out of affliction,
　　and makes their families like flocks.
The upright see it and are glad;
　　and all wickedness stops its mouth.
Whoever is wise, let him give heed
　　to these things;
　　let men consider the steadfast love
　　　　of the LORD.

My heart is steadfast, O God,
　　my heart is steadfast!

I will sing and make melody!
   Awake, my soul!
Awake, O harp and lyre!
   I will awake the dawn!
I will give thanks to thee, O LORD,
    among the peoples,
   I will sing praises to thee
    among the nations.
For thy steadfast love is great
    above the heavens,
   thy faithfulness reaches to the clouds.

Be exalted, thyself, O God,
    above the heavens!
   Let thy glory be over all the earth!
That thy beloved may be delivered,
   give help by thy right hand,
    and answer me!

God has promised in his sanctuary:
   "With exultation I will
    divide up Shechem,
and portion out the Vale of Succoth.
Gilead is mine; Manasseh is mine;
   Ephraim is my helmet;
   Judah my scepter.
Moab is my washbasin;

upon Edom I cast my shoe;
over Philistia I shout in triumph."

Who will bring me to the fortified city?
Who will lead me to Edom?
Hast thou not rejected us, O God?
Thou dost not go forth, O God,
with our armies.
O grant us help against the foe,
for vain is the help of man!
With God we shall do valiantly;
it is he who will tread down our foes.

The Lord says to my lord:
"Sit at my right hand,
till I make your enemies your footstool."
The Lord sends forth from Zion
your mighty scepter.
Rule in the midst of your foes!
Your people will offer themselves freely
on the day you lead your host
upon the holy mountains.
From the womb of the morning
like dew your youth will come to you.
The Lord has sworn
and will not change his mind,

"You are a priest for ever
    after the order of Melchizedek."
The Lord is at your right hand;
    he will shatter kings on the day
        of his wrath.
He will execute judgment
        among the nations,
    filling them with corpses;
he will shatter chiefs
    over the wide earth.
He will drink from the brook by the way;
    therefore he will lift up his head.

Praise the LORD.
I will give thanks to the LORD
        with my whole heart,
    in the company of the upright,
        in the congregation.
Great are the works of the LORD,
    studied by all who have pleasure
        in them.
Full of honor and majesty is his work,
    and his righteousness endures for ever.
He has caused his wonderful works
        to be remembered;
    the LORD is gracious and merciful.

He provides food for those who fear him;
  he is ever mindful of his covenant.
He has shown his people the power
    of his works,
  in giving them the heritage
  of the nations.
The works of his hands are faithful
    and just;
  all his precepts are trustworthy,
they are established for ever and ever,
  to be performed with faithfulness
  and uprightness.
He sent redemption to his people;
  he has commanded his covenant
    for ever.
  Holy and terrible is his name!
The fear of the LORD is the beginning
    of wisdom;
  a good understanding have all those
    who practice it.
  His praise endures for ever!

When Israel went forth from Egypt,
  the house of Jacob from a people
    of strange language,
Judah became his sanctuary,

Israel his dominion.
The sea looked and fled,
　　Jordan turned back.
The mountains skipped like rams,
　　the hills like lambs.
What ails you, O sea, that you flee?
　　O Jordan, that you turn back?
O mountains, that you skip like rams?
　　O hills, like lambs?
Tremble, O earth, at the presence
　　　of the LORD,
　　at the presence of the God of Jacob,
who turns the rock into a pool of water,
　　the flint into a spring of water.

I love the LORD, because he has heard
　　my voice and my supplications.
Because he inclined his ear to me,
　　therefore I will call on him
　　　　as long as I live.
The snares of death encompassed me;
　　the pangs of Sheol laid hold on me;
　　I suffered distress and anguish.
Then I called on the name of the LORD:
　　"O LORD, I beseech thee, save my life!"
Gracious is the LORD, and righteous;

our God is merciful.
The LORD preserves the simple;
    when I was brought low, he saved me.
Return, O my soul, to your rest;
    for the LORD has dealt
        bountifully with you.
For thou hast delivered my soul
        from death,
    my eyes from tears,
    my feet from stumbling;
I walk before the LORD
    in the land of the living.
I kept my faith, even when I said,
    "I am greatly afflicted";
I said in my consternation,
    "Men are all a vain hope."

What shall I render to the LORD
    for all his bounty to me?
I will lift up the cup of salvation
    and call on the name of the LORD,
I will pay my vows to the LORD
    in the presence of all his people.
Precious in the sight of the LORD
    is the death of his saints.
O LORD, I am thy servant;
    I am thy servant, the son
        of thy handmaid.

Thou hast loosed my bonds.
I will offer to thee the sacrifice
    of thanksgiving
  and call on the name of the LORD.
I will pay my vows to the LORD
  in the presence of all his people,
in the courts of the house of the LORD,
  in your midst, O Jerusalem.
Praise the LORD!

Praise the LORD, all nations!
  Extol him, all peoples!
For great is his steadfast love toward us;
  and the faithfulness of the LORD
    endures for ever.
Praise the LORD!

O give thanks to the LORD,
  for he is good;
  his steadfast love endures for ever!

Out of my distress I called on the LORD;
  the LORD answered me and set me free.
With the LORD on my side I do not fear.
  What can man do to me?

The LORD is on my side to help me;
  I shall look in triumph on those
    who hate me.
It is better to take refuge in the LORD
  than to put confidence in man.
It is better to take refuge in the LORD
  than to put confidence in princes.
All nations surrounded me on every side;
  they blazed like a fire of thorns;
  in the name of the LORD
    I cut them off!
I was pushed hard, so that I was falling,
  but the LORD helped me.
The LORD is my strength and my song;
  he has become my salvation.
Hark, glad songs of victory
  in the tents of the righteous.

I thank thee that thou hast answered me
  and hast become my salvation.
The stone which the builders rejected
  has become the head of the corner.
This is the LORD's doing;
  it is marvelous in our eyes.
This is the day which the LORD has made;
  let us rejoice and be glad in it.
Save us, we beseech thee, O LORD!

O LORD, we beseech thee, give
    us success!

Blessed be he who enters in the name
        of the LORD!
O give thanks to the LORD, for he is good;
    for his steadfast love endures for ever!

Blessed are those whose way is blameless,
    who walk in the law of the LORD!
Blessed are those who keep his testimonies,
    who seek him with their whole heart,
who also do no wrong,
    but walk in his ways!
Thou hast commanded thy precepts
    to be kept diligently.
O that my ways may be steadfast
    in keeping thy statutes!
Then I shall not be put to shame,
    having my eyes fixed on all
        thy commandments.
I will praise thee with an upright heart,
    when I learn thy righteous ordinances.
I will observe thy statutes;
    O forsake me not utterly!
Thy word is a lamp to my feet

and a light to my path.
I have sworn an oath and confirmed it,
  to observe thy righteous ordinances.
I am sorely afflicted;
  give me life, O LORD, according
    to thy word!
Accept my offerings of praise, O LORD,
  and teach me thy ordinances.
I hold my life in my hand continually,
  but I do not forget thy law.
The wicked have laid a snare for me,
  but I do not stray from thy precepts.
Thy testimonies are my heritage
    for ever;
  yea, they are the joy of my heart.
I incline my heart to perform thy statutes
  for ever, to the end.

Thy testimonies are wonderful;
  therefore my soul keeps them.
The unfolding of thy words gives light;
  it imparts understanding to the simple.
With open mouth I pant,
  because I long for thy commandments.
Turn to me and be gracious to me,
  as is thy wont toward those
    who love thy name.

Keep steady my steps according
   to thy promise,
  and let no iniquity get dominion over me.
Redeem me from man's oppression,
  that I may keep thy precepts.
Make thy face shine upon thy servant,
  and teach me thy statutes.
My eyes shed streams of tears,
  because men do not keep thy law.

Princes persecute me without cause,
  but my heart stands in awe
   of thy words.
I rejoice at thy word
  like one who finds great spoil.
I hate and abhor falsehood,
  but I love thy law.
Seven times a day I praise thee
  for thy righteous ordinances.
Great peace have those who love thy law;
  nothing can make them stumble.
I hope for thy salvation, O LORD,
  and I do thy commandments.
My soul keeps thy testimonies;
  I love them exceedingly.
I keep thy precepts and testimonies,
  for all my ways are before thee.

Let my cry come before thee, O LORD;
  give me understanding according
    to thy word!
Let my supplication come before thee;
  deliver me according to thy word.
My lips will pour forth praise
  that thou dost teach me thy statutes.
My tongue will sing of thy word,
  for all thy commandments are right.
Let thy hand be ready to help me,
  for I have chosen thy precepts.
I long for thy salvation, O LORD,
  and thy law is my delight.
Let me live, that I may praise thee,
  and let thy ordinances help me.
I have gone astray like a lost sheep;
  seek thy servant,
    for I do not forget thy commandments.

I lift up my eyes to the hills.
  From whence does my help come?
My help comes from the LORD,
  who made heaven and earth.
He will not let your foot be moved,
  he who keeps you will not slumber.
Behold, he who keeps Israel

will neither slumber nor sleep.
The LORD is your keeper;
   the LORD is your shade
   on your right hand.
The sun shall not smite you by day,
   nor the moon by night.
The LORD will keep you from all evil;
   he will keep your life.
The LORD will keep
   your going out and your coming in
   from this time forth and for evermore.

I was glad when they said to me,
   "Let us go to the house of the LORD!"
Our feet have been standing
   within your gates, O Jerusalem!
Jerusalem, built as a city
   which is bound firmly together,
to which the tribes go up,
   the tribes of the LORD,
as was decreed for Israel,
   to give thanks to the name of the LORD.
There thrones for judgment were set,
   the thrones of the house of David.

Pray for the peace of Jerusalem!
   "May they prosper who love you!

Peace be within your walls,
  and security within your towers!"
For my brethren and
    companions' sake
  I will say, "Peace be within you!"
For the sake of the house of the LORD
    our God,
  I will seek your good.

To thee I lift up my eyes,
  O thou who art enthroned
    in the heavens!
Behold, as the eyes of servants
  look to the hand of their master,
as the eyes of a maid
  to the hand of her mistress,
so our eyes look to the LORD our God,
  till he have mercy upon us.
Have mercy upon us, O LORD,
    have mercy upon us,
  for we have had more than enough
    of contempt.
Too long our soul has been sated
  with the scorn of those
    who are at ease,
  the contempt of the proud.

Unless the LORD builds the house,
   those who build it labor in vain.
Unless the LORD watches over the city,
   the watchman stays awake in vain.
It is in vain that you rise up early
   and go late to rest,
eating the bread of anxious toil;
   for he gives to his beloved sleep.
Lo, sons are a heritage from the LORD,
   the fruit of the womb a reward.
Like arrows in the hand of a warrior
   are the sons of one's youth.
Happy is the man who has
   his quiver full of them!
He shall not be put to shame
   when he speaks with his enemies
      in the gate.

Blessed is every one who fears the LORD,
   who walks in his ways!
You shall eat the fruit of the labor
      of your hands;
   you shall be happy, and it shall be well
      with you.
Your wife will be like a fruitful vine
   within your house;

your children will be like olive shoots
    around your table.
Lo, thus shall the man be blessed
    who fears the LORD.
The LORD bless you from Zion!
    May you see the prosperity of Jerusalem
    all the days of your life!
May you see your children's children!
    Peace be upon Israel!

Out of the depths I cry to thee, O LORD!
    Lord, hear my voice!
Let thy ears be attentive
    to the voice of my supplications!
If thou, O LORD, shouldst mark iniquities,
    Lord, who could stand?
But there is forgiveness with thee,
    that thou mayest be feared.

I wait for the LORD, my soul waits,
    and in his word I hope;
my soul waits for the LORD
    more than watchmen for the morning.
O Israel, hope in the LORD!
    For with the LORD there is
        steadfast love,

and with him is plenteous redemption.
And he will redeem Israel
    from all his iniquities.

O Lord, my heart is not lifted up,
    my eyes are not raised too high;
I do not occupy myself with things
    too great and too marvelous for me.
But I have calmed and quieted my soul,
    like a child quieted
      at its mother's breast;
    like a child that is quieted is my soul.
O Israel, hope in the Lord
    from this time forth and for evermore.

Behold, how good and pleasant it is
    when brothers dwell in unity!
It is like the precious oil upon the head,
    running down upon the beard,
upon the beard of Aaron,
    running down on the collar of his robes!
It is like the dew of Hermon,
    which falls on the mountains of Zion!
For there the Lord has commanded
    the blessing,
    life for evermore.

By the waters of Babylon,
  there we sat down and wept,
  when we remembered Zion.
On the willows there
  we hung up our lyres.
For there our captors required of us songs,
and our tormentors, mirth, saying,
  "Sing us one of the songs of Zion!"
How shall we sing the LORD's song
    in a foreign land?

If I forget you, O Jerusalem,
  let my right hand wither!
Let my tongue cleave to the roof
    of my mouth,
  if I do not remember you,
if I do not set Jerusalem
  above my highest joy!
Remember, O LORD, against the Edomites
  the day of Jerusalem,
how they said, "Raze it, raze it!
  Down to its foundations!"
O daughter of Babylon, you devastator!
  Happy shall he be who requites you
  with what you have done to us!
Happy shall he be who takes
    your little ones
  and dashes them against the rock!

O LORD, thou hast searched me
    and known me!
Thou knowest when I sit down and
    when I rise up;
  thou discernest my thoughts from afar.
Thou searchest out my path
    and my lying down,
  and art acquainted with all my ways.
Even before a word is on my tongue,
  lo, O LORD, thou knowest it altogether.
Thou dost beset me behind and before;
  and layest thy hand upon me.
Such knowledge is too wonderful for me;
  it is high, I cannot attain it.
Whither shall I go from thy Spirit?
  Or whither shall I flee
    from thy presence?
If I ascend to heaven, thou art there!
  If I make my bed in Sheol,
    thou art there!
If I take the wings of the morning
  and dwell in the uttermost parts
    of the sea,
even there thy hand shall lead me,
  and thy right hand shall hold me.
If I say, "Let only darkness cover me,
  and the light about me be night,"

even the darkness is not dark to thee,
 the night is bright as the day;
  for darkness is as light with thee.

For thou didst form my inward parts,
 thou didst knit me together
  in my mother's womb.
I praise thee, for thou art fearful
 and wonderful.
 Wonderful are thy works!
Thou knowest me right well;
 my frame was not hidden
  from thee,
when I was being made in secret,
 intricately wrought in the depths
  of the earth.
Thy eyes beheld my unformed substance;
 in thy book were written,
  every one of them,
the days that were formed for me,
 when as yet there was none of them.
How precious to me are thy thoughts,
 O God!
 How vast is the sum of them!
If I would count them, they are more
 than the sand.
 When I awake, I am still with thee.

O that thou wouldst slay the wicked,
　　O God,
　and that men of blood would depart
　　from me,
men who maliciously defy thee,
　who lift themselves up against thee
　　for evil!
Do I not hate them that hate thee,
　　O LORD?
　And do I not loathe them that rise up
　　against thee?
I hate them with perfect hatred;
　I count them my enemies.
Search me, O God, and know my heart!
　Try me and know my thoughts!
And see if there be any wicked way in me,
　and lead me in the way everlasting!

Blessed be the LORD, my rock,
who trains my hands for war,
　and my fingers for battle;
my rock and my fortress,
　my stronghold and my deliverer,
my shield and he in whom
　　I take refuge,
　who subdues the peoples under him.

I will sing a new song to thee, O God;
  upon a ten-stringed harp I will play
    to thee,
who givest victory to kings,
  who rescuest David thy servant.

May our sons in their youth
  be like plants full grown,
our daughters like corner pillars
  cut for the structure of a palace;
may our garners be full,
  providing all manner of store;
may our sheep bring forth thousands
  and ten thousands in our fields;
may our cattle be heavy with young,
  suffering no mischance or failure
    in bearing;
may there be no cry of distress
    in our streets!
Happy the people to whom
    such blessings fall!
  Happy the people whose God
    is the LORD!

I will extol thee, my God and King,
  and bless thy name for ever and ever.

Every day I will bless thee,
   and praise thy name for ever and ever.
Great is the LORD, and greatly
    to be praised,
   and his greatness is unsearchable.
One generation shall laud thy works
    to another,
   and shall declare thy mighty acts.
On the glorious splendor of thy majesty,
   and on thy wondrous works,
    I will meditate.
Men shall proclaim the might
    of thy terrible acts,
   and I will declare thy greatness.
They shall pour forth the fame
    of thy abundant goodness,
   and shall sing aloud of thy righteousness.

The LORD is gracious and merciful,
   slow to anger and abounding
    in steadfast love.
The LORD is good to all,
   and his compassion is over all
    that he has made.

All thy works shall give thanks to thee,
   O LORD,

and all thy saints shall bless thee!
They shall speak of the glory
    of thy kingdom,
  and tell of thy power,
to make known to the sons of men
    thy mighty deeds,
  and the glorious splendor
    of thy kingdom.
Thy kingdom is an everlasting kingdom,
  and thy dominion endures
    throughout all generations.

The LORD is faithful in all his words,
  and gracious in all his deeds.
The LORD upholds all who are falling,
  and raises up all who are bowed down.
The eyes of all look to thee,
  and thou givest them their food
    in due season.
Thou openest thy hand,
  thou satisfiest the desire
    of every living thing.
The LORD is just in all his ways,
  and kind in all his doings.
The LORD is near to all who call upon him,
  to all who call upon him in truth.
He fulfils the desire of all who fear him,

he also hears their cry, and saves them.
The LORD preserves all who love him;
but all the wicked he will destroy.
My mouth will speak the praise
of the LORD,
and let all flesh bless his holy name
for ever and ever.

Praise the LORD!
Praise the LORD from the heavens,
praise him in the heights!
Praise him, all his angels,
praise him, all his host!
Praise him, sun and moon,
praise him, all you shining stars!
Praise him, you highest heavens,
and you waters above the heavens!
Let them praise the name of the LORD!
For he commanded and they
were created.
And he established them for ever and ever;
he fixed their bounds which cannot
be passed.
Praise the LORD from the earth,
you sea monsters and all deeps,
fire and hail, snow and frost,

stormy wind fulfilling his command!
Mountains and all hills,
  fruit trees and all cedars!
Beasts and all cattle,
  creeping things and flying birds!
Kings of the earth and all peoples,
  princes and all rulers of the earth!
Young men and maidens together,
  old men and children!
Let them praise the name of the LORD,
  for his name alone is exalted;
  his glory is above earth and heaven.
He has raised up a horn for his people,
  praise for all his saints,
    for the people of Israel who are near
      to him.
Praise the LORD!

Praise the LORD!
Praise God in his sanctuary;
  praise him in his mighty firmament!
Praise him for his mighty deeds;
  praise him according to his
    exceeding greatness!
Praise him with trumpet sound;
  praise him with lute and harp!

Praise him with timbrel and dance;
  praise him with strings and pipe!
Praise him with sounding cymbals;
  praise him with loud clashing cymbals!
Let everything that breathes
    praise the LORD!
Praise the LORD!

PROVERBS

This book is a compendium of religious and moral instruction as given to Jewish youth by professional sages in the post-exilic period. The overall concept is "wisdom," but this does not mean merely knowing many things or being very clever. It means knowing the right thing to do *and doing it.* Wisdom is a practical thing of daily life; it is not nationalistic, but is individual and universal. As it stands, the book represents a gathering of several different collections of proverbs, stemming from various localities during the ninth to the third century B.C. Some sections offer extended admonition and warning, others provide pithy two-line maxims, all appealing to the lessons of experience. The frequent use of the book by New Testament writers (nearly a dozen quotations and more than twenty allusions) indicates the respect of early Christians for these wise thoughts of Israel's ancient sages.

———

THE PROVERBS OF Solomon, son of David, king of Israel:

That men may know wisdom, understand words of insight, receive instruction in wise dealing, righteousness, justice, and equity; that prudence may be given to the simple, knowledge and discretion to the youth—the man of understanding acquire skill, to understand a proverb and a figure, the words of the wise and their riddles.

The fear of the LORD is the beginning of knowledge; fools despise wisdom and instruction.

Hear, my son, your father's instruction, and reject not your mother's teaching; for they are a fair garland for your head. My son, if sinners entice you, if they say, "Come, let us lie in wait for blood, let us ambush the innocent; we shall fill our houses with spoil"—my son, hold back your foot from their paths. For in vain is a net spread in the sight of any bird; but these men set an ambush for their own lives. Such are the ways of all who get gain by violence; it takes away the life of its possessors.

Wisdom cries aloud in the street: "How long, O simple ones, will you love being simple? How long will fools hate knowledge? Give heed to my reproof. Because I have called and you refused to listen, I will laugh when panic strikes you like a storm. Then you will seek me, but you will not find me. Because you hated knowledge and did not choose the fear of the LORD, therefore you shall eat the fruit of your way and be sated with your own devices. For the complacence of fools destroys them; but he who listens to me will be at ease, without dread of evil."

My son, if you treasure up my commandments, if you cry out for insight and seek it like hidden treasure, you will understand the fear of the LORD and find the knowledge of God; for the LORD stores up sound wisdom for the upright, guarding the paths of justice and preserving the way of his saints. Then knowledge will be pleasant to your soul; discretion will watch over you, delivering you from the ways of darkness, from men of perverted speech, whose paths are crooked, and who are devious in their ways. You will be saved from the adventuress with her smooth words, who forsakes the companion of her youth and forgets the covenant of her God. You will walk in the way of good men, for the upright will inhabit the land.

My son, let not loyalty and faithfulness forsake you; write them on the tablet of your heart. So you will find favor and good repute in the sight of God and man. Trust in the LORD with all your heart, and do not rely on your own insight. In all your ways acknowledge him, and he will make straight your paths. Be not wise in your own eyes, and turn away from evil. It will be healing to your flesh and refreshment to your bones.

Do not despise the LORD's discipline or be weary of his reproof, for the LORD reproves him whom he loves, as a father the son in whom he delights.

Happy is the man who finds wisdom, for her profit is better than gold. Long life is in her right hand; in her left are riches and honor. Her ways are ways of pleasantness, and all her paths are peace. She is a tree of life to those who lay hold of her; those who hold her fast are called happy.

Do not withhold good from those to whom it is due, when it is in your power to do it. Do not say to your neighbor, "Go, and come again, tomorrow I will give it"— when you have it with you. Do not plan evil against your neighbor who dwells trustingly beside you. Do not envy a man of violence and do not choose any of his ways; for the perverse man is an abomination to the LORD, but the upright are in his confidence.

When I was a son with my father, tender, the only one in the sight of my mother, he taught me, "The beginning of wisdom is this: Get wisdom, and whatever you get, get insight. Prize her highly, and she will exalt you." I have taught you the way of wisdom, my son; guard her, for she is your life. Do not enter the path of the wicked; turn away from it and pass on. For the way of the wicked is like deep darkness; they do not know over what they stumble. But the path of the righteous is like the light of dawn, which shines brighter and brighter until full day.

The lips of a loose woman drip honey, and her speech is smoother than oil; but in the end she is bitter as wormwood, sharp as a two-edged sword. She does not take heed to the path of life; her feet go down to death. O sons, keep your way far from her; do not go near her door, lest you give your honor to others and your years to the merciless; and at the end of your life you groan, when your flesh and body are consumed, and you say, "How I hated discipline, and my heart despised reproof! I was at the point of utter ruin in the assembled congregation."

Drink water from your own cistern, flowing water from your own well. Let your fountain be blessed, and rejoice in the wife of your youth, a lovely hind, a graceful doe. Let her affection fill you with delight, be infatuated at all times with her love. Why should you embrace the bosom of an adventuress, my son? For a man's ways are before the eyes of the LORD, and he watches all his paths.

Go to the ant, O sluggard; consider her ways, and be wise. Without having any chief, officer or ruler, she prepares her food in summer, and gathers her sustenance in harvest. How long will you lie there, O sluggard? When will you arise from your sleep? A little sleep, a little slumber, a little folding of the hands to rest, and poverty will come upon you like a robber, and want like an armed man.

There are six things which the LORD hates, seven which are an abomination to him: haughty eyes, a lying tongue, and hands that shed innocent blood, a heart that devises wicked plans, feet that make haste to run to evil, a false witness who breathes out lies, and a man who sows discord among brothers.

Through the window of my house I have seen among the simple a young man passing along the street in the twilight, at the time of night and darkness. And lo, a woman meets him, dressed as a harlot, wily of heart. She is loud and wayward; her feet do not stay at home. Now in the street, now in the market, and at every corner she lies in wait. She seizes him and kisses him, and with impudent face she says: "I had to offer sacrifices, and today I have paid my vows; so now I have come to seek you. I have decked my couch with colored linen; I have perfumed my bed with myrrh. Come, let us delight ourselves with love till morning. For my husband has gone on a journey; only at full moon will he return."

With her smooth talk she persuades him. All at once he follows her, as an ox goes to the slaughter. He does not know that it will cost him his life. For many a victim has she laid low; yea, all her slain are a mighty host. Her house is the way to Sheol, going down to the chambers of death.

Does not wisdom call, does not understanding raise her voice? On the heights beside the way, beside the gates in front of the town, she cries aloud: "To you, O men, I call. O foolish ones, pay attention. Hear, for I will speak noble things; my mouth will utter truth. Take my instruction instead of silver, and knowledge rather than gold. I, wisdom, dwell in prudence, and I find knowledge and discretion. I have counsel, I have insight, I have strength. By me kings reign, and rulers decree what is just. I love those who love me, and those who seek me diligently find me. I walk in the way of righteousness, in the paths of justice, endowing with wealth those who love me, and filling their treasuries.

"The LORD created me at the beginning of his work, the first of his acts of old. Ages ago I was set up, before the beginning of the earth. When there were no depths, I was brought forth, before the mountains had been shaped. Before the LORD made the first dust of the world, when he established the heavens, I was there. When he made firm the skies above, when he assigned to the sea its limit, when he marked out the foundations of the earth, then I was beside him. Like a little child, I was daily his delight, rejoicing in his inhabited world, rejoicing in the sons of men.

"He who finds me finds life and obtains favor from the LORD; but he who misses me injures himself. All who hate me love death."

Wisdom has built her house, she has set up her seven pillars. She has slaughtered her beasts, she has mixed her wine, she has also set her table. She has sent out her maids to call from the highest places in the town, "Whoever is simple, let him turn in here!" To him who is without sense she says, "Come, eat of my bread and drink of the wine I have mixed. Leave simpleness, and live, and walk in the way of insight."

A foolish woman is noisy; she is wanton and knows no shame. She sits at the door of her house, calling to those who pass by, "Whoever is simple, let him turn in here!" And to those without sense she says, "Stolen water is sweet, and bread eaten in secret is pleasant." But they do not know that the dead are there, that her guests are in the depths of Sheol.

THE PROVERBS OF Solomon.

A wise son makes a glad father,
   but a foolish son is a sorrow
     to his mother.
The LORD does not let the righteous
    go hungry,
   but he thwarts the craving of the wicked.
A slack hand causes poverty,
   but the hand of the diligent makes rich.
The memory of the righteous is a blessing,
   but the name of the wicked will rot.
He who walks in integrity walks securely,
   but he who perverts his ways
    will stumble.
He who winks the eye causes trouble,
   but he who boldly reproves makes peace.
The mouth of the righteous is a fountain
    of life,
   but the mouth of the wicked
    conceals violence.
Hatred stirs up strife,
   but love covers all offenses.
The lips of the righteous feed many,
   but fools die for lack of sense.
The blessing of the LORD makes rich,
   and he adds no sorrow with it.

When the tempest passes, the wicked is
  no more,
   but the righteous is established for ever.
Like vinegar to the teeth, and smoke
  to the eyes,
   so is the sluggard to those
    who send him.
The fear of the LORD prolongs life,
   but the years of the wicked will be short.
A false balance is an abomination
   to the LORD,
   but a just weight is his delight.
When pride comes, then comes disgrace;
   but with the humble is wisdom.
Riches do not profit in the day of wrath,
   but righteousness delivers from death.
Where there is no guidance, a people falls;
   but in an abundance of counselors
    there is safety.
Like a gold ring in a swine's snout
   is a beautiful woman without discretion.
One man gives freely, yet grows
   all the richer;
   another withholds, and only suffers want.
He who trusts in his riches will wither,
   but the righteous will flourish
    like a green leaf.

If the righteous is requited on earth,
    how much more the wicked
      and the sinner!
A good wife is the crown of her husband,
    but she who brings shame is like
      rottenness in his bones.
Better is a man of humble standing
    who has bread
    than one who plays the great man
      but lacks it.
A righteous man has regard for the life
    of his beast,
    but the mercy of the wicked is cruel.
The strong tower of the wicked comes
    to ruin,
    but the root of the righteous stands firm.
The way of a fool is right in his own eyes,
    but a wise man listens to advice.
The vexation of a fool is known at once,
    but the prudent man ignores an insult.
Truthful lips endure for ever,
    but a lying tongue is but for a moment.
Anxiety in a man's heart
    weighs him down,
    but a good word makes him glad.
A wise son heeds his father's instruction,
    but a scoffer does not listen to rebuke.

The soul of the sluggard craves,
　　and gets nothing,
　while the soul of the diligent
　　is richly supplied.
Hope deferred makes the heart sick,
　　but a desire fulfilled is a tree of life.
The ground of the poor yields much food,
　　but it is swept away through injustice.
He who spares the rod hates his son,
　　but he who loves him is diligent
　　　to discipline him.
Wisdom builds her house,
　　but folly with her own hands
　　　tears it down.
The heart knows its own bitterness,
　　and no stranger shares its joy.
The house of the wicked will
　　　be destroyed,
　　but the tent of the upright will flourish.
There is a way which seems right to a man,
　　but its end is the way to death.
Even in laughter the heart is sad,
　　and the end of joy is grief.
A perverse man will be filled with the fruit
　　　of his ways,
　　and a good man with the fruit
　　　of his deeds.

The simple believes everything,
    but the prudent looks where he is going.
The evil bow down before the good,
    the wicked at the gates of the righteous.
In all toil there is profit,
    but mere talk tends only to want.
The fear of the LORD is a fountain of life,
    that one may avoid the snares of death.
A tranquil mind gives life to the flesh,
    but passion makes the bones rot.
He who oppresses a poor man
        insults his Maker,
    but he who is kind to the needy
        honors him.
A soft answer turns away wrath,
    but a harsh word stirs up anger.
The sacrifice of the wicked is an
        abomination to the LORD,
    but the prayer of the upright
        is his delight.
All the days of the afflicted are evil,
    but a cheerful heart has
        a continual feast.
Better is a little with the fear of the LORD
    than great treasure and trouble with it.
To make an apt answer is a joy to a man,
    and a word in season, how good it is!

The LORD tears down the house
   of the proud,
  but maintains the widow's boundaries.
The LORD is far from the wicked,
  but he hears the prayer of the righteous.
The light of the eyes rejoices the heart,
  and good news refreshes the bones.
The plans of the mind belong to man,
   but the answer of the tongue is
    from the LORD.
The LORD has made everything for its
    purpose,
  even the wicked for the day of trouble.
When a man's ways please the LORD,
  even his enemies will be at peace
   with him.
A just balance and scales are the LORD's;
  all the weights are his work.
It is an abomination to kings to do evil,
  for the throne is established
   by righteousness.
Pride goes before destruction,
  and a haughty spirit before a fall.
It is better to be of a lowly spirit
   with the poor
  than to divide the spoil with the proud.
Better is a dry morsel with quiet

than a house full of feasting with strife.
The crucible is for silver, and the furnace
    is for gold,
  and the LORD tries hearts.
Fine speech is not becoming to a fool;
  still less is false speech to a prince.
He who forgives an offense seeks love,
    but he who dwells on a matter alienates
    a friend.
A rebuke goes deeper into a man
    of understanding
  than a hundred blows into a fool.
Let a man meet a she-bear robbed
    of her cubs,
  rather than a fool in his folly.
If a man returns evil for good,
  evil will not depart from his house.
The beginning of strife is like
    letting out water;
  so quit before the quarrel breaks out.
A friend loves at all times,
  and a brother is born for adversity.
A cheerful heart is a good medicine,
  but a downcast spirit dries
    up the bones.
Even a fool who keeps silent
    is considered wise;

when he closes his lips, he is
deemed intelligent.
A fool takes no pleasure in understanding,
but only in expressing his opinion.
The words of a whisperer are like delicious
morsels;
they go down into the inner parts
of the body.
He who is slack in his work
is a brother to him who destroys.
If one gives answer before he hears,
it is his folly and shame.
A man's spirit will endure sickness;
but a broken spirit who can bear?
He who states his case first seems right,
until the other comes and examines him.
When a man's folly brings his way to ruin,
his heart rages against the LORD.
Wealth brings many new friends,
but a poor man is deserted by all.
It is not fitting for a fool to live in luxury,
much less for a slave to rule over princes.
A king's wrath is like the growling of a lion,
but his favor is like dew upon the grass.
A foolish son is ruin to his father,
and a wife's quarreling is a continual
dripping of rain.

House and wealth are inherited
    from fathers,
  but a prudent wife is from the LORD.
Many are the plans in the mind of a man,
    but it is the purpose of the LORD
    that will be established.
The sluggard buries his hand in the dish,
    and will not even bring it back
    to his mouth.
Who can say, "I have made my heart
    clean;
  I am pure from my sin"?
Even a child makes himself known
    by his acts,
  whether what he does is pure and right.
The hearing ear and the seeing eye,
  the LORD has made them both.
If one curses his father or his mother,
  his lamp will be put out in utter darkness.
Do not say, "I will repay evil";
  wait for the LORD, and he will help you.
A man's steps are ordered by the LORD;
  how then can man understand his way?
It is a snare for a man to say rashly,
    "It is holy,"
  and to reflect only after making
    his vows.

Blows that wound cleanse away evil;
   strokes make clean the innermost parts.
The king's heart is a stream of water
     in the hand of the LORD;
   he turns it wherever he will.
To do righteousness and justice
   is more acceptable to the LORD
     than sacrifice.
The getting of treasures by a lying tongue
   is a fleeting vapor and a snare of death.
He who closes his ear to the cry
     of the poor
   will himself cry out and not be heard.
A gift in secret conceals anger;
   and a bribe in the bosom,
     strong wrath.
A man who wanders from the way
     of understanding
   will rest in the assembly of the dead.
It is better to live in a desert land
   than with a fretful woman.
"Scoffer" is the name of the proud,
     haughty man
   who acts with arrogant pride.
All day long the wicked covets,
   but the righteous gives and does not
     hold back.

No wisdom, no understanding, no counsel
  can avail against the LORD.
The horse is made ready for the day
    of battle,
  but the victory belongs to the LORD.
A good name is to be chosen rather than
    great riches,
  and favor is better than silver or gold.
The rich and the poor meet together;
  the LORD is the maker of them all.
A prudent man sees danger
    and hides himself;
  but the simple go on, and suffer for it.
The reward for humility and fear
    of the LORD
  is riches and honor and life.
Train up a child in the way he should go,
  and when he is old he will not depart
    from it.
The rich rules over the poor,
  and the borrower is the slave
    of the lender.
He who loves purity of heart
  will have the king as his friend.
The sluggard says, "There is
    a lion outside!
    I shall be slain in the streets!"

He who oppresses the poor to increase
   his own wealth
  will only come to want.

HAVE I NOT written sayings of admonition
and knowledge, to show you what is right
and true, that you may give a wise answer
to those who ask you?

Do not rob the poor, because he is poor,
or crush the afflicted at the gate; for the
LORD will plead their cause and despoil of
life those who despoil them.

Make no friendship with a wrathful
man, lest you learn his ways and entangle
yourself in a snare.

Do you see a man skilful in his work?
He will stand before kings.

When you sit down to eat with a ruler,
observe carefully what is before you; and
put a knife to your throat if you are a man
given to appetite. Do not desire a king's
delicacies, for they are deceptive food.

Do not toil to acquire wealth; be wise
enough to desist. When your eyes light
upon it, it is gone; for suddenly it
takes wing, flying like an eagle toward
heaven.

Do not eat the bread of a man who is stingy; do not desire his delicacies; for he is like one who is inwardly reckoning. "Eat and drink!" he says to you; but his heart is not with you.

Do not remove an ancient landmark or enter the fields of the fatherless; for their Redeemer is strong; he will plead their cause against you.

My son, if your heart is wise, my heart too will be glad. My soul will rejoice when your lips speak what is right. Let not your heart envy sinners, nor desire to be with them, but continue in the fear of the LORD all the day. Surely there is a future, and your hope will not be cut off.

Who has sorrow? Who has strife? Who has wounds without cause? Those who tarry over wine, who try mixed wine. Do not look at wine when it sparkles in the cup. Though it goes down smoothly, at the last it stings like an adder. Your eyes will see strange sights, and your mind utter perverse things. You will be like one sleeping in a stormy sea, lying on top of the mast. "They struck me," you will say, "but

I was not hurt; they beat me, but I did not feel it. When shall I awake? I will seek another drink."

By wisdom a house is built; by knowledge the rooms are filled with all precious and pleasant riches.

A wise man is mightier than a strong man, and a man of knowledge than he who has strength; for by wise guidance you can wage war, and in abundance of counselors there is victory.

If you faint in the day of adversity, your strength is small. Rescue those who are being taken away to death. If you say, "Behold, we did not know this," does not he who weighs the heart perceive it, and will he not requite you according to your work?

Do not rejoice when your enemy falls, and let not your heart be glad when he stumbles; lest the LORD see it, and be displeased, and turn away his anger from him.

Fear the LORD and the king, and do not disobey either of them; for disaster from them will rise suddenly, and who knows the ruin that will come?

THESE ALSO ARE proverbs of Solomon which the men of Hezekiah king of Judah copied.

It is the glory of God to conceal things, but the glory of kings is to search things out. As the heavens for height, and the earth for depth, so the mind of kings is unsearchable. Take away the dross from the silver, and the smith brings forth a vessel; take away the wicked from the presence of the king, and his throne will be established in righteousness.

Do not put yourself forward in the king's presence or stand in the place of the great; for it is better to be told, "Come up here," than to be put lower in the presence of the prince.

What your eyes have seen, do not hastily bring into court; for what will you do in the end, when your neighbor puts you to shame? Argue your case with your neighbor himself, and do not disclose his secret; lest he bring shame upon you, and your ill repute have no end.

A word fitly spoken
  is like apples of gold in a setting of silver.
Like clouds without rain
  is a man who boasts of a gift he does
    not give.
With patience a ruler may be persuaded,
  and a soft tongue will break a bone.
A faithless man in time of trouble
  is like a bad tooth or a foot that slips.
He who sings songs to a heavy heart
  is like vinegar on a wound.
If your enemy is hungry, give him bread
    to eat;
  and if he is thirsty, give him water
    to drink;
for you will heap coals of fire
    on his head,
  and the LORD will reward you.
The north wind brings forth rain,
  and a backbiting tongue, angry looks.
Like cold water to a thirsty soul,
  so is good news from a far country.
Like a muddied spring or
    a polluted fountain
  is a righteous man who falters
    before the wicked.
Like snow in summer or rain in harvest,

so honor is not fitting for a fool.
Like a sparrow in its flitting, like a swallow
    in its flying,
    a curse that is causeless does not alight.
A whip for the horse, a bridle for the ass,
    and a rod for the back of fools.
Answer not a fool according to his folly,
    lest you be like him yourself.
Answer a fool according to his folly,
    lest he be wise in his own eyes.
Like a dog that returns to his vomit
    is a fool that repeats his folly.
Do you see a man who is wise
    in his own eyes?
    There is more hope for a fool than
    for him.
As a door turns on its hinges,
    so does a sluggard on his bed.
The sluggard is wiser in his own eyes
    than seven men who can
    answer discreetly.
He who meddles in a quarrel not his own
    is like one who takes a passing dog
    by the ears.
Like a madman who throws firebrands
    and arrows
    is the man who deceives his neighbor

and says, "I am only joking!"
For lack of wood the fire goes out;
and where there is no whisperer,
quarreling ceases.

He who hates, dissembles with his lips;
when he speaks graciously, believe him
not, for there are seven abominations in
his heart. Though his hatred be covered
with guile, his wickedness will be exposed.
He who digs a pit will fall into it, and a
stone will come back upon him who starts
it rolling.

Do not boast about tomorrow,
for you do not know what a day
may bring forth.
Let another praise you, and not your
own mouth;
a stranger, and not your own lips.
A stone is heavy, and sand is weighty,
but a fool's provocation is heavier
than both.
Wrath is cruel, anger is overwhelming;
but who can stand before jealousy?
Better is open rebuke
than hidden love.

Sincere are the wounds of a friend;
  perverse are the kisses of an enemy.
He who blesses his neighbor
    with a loud voice
  will be counted as cursing.
Iron sharpens iron,
  and one man sharpens another.
As in water face answers to face,
  so the mind of man reflects the man.
The wicked flee when no one pursues,
  but the righteous are bold as a lion.
A chieftain who oppresses the poor
  is a beating rain that leaves no food.
He who augments his wealth by interest
    and increase
  gathers it for him who is kind
    to the poor.
When the righteous triumph, there is
    great glory;
  but when the wicked rise,
    men hide themselves.
He who conceals his transgressions
    will not prosper,
  but he who confesses them
    will obtain mercy.
Like a roaring lion or a charging bear
  is a wicked ruler over a people.

If a man is burdened with the blood
   of another,
  let him be a fugitive until death.
A miserly man hastens after wealth,
   and does not know that want will come
    upon him.
He who is often reproved, yet stiffens
   his neck,
  will suddenly be broken beyond healing.
If a ruler listens to falsehood,
  all his officials will be wicked.
If a king judges the poor with equity,
  his throne will be established for ever.
When the wicked are in authority,
   transgression increases;
  but the righteous will look upon
   their downfall.
Do you see a man who is hasty
   in his words?
  There is more hope for a fool
   than for him.
Many seek the favor of a ruler,
  but from the LORD a man gets justice.

THE WORDS OF Agur son of Jakeh of Massa.

Surely I am too stupid to be a man. I

have not the understanding of a man. I
have not learned wisdom, nor have I
knowledge of the Holy One. Who has as-
cended to heaven and come down? Who
has gathered the wind in his fists? Who
has wrapped up the waters in a garment?
Who has established all the ends of the
earth? What is his name, and what is his
son's name? Surely you know!

Every word of God proves true. Do not
add to his words, lest he rebuke you, and
you be found a liar.

Two things I ask of thee; deny them not
to me before I die: Remove far from me
falsehood and lying; give me neither poverty nor riches; feed me with the food that
is needful for me, lest I be full and deny
thee, or lest I be poor and steal, and profane the name of my God.

The leech has two daughters; "Give,
give," they cry. Three things are never satisfied; four never say, "Enough": Sheol,
the barren womb, the earth ever thirsty for
water, and the fire which never says,
"Enough."

Three things are too wonderful for me;
four I do not understand: the way of an

eagle in the sky, the way of a serpent on a rock, the way of a ship on the high seas, and the way of a man with a maiden.

Under three things the earth trembles; under four it cannot bear up: a slave when he becomes king, a fool when he is filled with food, an unloved woman when she gets a husband, and a maid when she succeeds her mistress.

THE WORDS OF Lemuel, king of Massa, which his mother taught him:

What, my son? What, son of my womb? Give not your strength to women, my son, your ways to those who destroy. It is not for kings, O Lemuel, it is not for kings to drink wine, lest they forget what has been decreed, and pervert the rights of all. Give strong drink to him who is perishing, to those in bitter distress. Let them drink and remember their misery no more. Open your mouth for the dumb, my son, for the rights of the desolate. Open your mouth, maintain the rights of the poor.

A good wife who can find? She is far more precious than jewels. The heart of her husband trusts in her, and he will have no lack of gain. She does him good, and not harm, all the days of her life. She is like the ships of the merchant, she brings her food from afar. She rises while it is yet night and works with willing hands. She considers a field and buys it; with the fruit of her hands she plants a vineyard. She opens her hand to the poor, and reaches out her hands to the needy. She is not afraid of snow; all her household are clothed in wool. Her husband is known in the gates; he sits among the elders of the land. She makes fine linen and purple; her lamp does not go out at night. Strength and dignity are her clothing, and she laughs at the time to come. She opens her mouth with wisdom, and the teaching of kindness is on her tongue. Her children call her blessed; her husband also, and he praises her: "Many women have done excellently, but you surpass them all." Charm is deceitful, and beauty is vain, but a woman who fears the LORD is to be praised.

ECCLESIASTES

The author of this book has reflected deeply on the frustrations of human existence, and has become disappointed with the so-called good things of life. Yet, in spite of his pessimism, he advises his readers to work hard, to overdo nothing, and to enjoy the gifts of God as much and as long as they can. Although the first section is written in the person of Solomon, the son of David, the subject matter and language make it clear that the book is the work of an unknown writer who lived centuries later, perhaps 350 B.C. Ecclesiastes was thus one of the latest books to be admitted into the canon of Hebrew Scripture. Its title is an interpretation of the Hebrew word *Qoheleth,* meaning a teacher or preacher in an assembly. The New Testament contains no quotation of this book, and no certain allusion. Fragments of it have been found among the Dead Sea Scrolls at Qumran.

THE WORDS OF the Preacher, the son of David, king in Jerusalem.

VANITY OF VANITIES, says the Preacher, vanity of vanities! All is vanity. What does man gain by all the toil at which he toils under the sun? A generation goes, and a generation comes, but the earth remains for ever. The sun rises and the sun goes down, and hastens to the place where it rises. The wind blows to the south, and goes round to the north; round and round goes the wind, and on its circuits the wind returns. All streams run to the sea, but the sea is not full; to the place where the streams flow, there they flow again.

All things are full of weariness; a man cannot utter it; the eye is not satisfied with seeing, nor the ear filled with hearing. What has been is what will be, and what has been done is what will be done; and there is nothing new under the sun. Is there a thing of which it is said, "See, this is new"? It has been already, in the ages before us. There is no remembrance of former things, nor will there be any remembrance of things yet to happen among those who come after.

I the Preacher have been king over Israel in Jerusalem. And I applied my mind to search out by wisdom all that is done under heaven. It is an unhappy business that God has given to the sons of men to be busy with. I have seen everything that is done under the sun; and behold, all is vanity and a striving after wind. What is crooked cannot be made straight, and what is lacking cannot be numbered.

I said to myself, "I have acquired great wisdom, surpassing all who were over Jerusalem before me." I perceived that this also is but a striving after wind. For in much wisdom is much vexation, and he who increases knowledge increases sorrow.

I said to myself, "Come now, I will make a test of pleasure." But this also was vanity. I said of laughter, "It is mad," and of pleasure, "What use is it?" I searched with my mind how to cheer my body with wine and how to lay hold on folly, till I might see what was good for the sons of men to do under heaven during the few days of their life. I made great works; I built houses and planted vineyards for myself; I made gardens and parks, and pools from which to water the forest of growing trees. I had also great herds and flocks, more than any who had been before me in Jerusalem. I gathered silver and gold and the treasure of kings and provinces. I got singers, both men and women, and many concubines, man's delight. Whatever my eyes desired I did not keep from them. I kept my heart from no pleasure, and this was my reward for all my toil. Then I considered all that my hands had done, and behold, all was vanity and a striving after wind.

So I turned to consider wisdom and madness and folly. I saw that wisdom excels folly as light excels darkness. The wise man has his eyes in his head, but the fool walks in darkness; and yet I perceived that one fate comes to all of them. I said to myself, "Why then have I been so very wise?" So I hated all my toil in which I had toiled under the sun, seeing that I must leave it to the man who will come after me; and who knows whether he will be a wise man or a fool? This is vanity and a great evil.

FOR EVERYTHING THERE is a season, and a time for every matter under heaven: a time to be born, and a time to die; a time to plant, and a time to pluck up what is planted; a time to kill, and a time to heal; a time to break down, and a time to build up; a time to weep, and a time to laugh; a time to mourn, and a time to dance; a time to cast away stones, and a time to gather stones together; a time to embrace, and a time to refrain from embracing; a time to seek, and a time to lose; a time to keep, and a time to cast away; a time to rend, and a time to sew; a time to keep silence, and a time to speak; a time to love, and a time to hate; a time for war, and a time for peace. What gain has the worker from all his toil?

I have seen the business that God has

given to the sons of men to be busy with. He has made everything beautiful in its time; also he has put eternity into man's mind, yet so that he cannot find out what God has done from the beginning to the end. I know that there is nothing better for men than to be happy and enjoy themselves as long as they live. It is God's gift to man that every one should eat and drink and take pleasure in his toil. I know that whatever God does endures for ever; nothing can be added to it, nor anything taken from it. God has made it so, in order that men should fear before him. That which is, already has been; that which is to be, already has been; and God seeks what has been driven away.

I saw under the sun that in the place of justice there was wickedness, and in the place of righteousness there was wickedness. I said in my heart, God will judge the righteous and the wicked, for he has appointed a time for every matter, and for every work. I said in my heart that God is testing the sons of men to show them that they are but beasts. For their fate and the fate of beasts is the same. All have the same breath; all go to one place; all are from the dust, and all turn to dust again. Who knows whether the spirit of man goes upward and the spirit of the beast goes down to the earth? And who can bring man to see what will be after him?

Again I saw all the oppressions that are practiced under the sun. And behold, the tears of the oppressed, and they had no one to comfort them! Power was on the side of their oppressors. I thought the dead more fortunate than the living; but better than both is he who has not yet been, and has not seen the evil deeds that are done under the sun.

Then I saw that toil and skill in work come from a man's envy of his neighbor. I saw a person who has no one, either son or brother, yet there is no end to all his toil, and his eyes are never satisfied with riches. He never asks, "For whom am I toiling and depriving myself of pleasure?" This is vanity and an unhappy business.

He who loves money will not be satisfied with money; nor he who loves wealth, with gain. Sweet is the sleep of a laborer, whether he eats little or much; but the surfeit of the rich will not let him sleep.

There is a grievous evil under the sun: riches kept by their owner to his hurt are lost in a bad venture. He is father of a son, but he has nothing in his hand. As he came from his mother's womb he shall go again, naked as he came, and shall take nothing for his toil. What gain has he that he toiled for the wind, and spent all his days in darkness and grief, in much vexation and sickness and resentment? A man to whom God has given the power to accept his lot and find enjoyment in his toil—this is the gift of God. For he will not reflect much on the days of his life; God keeps him occupied with joy in his heart. But a man to whom God gives wealth, possessions, and honor, so that he lacks nothing that he desires, yet does not give him the power to enjoy them; this is a sore affliction. If a man begets a hundred children, and lives many years, but does not enjoy life's good things, I say that an untimely birth is better off than he. For it comes into vanity and goes into darkness; moreover it has not seen the sun or known anything, yet it finds rest rather than he.

All the toil of a man is for his mouth, yet his appetite is not satisfied. Better is the sight of the eyes than the wandering of desire; this also is a striving after the wind. Whatever has come to be has already been named, and it is known what man is, and that he is not able to dispute with one stronger than he. The more words, the more vanity, and what is man the better?

A GOOD NAME is better than precious ointment; and the day of death better than the day of birth. It is better to go to the house of mourning than to go to the house of feasting; for this is the end of all men, and the living will lay it to heart. Sorrow is better than laughter, for by sadness of countenance the heart is made glad. The heart of the wise is in the house of mourning; but the heart of fools is in the house of mirth. It is better for a man to hear the rebuke of the wise than to hear the song of fools. For as the crackling of thorns under a pot, so is the laughter of fools; this also is vanity.

Surely oppression makes the wise man foolish, and a bribe corrupts the mind.

Better is the end of a thing than its beginning; and the patient in spirit is better than the proud in spirit. Be not quick to anger, for anger lodges in the bosom of fools. Say not, "Why were the former days better than these?" For it is not from wisdom that you ask this. Wisdom is good with an inheritance, an advantage to those who see the sun. For the protection of wisdom is like the protection of money; and the advantage of knowledge is that wisdom preserves the life of him who has it. In the day of prosperity be joyful, and in the day of adversity consider; God has made the one as well as the other, so that man may not find out anything that will be after him.

In my vain life I have seen everything; there is a righteous man who perishes in his righteousness, and there is a wicked man who prolongs his life in his evil-doing. Be not righteous overmuch, and do not make yourself overwise; why should you destroy yourself? It is good that you should take hold of this, and from that withhold not your hand; for he who fears God shall come forth from them all. Wisdom gives strength to the wise man more than ten rulers that are in a city. Surely there is not a righteous man on earth who does good and never sins.

All this I have tested by wisdom; I said, "I will be wise"; but it was far from me. That which is, is far off, and deep, very deep; who can find it out? I turned my mind to know and to search out wisdom and the sum of things, and to know the wickedness of folly and the foolishness which is madness. Behold, this is what I found, says the Preacher, adding one thing to another to find the sum, which my mind has sought repeatedly, but I have not found. One man among a thousand I found, but a woman among all these I have not found. Behold, this alone I found, that God made man upright, but they have sought out many devices.

KEEP THE KING'S command, and go from his presence when the matter is unpleasant, for he does whatever he pleases. He who obeys a command will meet no harm, and the mind of a wise man will know the time and way. For every matter has its time and way, although man's trouble lies heavy upon him, for he does not know what is to be. No man has power to retain the spirit, or authority over the day of death; there is no discharge from war, nor will wickedness deliver those who are given to it. All this I observed while applying my mind to all that is done under the sun, while man lords it over man to his hurt. Then I saw all the work of God, that man cannot find out the work that is done under the sun. Even though a wise man claims to know, he cannot find it out.

All this I laid to heart, examining it, how the righteous and the wise and their deeds are in the hand of God; whether it is love or hate man does not know. Everything before them is vanity, since one fate comes to all, to the righteous and the wicked, to the clean and the unclean, to him who sacrifices and him who does not sacrifice.

The hearts of men are full of evil and madness while they live, and after that they go to the dead. But he who is joined with the living has hope, for a living dog is better than a dead lion. The living know that they will die, but the dead know nothing.

Go, eat your bread with enjoyment, and

drink your wine with a merry heart, for God has already approved what you do. Enjoy life with the wife whom you love all the days of your vain life which he has given you under the sun. Whatever your hand finds to do, do it with your might, for there is no work or thought or knowledge or wisdom in death, to which you are going.

Again I saw that the race is not to the swift, nor the battle to the strong, nor bread to the wise, nor riches to the intelligent, nor favor to the men of skill; but time and chance happen to them all. For man does not know his time. Like fish which are taken in an evil net, so the sons of men are snared at an evil time, when it suddenly falls upon them.

I have also seen this example of wisdom under the sun, and it seemed great to me. There was a little city with few men in it, and a great king besieged it. But there was found in it a poor wise man, and he by his wisdom delivered the city. Yet no one remembered that poor man. But I say that wisdom is better than might, though the poor man's wisdom is despised, and his words are not heeded. The words of the wise heard in quiet are better than the shouting of a ruler among fools. Wisdom is better than weapons of war, but one sinner destroys much good.

There is an evil under the sun, as it were an error proceeding from the ruler: folly is set in many high places, and the rich sit in a low place. I have seen slaves on horses, and princes walking on foot like slaves.

Cast your bread upon the waters, for you will find it after many days. Give a portion to seven, or even to eight, for you know not what evil may happen on earth. If the clouds are full of rain, they empty themselves on the earth, and where a tree falls, there it will lie. As you do not know how the spirit comes to the bones in the womb of a woman with child, so you do not know the work of God who makes everything. In the morning sow your seed, and at evening withhold not your hand; for you do not know which will prosper, this or that, or whether both alike will be good.

Light is sweet, and it is pleasant for the eyes to behold the sun. If a man lives many years, let him rejoice in them all; but let him remember that the days of darkness will be many. All that comes is vanity.

Rejoice, O young man, in your youth, and let your heart cheer you; walk in the ways of your heart and the sight of your eyes. But know that for all these things God will bring you into judgment.

Remember also your Creator before the evil days come, and the years draw nigh, when you will say, "I have no pleasure in them"; before the sun and the light and the moon and the stars are darkened and the clouds return after the rain; in the day when the keepers of the house tremble, and the strong men are bent, and the grinders cease because they are few, and those that look through the windows are dimmed, and the doors on the street are shut; when the sound of the grinding is low, and one rises up at the voice of a bird, and all the daughters of song are brought low. They are afraid also of what is high, and terrors are in the way; the almond tree blossoms, the grasshopper drags itself along and desire fails; because man goes to his eternal home, and the mourners go about the streets; before the silver cord is snapped, or the golden bowl is broken, or the pitcher is broken at the fountain, or the wheel broken at the cistern, and the dust returns to the earth as it was, and the spirit returns to God who gave it. Vanity of vanities, says the Preacher; all is vanity.

BESIDES BEING WISE, the Preacher also taught the people knowledge, weighing and studying and arranging proverbs with great care. The Preacher sought to find pleasing words, and uprightly he wrote words of truth. The sayings of the wise are like goads, and like nails firmly fixed are the collected sayings which are given by one Shepherd. My son, beware of anything beyond these. Of making many books there is no end, and much study is a weariness of the flesh.

The end of the matter; all has been heard. Fear God, and keep his commandments; for this is the whole duty of man. For God will bring every deed into judgment, with every secret thing, whether good or evil.

SONG OF SOLOMON

Different from all other books of the Bible, the Song of Solomon is more like love poetry. It contains no outright mention of religion, and the word God does not occur even once. Its inclusion in the Jewish and Christian canon is due to its acceptance as an allegory of God's love for Israel, or of Christ's love for the church. The book is not a single poem, but a collection of several rather disconnected poems, which are spoken by characters as in a play. In places the sense is difficult to follow, but the theme is clear: mainly it is a dialogue between a rustic Jewish maiden (the Shulammite) and her lover, with several other people present as onlookers. Also known as the Song of Songs or Canticles, the book had long

been ascribed to Solomon. Modern scholars see it as a product of the third or
fourth century B.C.

————

THE SONG OF SONGS, which is Solomon's.

O that you would kiss me with the kisses
of your mouth!
For your love is better than wine,
your anointing oils are fragrant,
your name is oil poured out;
therefore the maidens love you.
Draw me after you, let us make haste.
The king has brought me into his
chambers.
We will exult and rejoice in you;
we will extol your love more than wine;
rightly do they love you.

I AM VERY dark, but comely,
O daughters of Jerusalem,
like the tents of Kedar,
like the curtains of Solomon.
Do not gaze at me because I am swarthy,

because the sun has scorched me.
My mother's sons were angry with me,
 they made me keeper of the vineyards;
 but my own vineyard I have not kept!
Tell me, you whom my soul loves,
 where you pasture your flock,
 where you make it lie down at noon;
for why should I be like one who wanders
 beside the flocks of your companions?

If you do not know,
 O fairest among women,
follow in the tracks of the flock,
 and pasture your kids
 beside the shepherds' tents.

I COMPARE YOU, my love,
 to a mare of Pharaoh's chariots.
Your cheeks are comely with ornaments,
 your neck with strings of jewels.
We will make you ornaments of gold,
 studded with silver.

While the king was on his couch,
 my nard gave forth its fragrance.
My beloved is to me a bag of myrrh,

that lies between my breasts.
My beloved is to me a cluster
   of henna blossoms
  in the vineyards of Engedi.

Behold, you are beautiful, my love;
  behold, you are beautiful;
  your eyes are doves.
Behold, you are beautiful, my beloved,
  truly lovely.
Our couch is green;
  the beams of our house are cedar,
  our rafters are pine.

I am a rose of Sharon,
  a lily of the valleys.
As a lily among brambles,
  so is my love among maidens.

As an apple tree among the trees
   of the wood,
  so is my beloved among young men.
With great delight I sat in his shadow,
  and his fruit was sweet to my taste.
He brought me to the banqueting house,
  and his banner over me was love.
Sustain me with raisins,

refresh me with apples;
  for I am sick with love.
O that his left hand were under my head,
  and that his right hand embraced me!
I adjure you, O daughters of Jerusalem,
that you stir not up nor awaken love
  until it please.

THE VOICE OF my beloved!
  Behold, he comes,
leaping upon the mountains,
  bounding over the hills.
My beloved is like a gazelle,
  or a young stag.
Behold, there he stands
  behind our wall,
gazing in at the windows,
  looking through the lattice.
My beloved speaks and says to me:
"Arise, my love, my fair one,
  and come away;
for lo, the winter is past,
  the rain is over and gone.
The flowers appear on the earth,
  the time of singing has come,
and the voice of the turtledove

is heard in our land.
The fig tree puts forth its figs,
  and the vines are in blossom;
  they give forth fragrance.
Arise, my love, my fair one,
  and come away.
O my dove, in the clefts of the rock,
  in the covert of the cliff,
let me see your face,
  let me hear your voice,
for your voice is sweet,
  and your face is comely.
Catch us the foxes,
  the little foxes,
that spoil the vineyards,
  for our vineyards are in blossom."

My beloved is mine and I am his,
  he pastures his flock among the lilies.
Until the day breathes
  and the shadows flee,
turn, my beloved, be like a gazelle,
  or a young stag upon rugged mountains.

UPON MY BED by night
  I sought him whom my soul loves;

I sought him, but found him not;
  I called him, but he gave no answer.
"I will rise now and go about the city,
  in the streets and in the squares;
I will seek him whom my soul loves."
  I sought him, but found him not.
The watchmen found me,
  as they went about in the city.
"Have you seen him whom my soul loves?"
Scarcely had I passed them,
  when I found him whom my soul loves.
I held him, and would not let him go
    until I had brought him into my
      mother's house,
    and into the chamber of her
      that conceived me.
I adjure you, O daughters of Jerusalem,
that you stir not up nor awaken love
    until it please.

WHAT IS THAT coming up from the
      wilderness,
    like a column of smoke,
perfumed with myrrh and frankincense,
    with all the fragrant powders
      of the merchant?

Behold, it is the litter of Solomon!
About it are sixty mighty men
   of the mighty men of Israel,
all girt with swords
   and expert in war,
each with his sword at his thigh,
   against alarms by night.
King Solomon made himself a palanquin
   from the wood of Lebanon.
He made its posts of silver,
   its back of gold, its seat of purple;
it was lovingly wrought within
   by the daughters of Jerusalem.
Go forth and behold King Solomon,
   on the day of the gladness of his heart.

BEHOLD, YOU ARE beautiful, my love,
   behold, you are beautiful!
Your eyes are doves behind your veil.
Your hair is like a flock of goats,
   moving down the slopes of Gilead.
Your teeth are like a flock
     of shorn ewes
   that have come up from the washing.
Your lips are like a scarlet thread,
   and your mouth is lovely.

Your cheeks are like halves
    of a pomegranate
behind your veil.
Your neck is like the tower of David,
    built for an arsenal,
whereon hang a thousand bucklers,
    all of them shields of warriors.
Your two breasts are like two fawns,
    twins of a gazelle,
    that feed among the lilies.
Until the day breathes
    and the shadows flee,
I will hie me to the mountain of myrrh
    and the hill of frankincense.
You are all fair, my love;
    there is no flaw in you.
Come with me from Lebanon, my bride;
    come with me from Lebanon.
Depart from the peak of Amana,
    from the peak of Senir and Hermon.
You have ravished my heart, my sister,
    my bride,
    you have ravished my heart with
      a glance of your eyes,
    with one jewel of your necklace.
How sweet is your love, my sister,
    my bride!

how much better is your love than wine,
and the fragrance of your oils
    than any spice!
Your lips distil nectar, my bride;
    honey and milk are under your tongue;
the scent of your garments is like the scent
        of Lebanon.
A garden locked is my sister, my bride,
    a garden locked, a fountain sealed.
Your shoots are an orchard
    of pomegranates
    with all choicest fruits,
    with all trees of frankincense,
myrrh and aloes,
    with all chief spices—
a garden fountain, a well of living water,
    and flowing streams from Lebanon.

Awake, O north wind,
    and come, O south wind!
Blow upon my garden,
    let its fragrance be wafted abroad.
Let my beloved come to his garden,
    and eat its choicest fruits.

I come to my garden, my sister, my bride,
    I gather my myrrh with my spice,

I eat my honeycomb with my honey,
I drink my wine with my milk.

I SLEPT, BUT my heart was awake.
Hark! my beloved is knocking.
"Open to me, my sister, my love,
    my dove, my perfect one;
for my head is wet with dew,
    my locks with the drops of the night."
I had put off my garment,
    how could I put it on?
I had bathed my feet,
    how could I soil them?
My beloved put his hand to the latch,
    and my heart was thrilled within me.
I arose to open to my beloved,
    and my hands dripped with myrrh,
my fingers with liquid myrrh,
    upon the handles of the bolt.
I opened to my beloved,
    but my beloved had turned and gone.
My soul failed me when he spoke.
I sought him, but found him not;
    I called him, but he gave no answer.
The watchmen found me,
    as they went about in the city;

they beat me, they wounded me,
   they took away my mantle,
   those watchmen of the walls.
I adjure you, O daughters of Jerusalem,
   if you find my beloved,
that you tell him
   I am sick with love.

What is your beloved more
   than another beloved,
   O fairest among women?
What is your beloved more
   than another beloved,
   that you thus adjure us?

My beloved is all radiant and ruddy,
   distinguished among ten thousand.
His head is the finest gold;
   his locks are wavy,
   black as a raven.
His eyes are like doves
   beside springs of water.
His cheeks are like beds of spices,
   yielding fragrance.
His lips are lilies,
   distilling liquid myrrh.
His arms are rounded gold,

set with jewels.
His body is ivory work,
  encrusted with sapphires.
His legs are alabaster columns,
  set upon bases of gold.
His appearance is like Lebanon,
  choice as the cedars.
His speech is most sweet,
  and he is altogether desirable.
This is my beloved,
  O daughters of Jerusalem.

Whither has your beloved gone,
  O fairest among women?
Whither has your beloved turned,
  that we may seek him with you?

My beloved has gone down to his garden,
  to the beds of spices,
to pasture his flock in the gardens,
  and to gather lilies.
I am my beloved's and my beloved is mine;
  he pastures his flock among the lilies.

You ARE BEAUTIFUL as Tirzah, my love,
  comely as Jerusalem,

terrible as an army with banners.
Turn away your eyes from me,
for they disturb me.
There are sixty queens and eighty
concubines,
and maidens without number.
My dove, my perfect one, is only one,
the darling of her mother,
flawless to her that bore her.
The maidens saw her and
called her happy;
the queens and concubines also,
and they praised her.
"Who is this that looks forth
like the dawn,
fair as the moon, bright as the sun,
terrible as an army with banners?"

I WENT DOWN to the nut orchard,
to look at the blossoms
of the valley,
to see whether the vines had budded,
whether the pomegranates were
in bloom.
Before I was aware, my fancy set me
in a chariot beside my prince.

RETURN, RETURN, O Shulammite,
  return, return, that we may look
    upon you.
Why should you look upon
    the Shulammite,
  as upon a dance before two armies?

How graceful are your feet in sandals,
  O queenly maiden!
Your rounded thighs are like jewels,
  the work of a master hand.
Your navel is a rounded bowl
  that never lacks mixed wine.
Your belly is a heap of wheat,
  encircled with lilies.
Your two breasts are like two fawns,
  twins of a gazelle.
Your neck is like an ivory tower.
Your eyes are pools in Heshbon,
  by the gate of Bath-rabbim.
Your head crowns you like Carmel,
  and your flowing locks are like purple;
  a king is held captive in the tresses.

How fair and pleasant you are,
  O loved one, delectable maiden!
You are stately as a palm tree,

and your breasts are like its clusters.
I say I will climb the palm tree
   and lay hold of its branches.
Oh, may your breasts be like clusters
    of the vine,
   and the scent of your breath like apples,
and your kisses like the best wine
   that goes down smoothly,
   gliding over lips and teeth.

I AM MY beloved's,
   and his desire is for me.
Come, my beloved,
   let us go forth into the fields,
   and lodge in the villages;
let us go out early to the vineyards,
   and see whether the vines have budded,
whether the grape blossoms have opened
   and the pomegranates are in bloom.
There I will give you my love.
The mandrakes give forth fragrance,
   and over our doors are all
    choice fruits,
new as well as old,
   which I have laid up for you,
    O my beloved.

WHO IS THAT coming up from
   the wilderness,
  leaning upon her beloved?

Under the apple tree I awakened you.
There your mother was in travail with you,
   there she who bore you was in travail.

Set me as a seal upon your heart,
   as a seal upon your arm;
for love is strong as death,
   jealousy is cruel as the grave.
Its flashes are flashes of fire,
   a most vehement flame.
Many waters cannot quench love,
   neither can floods drown it.
If a man offered for love
   all the wealth of his house,
   it would be utterly scorned.

MAKE HASTE, MY beloved,
   and be like a gazelle
or a young stag
   upon the mountains of spices.

ISAIAH

Isaiah received his call to prophesy in the form of a vision in the temple at Jerusalem about 740 B.C. Thus he lived during the critical period in which Israel was annexed by the Assyrians, and Judah became a tributary, threatened with the same fate. The first part of the book warns the sinners of Israel and Judah that God will punish their faithlessness through the Assyrians, but it also forecasts the wonderful reign of the Prince of Peace. The next section tells of Sennacherib's attack in 701 and how God kept Jerusalem safe—the greatest event of Isaiah's time. The latter part of the book, which appears to be of a later date, emphasizes God's majesty and mercy. In it the writer declares that God has forgiven the sins of Israel so that the people's sufferings will be at an end.

The prominent part played by Isaiah in his country's affairs made him a national figure, but he was also a poet of genius. His brilliant style and fresh imagery make his work preeminent in the literature of the Bible. From New Testament times onward, his prophecies of the coming Messiah have frequently been referred by Christian writers to the historic Christ.

THE VISION OF Isaiah the son of Amoz, which he saw concerning Judah and Jerusalem in the days of Uzziah, Jotham, Ahaz, and Hezekiah, kings of Judah.

Hear, O heavens, and give ear, O earth; for the LORD has spoken: "Sons have I reared, but they have rebelled against me. The ox knows its owner, and the ass its master's crib; but Israel does not know, my people do not understand."

Ah, sinful nation, a people laden with iniquity, offspring of evildoers, sons who deal corruptly! They have forsaken the LORD, despised the Holy One of Israel;

they are utterly estranged. Why will you still be smitten, that you continue to rebel? The whole head is sick, and the whole heart faint. From the sole of the foot to the head, there is no soundness in it, but bruises and sores and bleeding wounds. Your country lies desolate, your cities are burned; in your very presence aliens devour your land; it is desolate, as overthrown by aliens. And the daughter of Zion is left like a booth in a vineyard, like a besieged city. If the LORD of hosts had not left us a few survivors, we should have been like Sodom and Gomorrah.

Hear the word of the LORD, you rulers of Sodom! Give ear to the teaching of our God, you people of Gomorrah!

"What to me is the multitude of your sacrifices? I have had enough of burnt offerings. I do not delight in the blood of bulls. When you appear before me, who requires of you this trampling of my courts? Bring no more vain offerings; incense is an abomination to me. New moon and sabbath and solemn assembly I cannot endure. When you spread forth your hands, I will hide my eyes from you;

though you make many prayers, I will not listen; your hands are full of blood.

"Wash yourselves; make yourselves clean; cease to do evil, learn to do good; seek justice, correct oppression; defend the fatherless, plead for the widow.

"Come now, let us reason together, says the LORD: though your sins are like scarlet, they shall be as white as snow; though they are red like crimson, they shall become like wool. If you are willing and obedient, you shall eat the good of the land; but if you refuse and rebel, you shall be devoured by the sword; for the mouth of the LORD has spoken."

How the faithful city has become a harlot, she that was full of justice! Righteousness lodged in her, but now murderers. Your silver has become dross, your wine mixed with water. Your princes are rebels and companions of thieves. Every one loves a bribe and runs after gifts. They do not defend the fatherless, and the widow's cause does not come to them. Therefore the LORD, the Mighty One of Israel, says: "Ah, I will vent my wrath on my enemies. I will turn my hand against you and smelt away your dross as with lye. And I will restore your judges as at the beginning. Afterward you shall be called the faithful city."

Zion shall be redeemed by justice, and those in her who repent, by righteousness. But rebels and sinners shall be destroyed together, and those who forsake the LORD shall be consumed. You shall be ashamed of the oaks in which you delighted, and blush for the gardens you have chosen. For you shall be like an oak whose leaf withers, and like a garden without water. The strong shall become straw, and his work a spark, and both of them shall burn together, with none to quench them.

THE WORD WHICH Isaiah the son of Amoz saw concerning Judah and Jerusalem.

It shall come to pass in the latter days that the mountain of the house of the LORD shall be established as the highest of the mountains, and all the nations shall flow to it. Many peoples shall come, and say: "Come, let us go up to the mountain of the LORD, that he may teach us his ways and that we may walk in his paths." For out of Zion shall go forth the law, and the word of the LORD from Jerusalem. He shall judge between the nations, and shall decide for many peoples; they shall beat their swords into plowshares, and their spears into pruning hooks; nation shall not lift up sword against nation, neither shall they learn war any more.

O HOUSE OF Jacob, come, let us walk in the light of the LORD.

FOR THOU HAST rejected thy people, the house of Jacob, because they are full of diviners and soothsayers like the Philistines; and they strike hands with foreigners. Their land is filled with silver and gold, with horses and chariots; and they bow down to idols their own fingers have made. So men are brought low—forgive them not!

Enter into the rock, and hide from the terror of the LORD. For the LORD of hosts has a day against all that is proud and lifted up; against all the cedars of Lebanon and all the lofty hills; against every high tower and fortified wall; against all the beautiful ships of Tarshish. And the haughtiness of man shall be humbled and the LORD alone exalted in that day. In that day men will cast forth their idols to the moles and the bats, to enter the caverns of the rocks from before the terror of the LORD and the glory of his majesty, when he rises to terrify the earth.

Turn away from man in whose nostrils is breath, for of what account is he?

For behold, the LORD enters into judgment with the elders and princes of his people: "It is you who have devoured the vineyard, the spoil of the poor is in your houses. What do you mean by crushing my people, by grinding the face of the poor?"

And the LORD said: Because the daughters of Zion are haughty and walk with outstretched necks, glancing wantonly with their eyes, mincing along as they go, tinkling with their feet; the Lord will smite with a scab the heads of the daughters of Zion.

In that day the Lord will take away the finery of the anklets, the headbands, and the crescents; the pendants, the bracelets, and the scarfs; the headdresses, the armlets, the sashes, the perfume boxes, and the amulets; the signet rings and nose rings; the festal robes, the mantles, the cloaks, and the handbags; the garments of gauze, the linen garments, the turbans, and the veils. Instead of perfume there will be rottenness; instead of a girdle, a rope; instead of well-set hair, baldness; and instead of a rich robe, a girding of sackcloth; instead of beauty, shame.

Your men shall fall by the sword and your mighty men in battle. Her gates shall lament and mourn; ravaged, she shall sit upon the ground. Seven women shall take hold of one man in that day, saying, "We will eat our own bread and wear our own clothes, only let us be called by your name; take away our reproach."

In that day the branch of the LORD shall be beautiful and glorious, and the fruit of the land shall be the pride and glory of the survivors of Israel.

LET ME SING for my beloved a love song concerning his vineyard: My beloved had a vineyard on a very fertile hill. He digged it and cleared it of stones, and planted it with choice vines; he built a watchtower in the midst of it, and hewed out a wine vat in it; and he looked for it to yield grapes, but it yielded wild grapes.

Now, O men of Judah, judge, I pray you, between me and my vineyard. What more was there to do for my vineyard that I have not done in it? When I looked for it to yield grapes, why did it yield wild grapes? Now I will tell you what I will do to my vineyard. I will remove its hedge, and it shall be devoured and trampled down. I will make it a waste; it shall not be pruned or hoed, and briers shall grow up; I will also command the clouds that they rain no rain upon it.

For the vineyard of the LORD of hosts is the house of Israel, and the men of Judah are his pleasant planting; and he looked for justice, but behold, bloodshed; for righteousness, but behold, a cry!

WOE TO THOSE who join house to house, who add field to field until there is no more room and you dwell alone in the land. The LORD of hosts has sworn in my hearing: "Surely many houses shall be desolate, large and beautiful houses, without inhabitant. For a field shall yield but a tenth of the seed put in."

Woe to those who rise early in the morning, that they may run after strong drink, who tarry late into the evening till wine inflames them! They have harp and flute and wine at their feasts; but they do not regard the deeds of the LORD, or see the work of his hands.

Therefore my people go into exile for want of knowledge; their honored men are dying of hunger, their multitude of thirst. Therefore the grave has enlarged its appetite beyond measure, and the nobility of Jerusalem and her multitude go down. Men are brought low, and the eyes of the haughty are humbled. But the LORD of hosts is exalted in justice, and holy in righteousness. Then shall lambs graze as in their pasture, fatlings and kids shall feed among the ruins.

Woe to those who draw iniquity with cords of falsehood, who draw sin as with cart ropes; who say: "Let him make haste, that we may see his work; let the purpose of the Holy One draw near, that we may

know it!" Woe to those who call evil good
and good evil! Woe to those who are wise
in their own eyes! Woe to those who are
heroes at drinking wine, but acquit the
guilty for a bribe and deprive the innocent
of his right!

Therefore, as the tongue of fire devours
the stubble, and dry grass sinks in the
flame, so their root will be as rottenness,
and their blossom go up like dust; for they
have despised the word of the Holy One of
Israel. Therefore the anger of the LORD
was kindled against his people, and he
stretched out his hand and smote them,
and the mountains quaked; and their
corpses were as refuse in the streets. For all
this his anger is not turned away and his
hand is stretched out still. He will raise a
signal for a nation afar off, and whistle for
it from the ends of the earth; and lo, speedily it comes! None stumbles, not a waistcloth is loose; their arrows are sharp, all
their bows are bent. Like young lions they
roar; they seize their prey, and none can
rescue. They will growl over it on that day,
like the roaring of the sea. And if one look
to the land, behold, darkness and distress.

IN THE YEAR that King Uzziah died I saw
the Lord sitting upon a throne, high and
lifted up; and his train filled the temple.
Above him stood the seraphim; each had
six wings: with two he covered his face,
and with two he covered his feet, and
with two he flew. And one called to another and said: "Holy, holy, holy is the
LORD of hosts; the whole earth is full of
his glory." And the foundations shook at
the voice of him who called, and the
house was filled with smoke. And I said:
"Woe is me! For I am lost; for I am a
man of unclean lips, and I dwell in the
midst of a people of unclean lips; for my
eyes have seen the King, the LORD of
hosts!"

Then flew one of the seraphim to me,
having in his hand a burning coal which
he had taken with tongs from the altar.
And he touched my mouth, and said:
"Behold, this has touched your lips; your
guilt is taken away, and your sin forgiven." And I heard the voice of the Lord
saying, "Whom shall I send, and who
will go for us?" Then I said, "Here am I!
Send me."

And he said, "Go, and say to this people: 'Hear and hear, but do not understand; see and see, but do not perceive.' Make the heart of this people fat, and their ears heavy, and shut their eyes; lest they see with their eyes, and hear with their ears, and understand with their hearts, and turn and be healed."

Then I said, "How long, O Lord?"

And he said: "Until cities lie waste without inhabitant, and houses without men, and the forsaken places are many in the midst of the land. And though a tenth remain in it, it will be burned again, like a terebinth or an oak, whose stump remains standing when it is felled." The holy seed is its stump.

IN THE DAYS of Ahaz the king of Judah, Rezin the king of Syria and Pekah the son of Remaliah, king of Israel, came up to Jerusalem to wage war against it, but they could not conquer it. When the house of David was told, "Syria is in league with Ephraim," his heart and the heart of his people shook as the trees of the forest shake before the wind.

And the LORD said to Isaiah, "Go forth
to meet Ahaz, you and Shear-jashub your
son, on the highway to the Fuller's Field.
Say to him, 'Do not let your heart be faint
because of these two smoldering stumps of
firebrands, Rezin and the son of Remaliah.
Because Syria, with Ephraim, has devised
evil against you, saying, "Let us go up
against Judah and conquer it for ourselves,
and set up the son of Tabe-el as king,"
thus says the Lord GOD: It shall not come
to pass. For the head of Syria is Damascus,
and the head of Damascus is Rezin. And
the head of Ephraim is Samaria, and the
head of Samaria is Pekah the son of Remaliah. If you will not believe, you shall not
be established.' "

Again the LORD spoke to Ahaz, "Ask a
sign of the LORD your God; let it be deep
as Sheol or high as heaven." But Ahaz
said, "I will not ask, and I will not put the
LORD to the test."

And Isaiah said, "O house of David! Is
it too little for you to weary men, that you
weary my God also? Therefore the LORD
himself will give you a sign. Behold, a
young woman shall conceive and bear a

son, and shall call his name Immanuel. He shall eat curds and honey when he knows how to refuse the evil and choose the good. For before the child knows evil from good, the land whose kings you dread will be deserted. The LORD will bring upon you and your father's house such days as have not come since Ephraim departed from Judah."

Then the LORD said to me, "Take a large tablet and write upon it, 'Belonging to Maher-shalal-hashbaz.' " ("The spoil speeds, the prey hastes.") I got reliable witnesses to attest for me. And I went to the prophetess, and she conceived and bore a son. Then the LORD said, "Call his name Maher-shalal-hashbaz; for before he knows how to cry 'Father' or 'Mother,' the wealth of Damascus and the spoil of Samaria will be carried away. Because this people have refused the waters of Shiloah that flow gently, and melt in fear before Rezin and the son of Remaliah; therefore, behold, the Lord is bringing up against them the waters of the mighty River, the king of Assyria and all his glory. It will rise over all its banks and sweep on into Judah,

reaching even to the neck; and its out-
spread wings will fill the breadth of your
land, O Immanuel."

Give ear, all you far countries; gird
yourselves and be dismayed. Take counsel
together, but it will come to nought; for
God is with us.

For the LORD spoke thus to me with his
strong hand upon me, and warned me:
"Do not call conspiracy all that this people
call conspiracy, nor fear what they fear.
But the LORD of hosts, him you shall regard as holy; let him be your fear. And he
will become a stone of offense, and a rock
of stumbling to both houses of Israel, a
trap to the inhabitants of Jerusalem. And
many shall stumble thereon; they shall fall
and be broken; they shall be snared and
taken."

BIND UP THE testimony, seal the teaching
among my disciples. I will wait for the
LORD, who is hiding his face from the
house of Jacob, and I will hope in him.
Behold, I and the children whom the LORD
has given me are signs and portents from
the LORD of hosts, who dwells on Mount

Zion. And when they say to you, "Consult the mediums and the wizards who chirp and mutter," should not a people consult their God? Should they consult the dead on behalf of the living? To the teaching and to the testimony! Surely for this which they speak there is no dawn. They will pass through the land, greatly distressed and hungry; and they will curse their king and their God, and turn their faces upward; and they will look to the earth, but behold, distress and the gloom of anguish; and they will be thrust into thick darkness.

But there will be no gloom for her that was in anguish. In the latter time he will make glorious the land beyond the Jordan, Galilee of the nations.

The people who walked in darkness have seen a great light; those who dwelt in a land of deep darkness, on them has light shined. Thou hast multiplied the nation, thou hast increased its joy; they rejoice before thee as with joy at the harvest. For the yoke of his burden and the rod of his oppressor thou hast broken. Every boot of the tramping warrior in battle tumult and every garment rolled in blood will be burned as fuel for the fire.

For to us a child is born, to us a son is given; and the government will be upon his shoulder, and his name will be called "Wonderful Counselor, Mighty God, Everlasting Father, Prince of Peace." Of the increase of his government and of peace there will be no end, upon the throne of David, and over his kingdom, to establish it, and to uphold it with justice and with righteousness from this time forth and for evermore. The zeal of the LORD of hosts will do this.

THE LORD HAS sent a word against Jacob, and it will light upon Israel; and all the people will know, Ephraim and the inhabitants of Samaria, who say in pride and in arrogance of heart: "The bricks have fallen, but we will build with dressed stones; the sycamores have been cut down, but we will put cedars in their place."

So the LORD stirs up their enemies. The Syrians on the east and the Philistines on the west devour Israel with open mouth. For all this his anger is not turned away and his hand is stretched out still.

The people did not turn to him who smote them. So the LORD cut off from Israel head and tail, palm branch and reed in one day—the elder is the head, and the prophet who teaches lies is the tail; for those who lead this people lead them astray. Therefore the Lord does not rejoice over their young men, and has no compassion on their fatherless and widows; for every one is godless and every mouth speaks folly. For all this his anger is not turned away and his hand is stretched out still.

Through the wrath of the LORD of hosts the land is burned, and the people are like fuel for the fire; no man spares his brother. Each devours his neighbor's flesh, Manasseh Ephraim, and Ephraim Manasseh, and together they are against Judah. For all this his anger is not turned away and his hand is stretched out still.

THERE SHALL COME forth a shoot from the stump of Jesse, and a branch shall grow out of his roots. And the Spirit of the LORD shall rest upon him, the spirit of wisdom and understanding, the spirit of counsel and might, the spirit of knowledge and the fear of the LORD. And his delight shall be in the fear of the LORD.

He shall not judge by what his eyes see, or decide by what his ears hear; but with righteousness he shall judge the poor and the meek of the earth; with the breath of his lips he shall slay the wicked. Righteousness shall be the girdle of his waist and faithfulness the girdle of his loins.

The wolf shall dwell with the lamb, and the leopard shall lie down with the kid, and the calf and the lion and the fatling together; and a little child shall lead them. The suckling child shall play over the hole of the asp, and the weaned child shall put his hand on the adder's den. They shall not hurt or destroy in all my holy mountain; for the earth shall be full of the knowledge of the LORD as the waters cover the sea.

In that day the root of Jesse shall stand as an ensign to the peoples; him shall the nations seek, and his dwellings shall be glorious. In that day the Lord will extend his hand yet a second time to assemble the outcasts of Israel, and gather the dispersed of Judah from the four corners of the earth. Ephraim shall not be jealous of Judah, and Judah shall not harass Ephraim. But together they shall swoop down upon the Philistines, and put forth their hand against Edom and Moab. The LORD will utterly destroy the tongue of the sea of Egypt. And there will be a highway from Assyria for the remnant which is left of his people, as there was for Israel when they came up from the land of Egypt.

You will say in that day: "I will give thanks to thee, O LORD, for though thou wast angry with me, thy anger turned away, and thou didst comfort me. Behold, God is my salvation; I will trust, and will not be afraid; for the Lord GOD is my strength and my song." With joy you will draw water from the wells of salvation. And you will say: "Give thanks to the LORD; make known his deeds among the nations, proclaim that his name is exalted. Shout, and sing for joy, O inhabitant of Zion, for great in your midst is the Holy One of Israel."

THE ORACLE CONCERNING Babylon which Isaiah the son of Amoz saw.

On a bare hill raise a signal, cry aloud to them; wave the hand for them to enter the gates of the nobles. I myself have commanded my consecrated ones, my mighty men, to execute my anger. Hark, a tumult on the mountains, an uproar of nations gathering together! The LORD of hosts is mustering a host for battle. They come from the end of the heavens, the LORD and the weapons of his indignation, to destroy the whole earth.

Wail, for the day of the LORD is near; as destruction from the Almighty it will come! Therefore every man's heart will melt; pangs and agony will seize them; they will be in anguish like a woman in travail. They will look aghast at one another; their faces will be aflame.

Behold, the day of the LORD comes, cruel, with fierce anger. The stars and the moon will not shed their light; and the sun will be dark at its rising. I will punish the world for its evil; I will put an end to the pride of the arrogant and lay low the ruthless. I will make men more rare than fine gold. Therefore I will make the heavens tremble, and the earth will be shaken out

of its place at the wrath of the LORD of
hosts in the day of his anger. And like
sheep with none to gather them, every
man will flee to his own land. Whoever is
caught will fall by the sword. Their infants
will be dashed in pieces, their houses plundered, their wives ravished.

The LORD will have compassion on Jacob and will again choose Israel, and will
set them in their own land, and aliens will
join them and will cleave to the house of
Jacob. The house of Israel will take captive
those who were their captors, and rule
over those who oppressed them. When the
LORD has given you rest from your pain
and turmoil and the hard service which
you were made to serve, you will take up
this taunt against the king of Babylon:

"How the oppressor has ceased! The
LORD has broken the scepter of rulers that
smote the peoples with unceasing blows.
The whole earth is at rest; they break forth
into singing. The cedars of Lebanon rejoice
at you, saying, 'Since you were laid low, no
hewer comes up against us.' Sheol beneath
is stirred up to meet you; it rouses the
shades to greet you. All who were kings of

the nations will say: 'You too have become as weak as we!' Your pomp is brought down; maggots are the bed beneath you, and worms are your covering.

"How you are fallen from heaven, O Day Star, son of Dawn! How you are cut to the ground, you who laid the nations low! You said in your heart, 'I will set my throne above the clouds, I will make myself like the Most High.' But you are brought down to the Pit. Those who see you will stare at you and ponder over you: 'Is this the man who shook kingdoms, who made the world like a desert and did not let his prisoners go home?' All the kings of the nations lie in glory, each in his own tomb; but you are cast out like a loathed untimely birth. You will not be joined with them in burial, because you have destroyed your land, you have slain your people.

"May the descendants of evildoers nevermore be named! Prepare slaughter for his sons because of the guilt of their fathers, lest they rise and possess the earth."

THE LORD OF hosts has sworn: "As I have planned, so shall it be, that I will break the

Assyrian in my land and upon my mountains trample him under foot; and his yoke shall depart from them, and his burden from their shoulder." This is the purpose that the LORD of hosts has purposed, and who will annul it? His hand is stretched out over all the nations, and who will turn it back?

IN THE YEAR that King Ahaz died came this oracle: "Rejoice not, O Philistia, all of you, that the rod which smote you is broken, for from the serpent's root will come forth an adder, and its fruit will be a flying serpent. The poor will feed and the needy lie down in safety, but I will kill your root with famine. Wail, O city, melt in fear, all of you! For smoke comes out of the north, and there is no straggler in his ranks."

What will one answer the messengers of the nation? "The LORD has founded Zion, and in her the afflicted of his people find refuge."

AN ORACLE CONCERNING Damascus.

Behold, Damascus will cease to be a city and become a heap of ruins. Her cities, deserted for ever, will be for flocks, which will lie down, and none will make them afraid. The fortress will disappear from Ephraim, and the kingdom from Damascus; and the remnant of Syria will be like the glory of the children of Israel.

And in that day the glory of Jacob will be brought low, and the fat of his flesh will grow lean. And it shall be as when the reaper gathers grain in the Valley of Rephaim. Gleanings will be left in it, as when an olive tree is beaten—two or three berries in the highest bough, four or five on a fruit tree, says the LORD God of Israel.

For you have forgotten the God of your salvation, and have not remembered the Rock of your refuge; therefore, though you plant pleasant plants and set out slips of an alien god, though you make them blossom on the day you plant them, yet the harvest will flee away in a day of grief and incurable pain.

Ah, the thunder of many peoples, they thunder like the thundering of the sea! The nations roar like the roaring of mighty waters; but he will rebuke them, and they

will flee, chased like whirling dust before
the storm. At evening time, behold, terror!
Before morning, they are no more! This is
the portion of those who plunder us.

AH, LAND OF whirring wings which is beyond the rivers of Ethiopia; which sends
ambassadors by the Nile, in vessels of pa-
pyrus upon the waters! Go, you swift messengers, to a nation tall and smooth, to a
people feared near and far, a nation mighty
and conquering, whose land the rivers
divide.

All you inhabitants of the world, when a
signal is raised on the mountains, look!
When a trumpet is blown, hear!

For thus the LORD said to me: "I will
quietly look from my dwelling like clear
heat in sunshine, like a cloud of dew in the
heat of harvest."

For before the harvest, when the blossom is over, and the flower becomes a
ripening grape, he will cut off the shoots
with pruning hooks, and the spreading
branches he will hew away. They shall all
of them be left to the birds of prey of the
mountains and to the beasts of the earth.

At that time gifts will be brought to the LORD of hosts from a people tall and smooth, whose land the rivers divide.

AN ORACLE CONCERNING Egypt.

Behold, the LORD is riding on a swift cloud and comes to Egypt; the idols of Egypt will tremble and the heart of the Egyptians melt within them. I will stir up Egyptians against Egyptians, and they will fight, every man against his brother; and the spirit within them will be emptied out, and I will confound their plans. They will consult the idols and the mediums and the wizards; and I will give over the Egyptians into the hand of a hard master, says the LORD of hosts. And the waters of the Nile will be dried up; its canals will become foul, reeds and rushes will rot away, and all that is sown on the brink of the Nile will dry up and be no more. The fishermen will lament, all who cast hook in the Nile and spread nets upon it. The workers in combed flax will be in despair, and the weavers of white cotton. Those who are the pillars of the land will be crushed.

The princes of Zoan and Memphis have

become fools; the wise counselors of Pharaoh give stupid counsel. How can you say to Pharaoh, "I am a son of the wise, a son of ancient kings"? Where then are your wise men? Let them tell you what the LORD of hosts has purposed against Egypt. Those who are the cornerstones of her tribes have led Egypt astray. The LORD has mingled within her a spirit of confusion; and they have made her stagger as a drunken man in all her doings. And there will be nothing for Egypt which head or tail, palm branch or reed, may do.

In that day the Egyptians will tremble with fear before the hand which the LORD of hosts shakes over them. And Judah will become a terror to them because of the purpose which the LORD has purposed against them.

In that day there will be five cities in the land of Egypt which speak the language of Canaan and swear allegiance to the LORD of hosts. There will be an altar to the LORD in the midst of Egypt, and a pillar to the LORD at its border. It will be a sign and a witness; when they cry to the LORD because of oppressors he will send them a savior, and will defend and deliver them. The LORD will make himself known to the Egyptians; and they will know him and worship with sacrifice; they will make vows to the LORD and perform them. And the LORD will smite Egypt, smiting and healing, and they will return to the LORD, and he will heed their supplications and heal them.

In that day there will be a highway from Egypt to Assyria, and the Assyrian will come into Egypt, and the Egyptian into Assyria, and the Egyptians will worship with the Assyrians. Israel will be the third with Egypt and Assyria, a blessing in the midst of the earth, whom the LORD of hosts has blessed, saying, "Blessed be Egypt my people, and Assyria the work of my hands, and Israel my heritage."

THE ORACLE CONCERNING Tyre and Sidon.

Wail, O ships of Tarshish, for Tyre is laid waste, without house or haven! From the land of Cyprus it is revealed. Be still, O merchants of Sidon; your messengers passed over the sea; your revenue was the harvest of the Nile; you were the merchant of the nations. Be ashamed, O Sidon, for the sea has spoken, saying: "I have neither travailed nor given birth."

When the report comes to Egypt, they will be in anguish over Tyre. Pass over to Tarshish, wail, O inhabitants of the coast! Is this your exultant city whose origin is from days of old, whose feet carried her to settle afar? Who has purposed this against Tyre, the bestower of crowns, whose traders were the honored of the earth?

The LORD of hosts has purposed it, to defile the pride of all glory, to dishonor all the honored of the earth. Overflow your land like the Nile, O daughter of Tarshish; there is no restraint any more. He has stretched out his hand over the sea, he has shaken the kingdoms; the LORD has given command concerning Canaan to destroy its strongholds.

Behold the land of the Chaldeans! This is the people; it was not Assyria. They destined Tyre for wild beasts. They erected their siege towers, they razed her palaces, they made her a ruin.

In that day Tyre will be forgotten for seventy years, like the days of one king. At the end of seventy years, it will happen to Tyre as in the song of the harlot: "Take a harp, go about the city, O forgotten harlot! Make sweet melody, sing many songs, that you may be remembered."

At the end of seventy years, the LORD will visit Tyre, and she will return to her hire, and will play the harlot with all the kingdoms of the world. Her merchandise and her hire will be dedicated to the LORD; it will supply abundant food and fine clothing for those who dwell before the LORD.

ON THIS MOUNTAIN the LORD of hosts will make a feast for all peoples. He will destroy the veil that is spread over all nations. He will swallow up death for ever, and the Lord GOD will wipe away tears from all faces, and the reproach of his people he will take away from all the earth; for the LORD has spoken.

This song will be sung in the land of Judah: "We have a strong city; he sets up salvation as walls and bulwarks. Open the gates, that the nation which keeps faith may enter in. Thou dost keep him in perfect peace, whose mind is stayed on thee, because he trusts in thee. Trust in the LORD for ever, for the LORD GOD is an everlasting rock. He has brought low the lofty city; he casts it to the dust, and the foot tramples it, the feet of the poor."

Thou dost make smooth the way of the righteous. In the path of thy judgments, O LORD, we wait for thee; thy memorial name is the desire of our soul. My soul yearns for thee. For when thy judgments are in the earth, the inhabitants learn righteousness. If favor is shown to the wicked, he does not learn; he deals perversely. O LORD, thy hand is lifted up, but they see it not. Let them be ashamed. Let the fire for thy adversaries consume them.

O LORD, thou wilt ordain peace for us, thou hast wrought for us all our works. O LORD our God, other lords besides thee have ruled over us, but thy name alone we acknowledge. They are dead, they will not live; they are shades, they will not arise; to that end thou hast wiped out all remembrance of them. But thou, O LORD, thou hast increased the nation; thou art glorified.

O Lord, in distress they sought thee when thy chastening was upon them. Like a woman with child, who writhes and cries out when she is near her time, so were we because of thee, O Lord; we were with child, we writhed, we have as it were brought forth wind. We have wrought no deliverance in the earth.

Thy dead shall live, their bodies shall rise. O dwellers in the dust, awake and sing for joy! For thy dew is a dew of light, and on the land of the shades thou wilt let it fall.

Come, my people, enter your chambers, and shut your doors behind you; hide yourselves for a little while. For behold, the Lord is coming forth out of his place to punish the inhabitants of the earth for their iniquity, and the earth will disclose the blood shed upon her, and will no more cover her slain.

In that day the Lord with his hard and great and strong sword will punish Leviathan the fleeing serpent; he will slay the dragon that is in the sea.

In that day: "A pleasant vineyard, sing of it! I the Lord am its keeper; every moment I water it. Lest any one harm it, I guard it night and day; I have no wrath. Would that I had thorns and briers to battle! I would set out against them, I would burn them up together. Or let them lay hold of my protection, let them make peace with me."

In days to come Jacob shall take root, Israel shall blossom and put forth shoots, and fill the whole world with fruit.

Have they been slain as their slayers were slain? He removed them with his fierce blast. Therefore by this the guilt of Jacob will be expiated, when no incense altars will remain standing.

In that day, O people of Israel, a great trumpet will be blown, and those who were lost in Assyria and those who were driven out to the land of Egypt will come and worship the LORD on the holy mountain at Jerusalem.

WOE TO THE proud crown of the drunkards of Ephraim, and to the fading flower on the head of the rich valley! Behold, the Lord has one who is mighty and strong, like a storm of hail. The proud crown of the drunkards of Ephraim will be trodden under foot; and the fading flower of its glorious beauty will be like a first-ripe fig before the summer: when a man sees it, he eats it up as soon as it is in his hand.

In that day the LORD of hosts will be a crown of glory to the remnant of his people, a spirit of justice to him who sits in judgment, and strength to those who turn back the battle at the gate.

These also stagger with strong drink, the priest and the prophet; they are confused with wine, they err in vision, they stumble in giving judgment. "Whom will he teach," they say, "to whom explain the message? Those weaned from the milk? For it is precept upon precept, precept upon precept, line upon line, line upon line, here a little, there a little."

Nay. By men of strange lips and alien tongue the LORD will speak to this people, to whom he has said, "This is rest; give rest to the weary; and this is repose"; yet they would not hear. Therefore the word of the LORD will be to them precept upon precept, precept upon precept, line upon line, line upon line, here a little, there a little; that they may fall backward, and be broken, and snared, and taken.

Hear the word of the LORD, you scoffers who rule this people in Jerusalem! Because you have said, "We have made a covenant with death and an agreement with Sheol; when the overwhelming scourge passes through, it will not come to us, for we have made lies our refuge, and in falsehood we have taken shelter"; therefore thus says the Lord GOD, "Behold, I am laying in Zion for a foundation a stone, a tested stone, a precious cornerstone, of a sure foundation: 'He who believes will not be in haste.' And I will make justice the line, and righteousness the plummet; and hail will sweep away the refuge of lies, and waters will overwhelm the shelter."

Then your covenant with death will be annulled, and when the overwhelming scourge passes through, you will be beaten down by it. As often as it passes through, it will take you, morning by morning, by day and by night; and it will be sheer terror to understand the message. For the bed is too short to stretch oneself on it, and the covering too narrow to wrap oneself in it.

Now therefore do not scoff, lest your bonds be made strong; for I have heard a decree of destruction from the Lord GOD of hosts upon the whole land.

Give ear, and hear my voice. Does he who plows for sowing plow continually? Does he continually harrow his ground? When he has leveled its surface, does he not scatter dill, sow cummin, and put in wheat in rows? For he is instructed aright; his God teaches him.

Dill is not threshed with a sledge, nor is a cart wheel rolled over cummin; but dill is beaten out with a stick, and cummin with a rod. Does one crush bread grain? No, he does not thresh it for ever. This also comes from the LORD of hosts; he is excellent in wisdom.

AND THE LORD said: "Because this people draw near with their mouth and honor me with their lips, while their hearts are far from me, and their fear of me is a commandment of men learned by rote; therefore, behold, I will again do marvelous things with this people, and the wisdom of their wise men shall perish." Woe to those

who hide deep from the LORD their counsel, whose deeds are in the dark, and who
say, "Who sees us? Who knows us?" You
turn things upside down! Shall the potter
be regarded as the clay; that the thing made
should say of its maker, "He did not make
me"; or the thing formed say of him who
formed it, "He has no understanding"?

"Woe to the rebellious children," says
the LORD, "who carry out a plan, but not
mine; who make a league, but not of my
spirit; who set out, without asking my
counsel, to take refuge in the protection of
Pharaoh! Shelter in the shadow of Egypt
shall turn to humiliation. For every one
comes to shame through a people that cannot profit them. And Egypt's help is
worthless and empty."

Now go, write it before them on a tablet, inscribe it in a book, that it may be for
the time to come as a witness for ever. For
they are a rebellious people, lying sons,
who say to the prophets, "Prophesy not
what is right; speak to us smooth things,
prophesy illusions; turn aside from the
path, let us hear no more of the Holy One
of Israel."

Therefore thus says the Holy One of Israel, "Because you despise this word, and trust in oppression and perverseness, this iniquity shall be to you like a break in a high wall, about to collapse, whose crash comes suddenly, its breaking like that of a potter's vessel smashed so ruthlessly that not a fragment is found with which to dip up water from the cistern."

For thus said the Lord God, "In returning and rest you shall be saved; in quietness and in trust shall be your strength." And you would not. You said, "No! We will speed away upon horses." Therefore your pursuers shall be swift. A thousand shall flee at the threat of one, at the threat of five you shall flee, till you are left like a flagstaff on the top of a mountain.

THEREFORE THE LORD waits to be gracious to you; he exalts himself to show mercy to you. For he is a God of justice; blessed are those who wait for him. O people in Jerusalem, you shall weep no more. Surely at the sound of your cry he will answer you. Though he give you the bread of adversity and the water of affliction, yet your Teacher will not hide himself any more, but your eyes shall see him. Your ears shall hear a word behind you, saying, "This is the way, walk in it," when you turn to the right or turn to the left. Then you will scatter your graven images as unclean things and say to them, "Begone!" And he will give rain for the seed you sow, and grain will be plenteous. Your cattle will graze in large pastures. And upon every high hill there will be brooks running with water. Moreover the light of the moon will be as the light of the sun, and the light of the sun sevenfold, in the day when the LORD binds up the hurt of his people.

Behold, the name of the LORD comes from far, burning with his anger; his breath is like an overflowing stream that reaches up to the neck.

You shall have a song as in the night when a holy feast is kept; and gladness of heart, as when one sets out to the sound of the flute to go to the mountain of the LORD. And the LORD will cause his majestic voice to be heard and the descending blow of his arm to be seen, in furious anger and a flame of devouring fire. The Assyrians will be terror-stricken at the voice of the LORD, when he smites with his rod. For a burning place has long been prepared; yea, for the king it is made ready, its pyre with fire and wood in abundance; the breath of the LORD, like a stream of brimstone, kindles it.

Woe to those who trust in chariots because they are many and in horsemen because they are strong, but do not consult the LORD! He does not call back his words, but will arise against evildoers and the helpers of those who work iniquity. The Egyptians are men, and not God; their horses are flesh, and not spirit. When the LORD stretches out his hand, the helper will stumble, and he who is helped will fall, and they will all perish together.

For thus the LORD said to me: As a lion growls over his prey, and when a band of shepherds is called forth against him is not daunted by their shouting, so the LORD of hosts will come down to fight upon Mount Zion. Like birds hovering, the LORD of hosts will protect Jerusalem.

And the Assyrian shall fall by a sword, not of man, and his officers desert the standard in panic.

DRAW NEAR, O peoples, to hear! Let the earth listen, and all that fills it. For the LORD is enraged against all the nations and has given them over for slaughter. Their slain shall be cast out, and the stench of their corpses shall rise. All the host of heaven shall rot away and fall like leaves falling from the fig tree, and the skies roll up like a scroll. For my sword has drunk its fill in the heavens; and behold, it descends for judgment upon Edom, the people I have doomed. Their land shall be soaked with blood.

For the LORD has a day of vengeance. The streams of Edom shall be turned into pitch, and her soil into brimstone; its smoke shall go up for ever. From generation to generation it shall lie waste; none shall pass through it. But the hawk and the porcupine shall possess it. They shall name it No Kingdom There, and all its princes shall be nothing. Thorns shall grow over its fortresses. It shall be the haunt of jackals, an abode for ostriches. The satyr shall cry to his fellow; yea, there shall the night hag alight and find a resting place. For the mouth of the LORD has commanded and his hand has portioned it out to them; from generation to generation they shall dwell in it.

THE WILDERNESS AND the dry land shall be glad, the desert shall rejoice and blossom; like the crocus it shall blossom abundantly, and rejoice with joy and singing. They shall see the glory of the LORD, the majesty of our God. Strengthen the weak hands, and make firm the feeble knees. Say to those who are of a fearful heart, "Be strong, fear not! Behold, your God will come with vengeance, with the recompense of God. He will come and save you."

Then the eyes of the blind shall be opened, and the ears of the deaf unstopped; then shall the lame man leap like a hart, and the tongue of the dumb sing for joy. For waters shall break forth in the wilderness, and streams in the desert; the burning sand shall become a pool, and the thirsty ground springs of water. And a highway shall be there, and it shall be called the Holy Way; the unclean shall not pass over it, and fools shall not err therein. No lion nor any ravenous beast shall come up on it, but the redeemed shall walk there. And the ransomed of the LORD shall return to Zion with singing; everlasting joy shall be upon their heads, and sorrow and sighing shall flee away.

IN THE FOURTEENTH year of King Hezekiah, Hezekiah became sick and was at the point of death. And Isaiah the prophet, the son of Amoz, came to him and said, "Thus says the LORD: 'Set your house in order; for you shall die, you shall not recover.' " Then Hezekiah turned his face to the wall, and prayed to the LORD, saying, "Remember now, O LORD, I beseech thee, how I have walked before thee in faithfulness and with a whole heart, and have done what is good in thy sight." And he wept bitterly.

Then the word of the LORD came to Isaiah: "Go and say to Hezekiah, 'Thus says the LORD: I have heard your prayer, I have seen your tears; behold, I will add fifteen years to your life.' " And Isaiah said, "Bring a cake of figs, and apply it to the boil, that he may recover. And this is the sign to you from the LORD: Behold, I will make the shadow cast by the declining sun on the dial of Ahaz turn back ten steps." So the sun turned back on the dial ten steps.

A writing of Hezekiah king of Judah, after he had recovered:

I said, In the noontide of my days I must depart; I am consigned to the grave. I said, I shall not see the LORD in the land of the living; I shall look upon man no more. Like a weaver I have rolled up my life; he cuts me off from the loom; from day to night thou dost bring me to an end; I cry for help until morning. O Lord, I am op- pressed; be thou my security! But what can I say? For he himself has done it. All my sleep has fled because of the bitterness of my soul.

O Lord, in these things is the life of my spirit. Oh, restore me to health! Lo, it was for my welfare that I had great bitterness; but thou hast held back my life from the Pit, thou hast cast my sins behind thy back. For the dead cannot thank thee; those who go down to the Pit cannot hope for thy faithfulness. The living, the living, he thanks thee, as I do this day; the father makes known to the children thy faithfulness. And we will sing to stringed instruments all the days of our life, at the house of the LORD.

SENNACHERIB KING OF Assyria came up against all the fortified cities of Judah and took them. Then he sent the Rabshakeh, his chief of staff, with a great army to Jerusalem. And he stood by the water conduit. There came out to him Eliakim the son of Hilkiah, who was over the household.

The Rabshakeh said to him, "Say to Hezekiah, 'Thus says the great King Sennacherib: On what do you rest this confidence of yours, that you have rebelled against me? Do you think mere words are strategy and power? Behold, you are relying on Egypt, that broken reed of a staff, which will pierce the hand of any man who leans on it. How then can you repulse the least of my captains? But if you say to me, "We rely on the LORD our God," is it without the LORD that I have come up against this land to destroy it? The LORD said to me, Go up against this land, and destroy it.' "

"Pray, speak to your servant in Aramaic," said Eliakim, "for I understand it. Do not speak in the language of Judah within hearing of the people on the wall." The Rabshakeh replied, "Has my master sent me to speak these words to your master and not to the men sitting on the wall, who are doomed with you to eat their own dung and drink their own urine?"

Then the Rabshakeh stood and called out in a loud voice in the language of Judah: "Hear the word of the great king, the king of Assyria! Thus says the king: 'Do not let Hezekiah deceive you, for he will not be able to deliver you. And do not listen when he misleads you by saying, "The LORD will surely deliver us." Has any of the gods of the nations delivered his land out of the hand of the king of Assyria? Where are the gods of Samaria? Have they delivered Samaria out of my hand, that the LORD should deliver Jerusalem?' "

But Eliakim was silent, for the king's command was, "Do not answer him." Then he came to Hezekiah and told him the words of the Rabshakeh. Hezekiah rent his clothes and covered himself with sackcloth and went into the house of the LORD. He sent Eliakim and the senior priests, clothed with sackcloth, to the prophet Isaiah. "Thus says Hezekiah," they said to him. " 'It may be that the LORD your God heard the words of the Rabshakeh, whom the king of Assyria has sent to mock the living God, and will rebuke them; therefore lift up your prayer for the remnant that is left.' "

Isaiah replied, "Say to your master, 'Thus says the LORD concerning the king of Assyria: He shall not come into this city, or shoot an arrow there, or come before it with a shield or cast up a siege mound against it. By the way that he came, he shall return, says the LORD, and I will make him fall by the sword in his own land. For I will defend this city to save it, for my own sake and for the sake of my servant David.' "

And the angel of the LORD went forth

and slew a hundred and eighty-five thousand in the camp of the Assyrians; and when men arose early in the morning, behold, these were all dead bodies. Then Sennacherib king of Assyria departed and went home to Nineveh. And as he was worshiping in the house of his god, two of his sons slew him with the sword and escaped into Ararat. And Esarhaddon his son reigned in his stead.

COMFORT, COMFORT MY people, says your God. Speak tenderly to Jerusalem, and cry to her that her warfare is ended, that her iniquity is pardoned, that she has received from the LORD's hand double for all her sins.

A voice cries: "In the wilderness prepare the way of the LORD, make straight in the desert a highway for our God. Every valley shall be lifted up, and every hill made low; and the glory of the LORD shall be revealed, and all flesh shall see it together, for the mouth of the LORD has spoken."

A voice says, "Cry!" And I said, "What shall I cry?" All flesh is grass, and all its beauty is like the flower of the field. The grass withers, the flower fades, when the breath of the LORD blows upon it; surely the people is grass. The grass withers, the flower fades; but the word of our God will stand for ever.

Get you up to a high mountain, O Zion, herald of good tidings, lift up your voice, fear not; say to the cities of Judah, "Behold your God!" Behold, the Lord GOD comes with might, and his arm rules for him; behold, his recompense is with him. He will feed his flock like a shepherd; he will carry the lambs in his bosom and gently lead those that are with young.

Who has measured the waters in the hollow of his hand, marked off the heavens with a span, and weighed the mountains in scales? Who has directed the Spirit of the LORD, or as his counselor has instructed him? Who taught him knowledge and showed him the way of understanding? Behold, the nations are like a drop from a bucket, and accounted as dust on the scales. Lebanon would not suffice for fuel, nor are its beasts enough for a burnt offering. All the nations are as nothing before him.

To whom then will you liken God, what likeness compare with him? The idol! a workman casts it, a goldsmith overlays it with gold; he who is impoverished chooses wood that will not rot and seeks out a craftsman to set up an image.

Have you not known? Have you not heard? Has it not been told you from the beginning? Have you not understood from the foundations of the earth? It is he who sits above the circle of the earth, and its inhabitants are like grasshoppers; he who stretches out the heavens like a curtain.

To whom then will you compare me, that I should be like him? says the Holy One. Lift up your eyes on high and see: who created these? He who brings out their host by number, calling them all by name; and because he is strong in power, not one is missing.

Why do you say, O Jacob, O Israel, "My way is hid from the LORD, and my right is disregarded by my God"?

Have you not known? Have you not heard? The LORD is the everlasting God, the Creator of the ends of the earth. He does not faint or grow weary, his understanding is unsearchable. He gives power to the faint, and to him who has no might he increases strength. Even youths shall faint and be weary, and young men shall fall exhausted; but they who wait for the LORD shall renew their strength, they shall mount up with wings like eagles, they shall run and not be weary, they shall walk and not faint.

BEHOLD MY SERVANT, whom I uphold, my chosen, in whom my soul delights; I have put my Spirit upon him, he will bring forth justice to the nations. He will not cry or lift up his voice, or make it heard in the street; a bruised reed he will not break, and a dimly burning wick he will not quench. He will not fail or be discouraged till he has established justice in the earth; and the coastlands wait for his law.

Thus says the LORD, who created the heavens, who spread forth the earth, who gives breath and spirit to those who walk in it: "I am the LORD, I have called you in righteousness, I have taken you by the hand; I have given you as a covenant to the people, a light to the nations, to open eyes that are blind, to bring out from prison those who sit in darkness. I am the LORD, that is my name; my glory I give to no other, nor my praise to graven images. Behold, the former things have come to pass, and new things I now declare; before they spring forth I tell you of them."

Sing to the LORD a new song, his praise from the end of the earth! Let the sea roar and all that fills it, the coastlands and their inhabitants. Let the desert and its cities lift up their voice. Let them shout from the top of the mountains. Let them give glory to the LORD. The LORD goes forth like a man of war; he shows himself mighty against his foes.

For a long time I have held my peace, I have kept still and restrained myself. Now I will cry out like a woman in travail. I will lay waste mountains; I will turn the rivers into islands and dry up the pools. And I will lead the blind in paths they have not known. I will turn the darkness before them into light, the rough places into level ground. These are the things I will do. And they shall be turned back and utterly put to shame, who trust in graven images, who say to molten images, "You are our gods."

Hear, you deaf; look, you blind, that you may see! Who is blind but my servant, or deaf as my messenger? Who is blind as my dedicated one, blind as the servant of the LORD? He sees many things, but does not observe them; his ears are open, but he does not hear. The LORD was pleased, for his righteousness' sake, to magnify his teaching and make it glorious. But this is a people robbed and plundered, trapped in holes, hidden in prisons; they have become a prey with none to rescue. Who among you will listen for the time to come? Who gave up Jacob to the spoiler and Israel to the robbers? Was it not the LORD, whose law they would not obey? So he poured upon Jacob the heat of his anger; it set him on fire round about, but he did not understand.

BUT NOW THUS says the LORD, he who created you, O Jacob, O Israel: "Fear not, for I have redeemed you; I have called you by name, you are mine. When you pass through the waters, I will be with you; when you walk through fire, the flame shall not consume you. For I am the LORD your God, the Holy One of Israel, your Savior.

"I give Egypt and Ethiopia as your ransom. Because you are precious in my eyes, and honored, and I love you, I give peoples in exchange for your life. Fear not, for I am with you; I will gather your offspring from east and west; I will say to the north and the south, Give up; bring my sons from afar and my daughters from the end of the earth, every one who is called by my name, whom I created for my glory."

Bring forth the people who are blind, yet have eyes, who are deaf, yet have ears! Let the nations assemble. Who among them can show us the former things? Let them bring their witnesses to justify them, and let them hear and say, It is true.

"You are my witnesses," says the LORD, "and my servant whom I have chosen, that you may know and believe me and understand that I am He. Before me no god was formed, nor shall there be any after me. I, I am the LORD. Besides me there is no savior. I declared and saved when there was no strange god among you. I am God, and also henceforth I am He; there is none who can deliver from my hand; I work and who can hinder it?"

Thus says the LORD, your Redeemer: "For your sake I will send to Babylon and break down all the bars, and the shouting of the Chaldeans will be turned to lamentations. I am the LORD, the Creator of Israel, your King." Thus says the LORD, who makes a way in the sea, who brings forth army and warrior: "Remember not the things of old. Behold, I am doing a new thing; now it springs forth, do you not perceive it? I will make a way in the wilderness. The wild beasts will honor me, for I make rivers in the desert to give drink to my people, the people I formed for myself, that they might declare my praise.

"Yet you did not call upon me, O Jacob; you have been weary of me, O Israel! You have not brought me your sheep for burnt offerings. You have not bought me sweet cane with money or honored me with your sacrifices. But you have burdened me with your sins.

"I, I am He who blots out your transgressions for my own sake; I will not remember your sins. Let us argue together; set forth your case. Your first father sinned, and your mediators transgressed against me. Therefore I profaned the princes of the sanctuary, I delivered Jacob to utter destruction.

"But now hear, O Jacob my servant, Israel whom I have chosen! Thus says the LORD who made you: Fear not, for I will pour water on the thirsty land; I will pour my Spirit upon your descendants, and they shall spring up like willows by flowing streams. This one will say, 'I am the LORD's,' another will call himself Jacob, and another will write on his hand, 'The LORD's' and surname himself Israel."

Thus says the LORD of hosts: "I am the first and I am the last; besides me there is no God. Who is like me? Let him declare it before me. Who has announced from of old the things to come? Let them tell us what is yet to be. Fear not; have I not told you from of old? And you are my witnesses! Is there a God besides me? There is no Rock; I know not any."

All who make idols are nothing, and the things they delight in do not profit; their witnesses neither see nor know, that they may be put to shame. Who fashions a god or casts an image that is profitable for nothing? The craftsmen are but men; let them stand forth, they shall be put to shame together. The ironsmith fashions it over the coals; he shapes it with hammers and forges it with his strong arm; he becomes hungry and his strength fails. The carpenter marks it out with a pencil and fashions it with planes; he shapes it into the figure of a man, with the beauty of a man, to dwell in a house. He chooses an oak and lets it grow strong in the forest; he plants a cedar and the rain nourishes it. Then it becomes fuel for a man; he takes a part of it and kindles a fire and bakes bread. Over half of it he roasts meat; also he warms himself. And the rest of it he makes into a god, his idol, and worships it; he prays, "Deliver me, for thou art my god!" They know not, nor do they discern; for he has shut their eyes and their minds. No one considers, nor is there discernment to say, "Half of it I burned in the fire, I baked bread, I roasted flesh and have eaten; and shall I make the residue an abomination? Shall I fall down before a block of wood?" A deluded mind has led him astray. He cannot deliver himself or say, "Is there not a lie in my right hand?"

Remember these things, O Jacob, and Israel, for you are my servant; I have swept away your transgressions like a cloud; return to me, for I have redeemed you. Sing, O heavens, shout, O earth; break forth into singing, O forest, and every tree in it! For the LORD has redeemed Jacob, and will be glorified in Israel.

THUS SAYS THE LORD, your Redeemer: "I am the LORD, who stretched out the heavens alone—Who was with me?—who frustrates the omens of liars; who turns wise men back and makes their knowledge foolish; who confirms the word of his servant and performs the counsel of his messengers; who says of Jerusalem, 'She shall be inhabited,' and of the cities of Judah, 'I will raise up their ruins'; who says of Cyrus, 'He is my shepherd, he shall fulfil my purpose'; and of the temple, 'Your foundation shall be laid.' "

Thus says the LORD to his anointed, to

Cyrus, whose right hand I have grasped, to subdue nations and ungird the loins of kings:

"I will go before you and level the mountains, I will break in pieces the doors of bronze, I will give you the treasures in secret places, that you may know that it is I, the LORD, the God of Israel, who call you by your name. For the sake of my servant Jacob, and Israel my chosen, I call you by your name, I surname you, though you do not know me.

"I am the LORD, and there is no other, besides me there is no God; I gird you, though you do not know me, that men may know, from the rising of the sun and from the west, that there is none besides me. I form light and create darkness, I make weal and create woe.

"Woe to him who strives with his Maker, an earthen vessel with the potter! Does the clay say to him who fashions it, 'What are you making?' or 'Your work has no handles'? Woe to him who says to a father, 'What are you begetting?' or to a woman, 'With what are you in travail?' "

Therefore thus says the LORD: "Will you

question me, or command me, concerning
the work of my hands? I made the earth
and created man upon it; I have aroused
Cyrus in righteousness, and he shall build
my city and set my exiles free, not for price
or reward," says the LORD of hosts.

Thus says the LORD: "The wealth of
Egypt and the merchandise of Ethiopia,
and the Sabeans, men of stature, shall
come over to you and be yours; they shall
come over in chains and make supplication
to you, saying: 'God is with you only, and
there is no other, no god besides him.' "

Israel is saved by the LORD with everlasting salvation. For thus says the LORD,
who formed the earth (he established it;
he did not create it a chaos, he formed it to
be inhabited!): "I am the LORD, and there
is no other. I did not speak in secret, in a
land of darkness; I did not say to the offspring of Jacob, 'Seek me in chaos.' I the
LORD speak the truth, I declare what is
right. There is no other god besides me, a
righteous God and a Savior. Turn to me
and be saved, all the ends of the earth! By
myself I have sworn, from my mouth has
gone forth in righteousness a word that

shall not return: 'To me every knee shall bow, every tongue shall swear.' In the LORD all the offspring of Israel shall triumph and glory."

LISTEN TO ME, O coastlands, and peoples from afar. The LORD called me from the womb, from the body of my mother he named my name. He made my mouth like a sharp sword, in the shadow of his hand he hid me; he made me a polished arrow, in his quiver he hid me away. And he said to me, "You are my servant, Israel, in whom I will be glorified."

But I said, "I have labored in vain, I have spent my strength for nothing and vanity; yet surely my right is with the LORD, and my recompense with my God."

And now the LORD says, who formed me from the womb to be his servant, to bring Jacob back to him, and that Israel might be gathered to him, for I am honored in the eyes of the LORD, and my God has become my strength—he says: "It is too light a thing that you should be my servant to restore the preserved of Israel; I will give you as a light to the nations, that my salvation may reach to the end of the earth."

But Zion said, "The LORD has forsaken me, my Lord has forgotten me."

"Can a woman forget her sucking child, that she should have no compassion on the son of her womb? Even these may forget, yet I will not forget you."

Thus says the LORD: "Where is your mother's bill of divorce, with which I put her away? Or which of my creditors is it to whom I have sold you? Behold, for your iniquities you were sold, and for your transgressions your mother was put away. Why, when I called, was there no one to answer? Is my hand shortened, that it cannot redeem? Or have I no power to deliver?"

THE LORD GOD has given me the tongue of those who are taught, that I may know how to sustain with a word him that is weary. Morning by morning he wakens my ear to hear as those who are taught. The Lord GOD has opened my ear, and I was not rebellious, I turned not backward. I gave my back to the smiters, and my

cheeks to those who pulled out the beard;
I hid not my face from shame and spitting.
For the Lord GOD helps me; therefore I
have not been confounded; I have set my
face like a flint and I know I shall not be
put to shame; he who vindicates me is
near.

Who will contend with me? Let us stand
up together. Who is my adversary? Behold, the Lord GOD helps me; who will
declare me guilty? Behold, all of them will
wear out like a garment; the moth will eat
them up. Who among you fears the LORD
and obeys the voice of his servant, who
walks in darkness and has no light, yet
trusts in the name of the LORD and relies
upon his God? Behold, all you who kindle
a fire, who set brands alight! Walk by the
light of your fire, and by the brands which
you have kindled! This shall you have from
my hand: you shall lie down in torment.

"HEARKEN TO ME, you who pursue deliverance, you who seek the LORD; look to the
rock from which you were hewn. Look to
Abraham your father and to Sarah who
bore you; when he was but one I called

him, and I blessed him and made him many. For the LORD will comfort Zion; he will make her wilderness like Eden; and gladness will be found in her, thanksgiving, and the voice of song.

"Listen to me, my nation; for a law will go forth from me for a light to the peoples. My deliverance draws near speedily, my salvation has gone forth; the coastlands wait for me, for my arm they hope. Lift up your eyes to the heavens, and look at the earth beneath; for the heavens will vanish like smoke, and the earth will wear out like a garment, but my salvation will be for ever.

"Hearken, you who know righteousness, you in whose heart is my law; fear not the reproach of men, be not dismayed at their revilings, for the moth will eat them up like wool; but my deliverance will be for all generations."

Awake, awake, O arm of the LORD, as in days of old. Was it not thou that didst cut the sea monster Rahab in pieces, thou that didst dry up the sea for the redeemed to pass over? And the ransomed of the LORD shall return to Zion with singing; everlasting joy shall be upon their heads, and sorrow and sighing shall flee away.

"I, I am he that comforts you; who are you that you are afraid of man who dies, and have forgotten the LORD, your Maker; you who fear continually all the day because of the fury of the oppressor, when he sets himself to destroy? And where is the fury of the oppressor? He who is bowed down shall speedily be released; he shall not die and go down to the Pit, neither shall his bread fail. For I am the LORD your God, who stirs up the sea so that its waves roar—the LORD of hosts is his name. And I have hid you in the shadow of my hand, saying to Zion, 'You are my people.' "

Rouse yourself, rouse yourself, O Jerusalem, you who have drunk at the hand of the LORD the cup of his wrath, who have drunk to the dregs the bowl of staggering. There is none to guide her among all the sons she has borne, none to take her by the hand. These things have befallen you— devastation, famine, and sword; who will comfort you? Your sons have fainted, they lie at the head of every street like an antelope in a net, full of the wrath of your God.

Therefore hear this, you who are drunk, but not with wine: Thus says your God who pleads the cause of his people: "Behold, I have taken from your hand the bowl of my wrath. I will put it into the hand of your tormentors, who have said to you, 'Bow down, that we may pass over'; and you have made your back like the street for them to pass over."

Awake, awake, put on your strength, O Zion; put on your beautiful garments, O Jerusalem, the holy city; for there shall no more come into you the uncircumcised and the unclean. Shake yourself from the dust, arise, loose the bonds from your neck, O captive daughter of Zion.

For thus says the LORD: "You were sold for nothing, and you shall be redeemed without money. My people went down at first into Egypt to sojourn there; and the Assyrian oppressed them for nothing. Now therefore what have I here, seeing that my people are taken away for nothing? Their rulers wail, and my name is despised. Therefore my people shall know my name;

in that day they shall know that it is I who speak; here am I."

How beautiful upon the mountains are the feet of him who brings good tidings, who publishes peace, who brings good tidings of good, who publishes salvation, who says to Zion, "Your God reigns." Hark, your watchmen lift up their voice, together they sing for joy; for eye to eye they see the return of the LORD to Zion. Break forth together into singing, you waste places of Jerusalem; for the LORD has comforted his people, he has redeemed Jerusalem. The LORD has bared his holy arm, and all the ends of the earth shall see the salvation of our God.

Depart, depart, go out thence, purify yourselves, you who bear the vessels of the LORD. And you shall not go in flight, for the LORD will go before you, and the God of Israel will be your rear guard.

BEHOLD, MY SERVANT shall prosper, he shall be exalted and lifted up. As many were astonished at him—his appearance was so marred, beyond human semblance, and his form beyond that of the sons of

men—so shall he startle many nations;
kings shall shut their mouths because of
him; for that which has not been told
them they shall see, and that which they
have not heard they shall understand.

Who has believed what we have heard?
And to whom has the arm of the LORD
been revealed? For he grew up before him
like a root out of dry ground; he had no
form or comeliness that we should look at
him, and no beauty that we should desire
him. He was despised and rejected by
men; a man of sorrows, and acquainted
with grief; and as one from whom men
hide their faces he was despised, and we
esteemed him not.

Surely he has borne our griefs and carried our sorrows; yet we esteemed him
stricken, smitten by God. But he was
wounded for our transgressions; upon him
was the chastisement that made us whole,
and with his stripes we are healed. All we
like sheep have gone astray; we have
turned every one to his own way; and the
LORD has laid on him the iniquity of us all.

He was oppressed, and he was afflicted,
yet he opened not his mouth; like a lamb

that is led to the slaughter, like a sheep that before its shearers is dumb, so he opened not his mouth. By oppression and judgment he was taken away; and as for his generation, who considered that he was cut off out of the land of the living, stricken for the transgression of my people? And they made his grave with the wicked and with a rich man in his death, although he had done no violence, and there was no deceit in his mouth.

Yet it was the will of the LORD to bruise him; he has put him to grief; when he makes himself an offering for sin, he shall see his offspring, he shall prolong his days; the will of the LORD shall prosper in his hand; he shall see the fruit of the travail of his soul and be satisfied; by his knowledge shall the righteous one, my servant, make many to be accounted righteous; and he shall bear their iniquities. Therefore I will divide him a portion with the great, and he shall divide the spoil with the strong; because he poured out his soul to death, and was numbered with the transgressors; yet he bore the sin of many, and made intercession for the transgressors.

"Sing, O barren one, who did not bear! For the children of the desolate one will be more than the children of her that is married, says the Lord. Enlarge the place of your tent, for you will spread abroad to right and left, and your descendants will possess the nations. You will forget the shame of your youth and the reproach of your widowhood. For your Maker is your husband, the Lord of hosts is his name; and the Holy One of Israel is your Redeemer, the God of the whole earth he is called. He has called you like a wife forsaken and grieved in spirit. For a brief moment I forsook you, in overflowing wrath, but with everlasting love I will have compassion on you, says the Lord, your Redeemer. This is like the days of Noah to me: as I swore that the waters of Noah should no more go over the earth, so I have sworn that I will not be angry with you. The mountains may be removed, but my steadfast love, my covenant of peace, shall not be removed.

"O afflicted one, storm-tossed, behold, I will set your stones in antimony, and lay your foundations with sapphires. I will make your pinnacles of agate, your gates of carbuncles, and all your wall of precious stones. All your sons shall be taught by the LORD, and great shall be their prosperity. In righteousness you shall be established; oppression and terror shall not come near you. If any one stirs up strife, it is not from me; whoever stirs up strife with you shall fall because of you. Behold, I have created the smith who produces a weapon; I have also created the ravager. No weapon that is fashioned against you shall prosper; you shall confute every tongue that rises against you in judgment. This is the heritage of the servants of the LORD, says the LORD."

"HO, EVERY ONE who thirsts, come to the waters; and he who has no money, come, buy and eat! Buy wine and milk without money and without price. Why do you spend your money for that which is not bread, and your labor for that which does not satisfy? Hearken diligently to me, and eat what is good, and delight yourselves in fatness. Come to me; hear, that your soul may live, and I will make with you an everlasting covenant, my steadfast, sure love for David. Behold, I made him a witness to the peoples, a leader for the peoples. You shall call nations that you know not, and nations that knew you not shall run to you because of the LORD your God, for he has glorified you.

"Seek the LORD while he may be found, call upon him while he is near; let the wicked forsake his way and the unrighteous man his thoughts; let him return to the LORD, that he may have mercy on him, and to our God, for he will abundantly pardon. My thoughts are not your thoughts, neither are your ways my ways, says the LORD. As the heavens are higher than the earth, so are my ways higher than your ways, and my thoughts than your thoughts. As rain and snow come down from heaven, and return not thither but water the earth, making it bring forth and sprout, giving seed to the sower and bread to the eater, so shall my word that goes forth from my mouth not return to me empty; but it shall accomplish that which I purpose.

"You shall go out in joy and peace; the mountains before you shall break forth into singing, and all the trees shall clap their hands. Instead of the thorn shall come up the cypress, instead of the brier, the myrtle; and it shall be to the LORD for an everlasting sign which shall not be cut off."

THUS SAYS THE LORD: "Keep justice, and do righteousness, for soon my salvation will come, and my deliverance be revealed. Blessed is the man who does this, who keeps the sabbath, not profaning it, and keeps his hand from doing any evil."

Let not the foreigner who has joined himself to the LORD say, "The LORD will surely separate me from his people"; and let not the eunuch say, "Behold, I am a dry tree." For thus says the LORD: "To the eunuchs who keep my sabbaths, and hold fast my covenant, I will give within my walls a monument and a name better than sons and daughters; an everlasting name which shall not be cut off.

"The foreigners who join themselves to the LORD, to minister to him, and to be his servants, every one who keeps the sabbath, and does not profane it, and holds fast my covenant—these I will bring to my holy mountain, and make them joyful in my house of prayer; their burnt offerings and their sacrifices will be accepted on my altar; for my house shall be called a house of prayer for all peoples."

All you beasts of the field, come to devour. His watchmen are blind, without knowledge; they are all dumb dogs, they cannot bark; dreaming, lying down, loving to slumber. The dogs have a mighty appetite; they never have enough. The shepherds also have no understanding; they have all turned to their own way, each to his own gain. "Come," they say, "let us fill ourselves with strong drink; tomorrow will be like this day, great beyond measure."

"CRY ALOUD, SPARE not, lift up your voice like a trumpet; declare to my people their transgression. Yet they seek me daily, as if they were a nation that did righteousness, and they ask of me righteous judgments. 'Why have we fasted, and thou seest it not? Why have we humbled ourselves, and

thou takest no knowledge of it?' Behold, in
the day of your fast you seek your own
pleasures and oppress all your workers.
You fast only to quarrel and to fight and to
hit with wicked fist. Fasting like yours this
day will not make your voice to be heard
on high. Is such the fast that I choose, a
day for a man to humble himself? Is it to
bow down his head, and spread sackcloth
and ashes under him? Will you call this a
fast, and a day acceptable to the LORD?

"Is not this the fast that I choose: to
loose the bonds of wickedness, to let the
oppressed go free, and to break every
yoke? Is it not to share your bread with
the hungry, and bring the homeless poor
into your house; when you see the naked,
to cover him? Then shall your light break
forth like the dawn, and your righteousness go before you. Then you shall call,
and the LORD will answer, Here I am.

"If you take away from the midst of you
the yoke, the pointing of the finger, and
speaking wickedness, if you pour yourself
out for the hungry and the afflicted, then
the LORD will guide you continually and
satisfy your desire with good things; you

shall be like a spring whose waters fail not. And your ancient ruins shall be rebuilt; you shall raise up the foundations of many generations; you shall be called the repairer of the breach, the restorer of streets to dwell in.

"If you turn back your foot from doing your pleasure on my holy day and call the sabbath a delight; if you honor it, not going your own ways, then I will make you ride upon the heights of the earth; I will feed you with the heritage of Jacob your father, for the mouth of the LORD has spoken."

BEHOLD, THE LORD'S hand is not shortened, that it cannot save; but your sins have made a separation between you and your God. For your hands are defiled with blood, and your tongue mutters wickedness. No one goes to law honestly; they speak lies, they conceive mischief and bring forth iniquity. They hatch adders' eggs, they weave the spider's web; he who eats their eggs dies, and their webs will not serve as clothing. Deeds of violence are in their hands, and their feet run to evil; their thoughts are thoughts of iniquity. Desolation and destruction are in their highways; they have made their roads crooked, no one who goes in them knows peace.

Therefore justice and righteousness are far from us; we look for light, but we walk in gloom and grope for the wall like the blind. We all growl like bears, we moan and moan like doves; we look for justice, but there is none; for salvation, but it is far from us.

For our sins are multiplied before thee and testify against us. We know our iniquities: transgressing, and turning away from following our God, speaking oppression and revolt, conceiving and uttering from the heart lying words. Justice is turned back, and righteousness stands afar off; for truth has fallen in the public squares, and uprightness cannot enter. Truth is lacking, and he who departs from evil makes himself a prey.

The LORD saw it, and it displeased him that there was no justice. He wondered that there was no man to intervene; then his own arm brought him victory. He put on righteousness as a breastplate, and a helmet of salvation upon his head; he put on garments of vengeance for clothing, and wrapped himself in fury as a mantle. According to their deeds will he repay. So they shall fear the name of the LORD from the west, and his glory from the rising of the sun; for he will come like a rushing stream which the wind of the LORD drives.

"He will come to Zion as Redeemer, to those in Jacob who turn from transgression, says the LORD.

"This is my covenant, says the LORD: my Spirit which is upon you, and my words which I have put in your mouth, shall not depart out of your mouth, or out of the mouth of your children, or out of the mouth of your children's children, from this time forth and for evermore."

ARISE, SHINE; FOR your light has come, and the glory of the LORD has risen upon you. For behold, darkness shall cover the earth, and thick darkness the peoples; but the LORD will arise upon you, and his glory will be seen upon you. And nations shall come to your light, and kings to the brightness of your rising.

Lift up your eyes and see; they all gather together, your sons from far, your daughters carried in the arms. Then you shall see and be radiant, your heart shall thrill and rejoice; because the abundance of the sea and the wealth of the nations shall come to you. A multitude of camels shall come, the young camels of Midian and Sheba. They shall bring gold and frankincense, and proclaim the praise of the LORD. All the flocks of Kedar shall come up with acceptance on my altar; and I will glorify my glorious house.

Who are these that fly like a cloud, like doves to their windows? The ships of Tarshish first, to bring your sons from far, their silver and gold with them, for the name of the LORD your God, because he has glorified you.

Foreigners shall build up your walls, and their kings shall minister to you; for in my wrath I smote you, but in my favor I have had mercy on you. Your gates shall be open day and night, that men may bring you the wealth of the nations, with their kings led in procession. For the nation and kingdom that will not serve you shall perish. The glory of Lebanon shall come to you, the cypress, the plane, and the pine, to beautify the place of my sanctuary; and I will make the place of my feet glorious. The sons of those who oppressed you shall bow down at your feet; they shall call you the City of the LORD.

Whereas you have been forsaken and hated, I will make you majestic for ever, a joy from age to age. You shall suck the milk of nations; and you shall know that I, the LORD, am your Savior and your Redeemer, the Mighty One of Jacob. Instead of bronze I will bring gold, and instead of iron I will bring silver; instead of wood, bronze, instead of stones, iron. I will make your overseers peace and righteousness. Violence shall no more be heard in your land; you shall call your walls Salvation and your gates Praise.

The sun shall be no more your light by day, nor the moon by night; but the LORD will be your everlasting light, and your days of mourning shall be ended. Your people shall all be righteous; they shall possess the land for ever, the shoot of my planting, that I might be glorified. The

least one shall become a clan, the smallest
a mighty nation; I am the LORD; in its time
I will hasten it.

THE SPIRIT OF the Lord GOD is upon me,
because the LORD has anointed me to
bring good tidings to the afflicted; he has
sent me to bind up the brokenhearted, to
proclaim liberty to the captives, and the
opening of the prison to those who are
bound; to proclaim the year of the LORD's
favor and the day of vengeance of our
God; to grant to those who mourn in Zion
a garland instead of ashes, the mantle of
praise instead of a faint spirit, that they
may be called oaks of righteousness, the
planting of the LORD, that he may be glorified. They shall build up the ancient ruins
and repair the devastations.

Aliens shall stand and feed your flocks,
foreigners shall be your plowmen; but you
shall be called the priests of the LORD, the
ministers of our God; you shall eat the
wealth of the nations and in their riches
you shall glory. Instead of dishonor you
shall rejoice in your lot; yours shall be
everlasting joy.

I the LORD love justice, I hate robbery
and wrong; I will faithfully give them their
recompense, and I will make an everlasting
covenant with them. Their descendants
shall be known among the nations; all who
see them shall acknowledge that they are a
people whom the LORD has blessed.

My soul shall exult in my God, for he
has clothed me with the garments of salvation, he has covered me with the robe of
righteousness, as a bridegroom decks himself with a garland, and a bride with her
jewels. As the earth brings forth its shoots,
so the Lord GOD will cause righteousness
and praise to spring forth before all the
nations.

WHO IS THIS that comes from Edom, in
crimsoned garments from Bozrah, he that
is glorious in his apparel, marching in the
greatness of his strength?

"It is I, announcing vindication, mighty
to save."

Why is thy apparel red, thy garments
like his that treads in the wine press?

"I have trodden the wine press alone;
from the peoples no one was with me; I

trod them in my anger and trampled them in my wrath; their lifeblood is sprinkled upon my garments and I have stained all my raiment. For the day of vengeance was in my heart and my year of redemption has come. I looked, but there was no one to help; I was appalled, but there was no one to uphold me, so my own arm brought me victory. I trod down the peoples in my anger, I made them drunk in my wrath, and I poured out their blood on the earth."

I WILL RECOUNT the steadfast love of the LORD, the praises of the LORD, according to the great goodness to the house of Israel which he has granted them. For he said, Surely they are my people, sons who will not deal falsely; and he became their Savior. In their affliction he was afflicted, and the angel of his presence saved them; in his love and pity he redeemed them; he lifted them up and carried them all the days of old.

But they rebelled and grieved his holy Spirit; therefore he himself fought against them. Then he remembered the days of Moses his servant. Where is he who brought up out of the sea the shepherds of his flock? Where is he who put in the midst of them his holy Spirit, who caused his glorious arm to go at the right hand of Moses, who divided the waters before them? So thou didst lead thy people, to make for thyself a glorious name.

Look down and see, from thy holy habitation. Where are thy zeal and thy compassion? For thou art our Father, though Abraham does not know us; thou, O LORD, art our Father, our Redeemer from of old. O LORD, why dost thou make us err from thy ways and harden our heart, so that we fear thee not? Return for the sake of thy servants. Thy holy people possessed thy sanctuary a little while; our adversaries have trodden it down. We have become like those over whom thou hast never ruled, like those who are not called by thy name.

Yet, O LORD, thou art our Father; we are the clay, and thou art our potter; we are all the work of thy hand. O LORD, remember not iniquity for ever. Consider, we are all thy people. Thy holy cities have become a wilderness. Our holy and beautiful house, where our fathers praised thee, has been burned by fire; all our pleasant places are ruins. Wilt thou keep silent, O LORD, and afflict us sorely?

I WAS READY to be sought by those who did not ask for me; I was ready to be found by those who did not seek me. I said, "Here am I, here am I," to a nation that did not call on my name.

I spread out my hands all day to a rebellious people, who provoke me continually, sacrificing in gardens and burning incense; who sit in tombs; who eat swine's flesh and broth of abominable things; who say, "Keep to yourself, I am set apart from you." These are a smoke in my nostrils, a fire that burns all the day.

Behold, it is written before me: "I will not keep silent, but I will repay their iniquities and their fathers' iniquities together, says the LORD; because they burned incense upon the mountains and reviled me upon the hills, I will measure into their bosom payment for their former doings."

Thus says the LORD: "As the wine is

found in the cluster, and they say, 'Do not destroy it, for there is a blessing in it,' so I will do for my servants' sake, and not destroy them all. I will bring forth descendants from Jacob, and from Judah inheritors of my mountains, and my servants shall dwell there.

"For behold, I create new heavens and a new earth; and the former things shall not come into mind. Be glad, for I create Jerusalem a rejoicing, and her people a joy. I will rejoice in Jerusalem; no more shall be heard in it the sound of weeping; no more shall there be in it an infant that lives but a few days, or an old man who does not fill out his days.

"They shall build houses and inhabit them; they shall plant vineyards and eat their fruit. They shall not build and another inhabit, or plant and another eat. They shall not labor in vain, or bear children for calamity; for they shall be the offspring of the blessed of the LORD. Before they call I will answer, while they are yet speaking I will hear. The wolf and the lamb shall feed together, the lion shall eat straw like the ox; and dust shall be the serpent's food.

They shall not hurt or destroy in all my holy mountain, says the LORD."

THUS SAYS THE LORD: "Heaven is my throne and the earth is my footstool; what is the house which you would build for me, and what is the place of my rest? All these things my hand has made, so all these things are mine. But this is the man to whom I will look, he that is humble and contrite in spirit, and trembles at my word.

"He who slaughters an ox is like him who kills a man; he who sacrifices a lamb, like him who breaks a dog's neck; he who presents a cereal offering, like him who offers swine's blood; he who makes an offering of frankincense, like him who blesses an idol. These have chosen their own ways; their soul delights in abominations. I also will choose affliction for them, because when I spoke they did not listen, but did what was evil in my eyes."

Hear the word of the LORD, you who tremble at his word: "Your brethren who hate you and cast you out for my name's sake have said, 'Let the LORD be glorified, that we may see your joy'; but it is they who shall be put to shame.

"Hark, an uproar from the city! A voice from the temple! The voice of the LORD, rendering recompense to his enemies!

"Before she was in labor she gave birth; before her pain came upon her she was delivered of a son. Who has heard such a thing? Shall a land be born in one day? For as soon as Zion was in labor she brought forth her sons. Shall I bring to the birth and not cause to bring forth? says the LORD; shall I, who cause to bring forth, shut the womb?

"Rejoice with Jerusalem, all you who love her; rejoice, that you may drink deeply from the abundance of her glory. Behold, I will extend prosperity to her like an overflowing stream; and you shall suck and be carried upon her hip, and dandled upon her knees. As one whom his mother comforts, so I will comfort you; your heart shall rejoice; your bones shall flourish; and it shall be known that the hand of the LORD is with his servants, and his indignation is against his enemies.

"Behold, the LORD will come in fire, and his chariots like the stormwind, to render his anger in fury. By fire will the LORD execute judgment, and by his sword, upon all flesh; and those slain by the LORD shall be many.

"Those who sanctify and purify themselves to go into the gardens, following one in the midst, eating swine's flesh and the abomination and mice, shall come to an end together, says the LORD.

"I am coming to gather all nations and tongues; they shall come and shall see my glory, and I will set a sign among them. And from them I will send survivors to the nations, to Tarshish, and to the coastlands afar off that have not seen my glory; and they shall declare my glory among the nations. And they shall bring all your brethren from all the nations as an offering to the LORD, upon horses, and in chariots, and in litters, and upon mules, and upon dromedaries, to my holy mountain Jerusalem, says the LORD, just as the Israelites bring their cereal offering in a clean vessel to the house of the LORD. And some of them also I will take for priests and for Levites, says the LORD.

"For as the new heavens and the new

earth which I will make shall remain before me, so shall your descendants and
your name remain. From new moon to
new moon, and from sabbath to sabbath,
all flesh shall come to worship before me,
says the LORD.

"And they shall go forth and look on the
dead bodies of the men that have rebelled
against me; for their worm shall not die,
their fire shall not be quenched, and they
shall be an abhorrence to all flesh."

JEREMIAH

The life of Jeremiah is much better known than that of any other Old Testament prophet. He was called by God in 627 B.C., while still a young man. With great eloquence, backed by threats of judgment and doom, he summoned his people to moral reform, proclaiming the goodness and power of the Lord. He warned the people of Judah to forsake idols, return to righteousness, and cultivate purity of heart, lest God's justice bring them catastrophe. Eventually he aroused the hostility of the Jewish establishment, and he was imprisoned. When Jerusalem fell, in 586 B.C., he was not among those taken into exile in Babylon, but later a band of conspirators took him with them to Egypt, where his story ends.

The influence of Jeremiah increased after his death, when his secretary, Baruch, gathered his prophecies together, though not in strict chronological order. Despite the thundering associated with his name, he was a man of great sensitivity, even tenderness. One of the high points of his teaching is the promise that God will make a new covenant with his people, writing his law on their hearts. Then, he predicts, both Jews and Gentiles will enjoy a new day under the rule of a messianic king.

———

THE WORDS OF Jeremiah, the son of Hilkiah, of the priests who were in Anathoth in the land of Benjamin, to whom the word of the LORD came in the days of Josiah, king of Judah, in the thirteenth year of his reign. It came also in the days of Jehoiakim the son of Josiah, and until the end of the eleventh year of Zedekiah the son of Josiah, until the captivity of Jerusalem in the fifth month.

Now the word of the LORD came to me, saying, "Before I formed you in the womb

I knew you, and before you were born I consecrated you; I appointed you a prophet to the nations."

Then I said, "Ah, Lord GOD! Behold, I do not know how to speak, for I am only a youth." But the LORD said to me, "Do not say, 'I am only a youth'; for to all to whom I send you you shall go, and whatever I command you you shall speak. Be not afraid of them, for I am with you to deliver you." Then the LORD put forth his hand and touched my mouth, and said, "Behold, I have put my words in your mouth. See, I have set you this day over nations and over kingdoms, to pluck up and to break down, to destroy and to overthrow, to build and to plant."

The word of the LORD came to me, saying, "Jeremiah, what do you see?" I said, "I see a rod of almond." The LORD said, "You have seen well, for I am watching over my word to perform it."

The word of the LORD came to me a second time, saying, "What do you see?" And I said, "I see a boiling pot, facing away from the north." The LORD said, "Out of the north evil shall break forth upon all the inhabitants of the land. For lo, I am calling all the tribes of the kingdoms of the north, says the LORD; and they shall come and every one shall set his throne at the entrance of the gates of Jerusalem, against all its walls round about, and against all the cities of Judah. And I will utter my judgments against them, for all their wickedness in forsaking me; they have burned incense to other gods, and worshiped the works of their own hands.

"But you, gird up your loins; arise, and say to them everything that I command you. Do not be dismayed by them, lest I dismay you before them. And I, behold, I make you this day a fortified city, an iron pillar, and bronze walls, against the whole land, against the kings of Judah, its princes, its priests, and the people of the land. They will fight against you; but they shall not prevail against you, for I am with you, says the LORD, to deliver you."

THE WORD OF the LORD came to me, saying, "Go and proclaim in the hearing of Jerusalem, Thus says the LORD, I remember the devotion of your youth, your love

as a bride, how you followed me in the
wilderness, in a land not sown. Israel was
holy to the LORD, the first fruits of his
harvest. What wrong did your fathers find
in me that they went far from me, and
went after worthlessness? I brought you
into a plentiful land to enjoy its fruits and
good things; but you made my heritage an
abomination. The priests did not say,
'Where is the LORD?' Those who handle
the law did not know me; the rulers transgressed against me; the prophets prophesied by Baal.

"Therefore I still contend with you, says
the LORD, and with your children's children I will contend. Has a nation changed
its gods, even though they are no gods?
My people have changed their glory for
that which does not profit. Be appalled, O
heavens, for my people have committed
two evils: they have forsaken me, the fountain of living waters, and hewed out cisterns for themselves, broken cisterns, that
can hold no water.

"How can you say, 'I am not defiled, I
have not gone after the Baals'? Look at
your way in the valley; know what you

have done. As a thief is shamed when caught, so the house of Israel shall be shamed: they, their kings, their princes, their priests, and their prophets, who say to a tree, 'You are my father,' and to a stone, 'You gave me birth.' For they have turned their back to me, and not their face. But in the time of their trouble they say, 'Arise and save us!' Where then are your gods that you made for yourself? Let them arise, if they can save you; for as many as your cities are your gods, O Judah."

"IF A MAN divorces his wife and she goes from him and becomes another man's wife, will he return to her? Would not that land be greatly polluted? You have played the harlot with many lovers; and would you return to me? says the LORD. Lift up your eyes to the bare heights, and see! Where have you not been lain with? You have polluted the land with your vile harlotry. Therefore the showers have been withheld, and the spring rain has not come; yet you refuse to be ashamed. "Have you not just now called to me, 'My father, thou art the friend of my youth—will he be angry for ever?' Behold, you have spoken, but you have done all the evil that you could."

The LORD said to me in the days of King Josiah: "Have you seen what she did, that faithless one, Israel, how on every high hill and under every green tree she played the harlot? I thought, 'After she has done all this she will return to me'; but she did not. Her false sister Judah saw it; she saw that for all the adulteries I had sent Israel away with a decree of divorce. Yet Judah did not fear, but she too went and played the harlot, polluting the land, committing adultery with stone and tree. Yet for all this, Judah did not return to me with her whole heart, but in pretense.

"Faithless Israel has shown herself less guilty than false Judah. Go, proclaim these words toward the north: 'Return, faithless Israel, for I am merciful, says the LORD; I will not be angry for ever. Only acknowledge your guilt, that you rebelled against the LORD your God and have not obeyed my voice. Return, O faithless children, says the LORD; for I am your master; I will take you, one from a city and two from a family, and I will bring you to Zion. I will give you shepherds after my own heart, who will feed you with knowledge and understanding. And when you have multiplied and increased in the land, Jerusalem shall be called the throne of the LORD, and all nations shall gather to it, to the presence of the LORD, and they shall no more stubbornly follow their own evil heart. The house of Judah shall join the house of Israel, and together they shall come from the north to the land that I gave your fathers.

" 'I thought how I would set you among my sons, and give you a pleasant land, a heritage most beauteous of all nations. And I thought you would call me, My Father, and would not turn from following me. Surely, as a faithless wife leaves her husband, so have you been faithless to me, O house of Israel, says the LORD.' "

A voice on the bare heights is heard, the weeping and pleading of Israel's sons, because they have perverted their way. They have forgotten the LORD their God.

"Return, O faithless sons, I will heal your faithlessness."

"Behold, we come to thee; for thou art

the LORD our God. Truly the hills are a delusion, the orgies on the mountains. Truly in the LORD our God is the salvation of Israel. But from our youth Baal has devoured all for which our fathers labored. Let us lie down in our shame, and let our dishonor cover us; for we have sinned against the LORD our God, we and our fathers, from our youth even to this day."

"If you return, O Israel, says the LORD, to me you should return. If you remove your abominations and do not waver, if you swear, 'As the LORD lives,' in truth, in justice, and in uprightness, then nations shall bless themselves in him, and in him shall they glory."

For thus says the LORD to the men of Judah: "Break up your fallow ground, and sow not among thorns. Circumcise yourselves to the LORD, remove the foreskin of your hearts; lest my wrath go forth like fire, and burn with none to quench it, because of the evil of your doings."

PROCLAIM IN JERUSALEM: "Blow the trumpet through the land; cry aloud, 'Assemble, and let us go into the fortified cities!'

Flee for safety, for I bring evil from the north. A lion has gone up from his thicket, a destroyer of nations has set out from his place to make your land a waste; your cities will be ruins without inhabitant. Gird you with sackcloth, lament and wail; for the fierce anger of the LORD has not turned back from us."

"In that day, says the LORD, courage shall fail both king and princes; the priests and the prophets shall be astounded." Then I said, "Ah, Lord GOD, surely thou hast utterly deceived this people, saying, 'It shall be well with you'; whereas the sword has reached their very life."

At that time it will be said to Jerusalem, "A hot wind from the desert toward the daughter of my people—not to winnow or cleanse, a wind too full for this—comes for me. Now it is I who speak in judgment upon them."

Behold, he comes up like clouds, his chariots like the whirlwind; his horses swifter than eagles—woe to us! O Jerusalem, wash your heart from wickedness, that you may be saved. How long shall your evil thoughts lodge within you? For a voice proclaims from Mount Ephraim: "Besiegers come from a distant land; they shout against Judah. Like keepers of a field are they against her round about, because she has rebelled against me, says the LORD. Your ways and your doings have brought this upon you. This is your doom; it has reached your very heart."

My anguish, my anguish! I writhe in pain! Oh, the walls of my heart! My heart is beating wildly; I cannot keep silent; for I hear the alarm of war. Disaster follows disaster, the whole land is laid waste. How long must I hear the sound of the trumpet?

"My people are foolish, they know me not; they have no understanding. They are skilled in doing evil, but how to do good they know not."

I looked on the earth, and lo, it was void; and to the heavens, and they had no light. I looked on the mountains, and they were quaking. I looked, and there was no man, and all the birds of the air had fled. I looked, and the fruitful land was a desert, and its cities were laid in ruins before the LORD, before his fierce anger.

For thus says the LORD, "The whole land shall be a desolation; yet I will not make a full end. The earth shall mourn, and the heavens be black; for I have spoken; I have not relented nor will I turn back."

At the noise of horseman and archer every city takes to flight; they enter thickets; they climb among rocks. And you, O desolate one, what do you mean that you dress in scarlet, deck yourself with ornaments of gold, enlarge your eyes with paint? In vain you beautify yourself. Your lovers despise you; they seek your life. I heard a cry as of one bringing forth her first child, the daughter of Zion gasping for breath, stretching out her hands, "Woe is me! I am fainting before murderers."

THE WORD THAT came to Jeremiah from the LORD: "Stand in the gate of the LORD's house, and proclaim there, Hear the word of the LORD, all you men of Judah who enter these gates to worship. Amend your ways, and I will let you dwell in this place. Do not trust in these deceptive words: 'This is the temple of the LORD, the temple of the LORD, the temple of the LORD.' For if you truly amend your doings, if you truly execute justice one with another, if you do not oppress the alien, the fatherless, or the widow, or shed innocent blood in this place, and if you do not go after other gods to your own hurt, then I will let you dwell in this land that I gave to your fathers for ever.

"Behold, you trust in deceptive words to no avail. Will you steal, murder, commit adultery, swear falsely, burn incense to Baal, and then stand before me in this house, which is called by my name, and say, 'We are delivered!'—only to go on doing all these abominations?

"Has this house become a den of robbers in your eyes? Behold, I myself have seen it, says the LORD. Go now to my place that was in Shiloh, where I made my name dwell at first, and see what I did to it for the wickedness of my people Israel. And now, because you have done all these things, says the LORD, and when I called you, you did not answer, therefore I will do to this house as I did to Shiloh. And I will cast you out of my sight, as I cast out your kinsmen of Ephraim.

"As for you, do you pray for this people, and do not intercede for them with me, for I do not hear you. Do you not see what they are doing in the streets of Jerusalem? The children gather wood, the fathers kindle fire, and the women knead dough to make cakes for the queen of heaven; and they pour out drink offerings to other gods, to provoke me to anger. Is it I whom they provoke? says the LORD. Is it not themselves, to their own confusion? Therefore my wrath will be poured out on this place, upon man and beast, upon the trees of the field and the fruit of the ground; it will burn and not be quenched."

Thus says the LORD of hosts, the God of Israel: "Add your burnt offerings to your sacrifices, and eat the flesh. For in the day that I brought them out of Egypt, I did not speak to your fathers concerning burnt offerings. But this command I gave them, 'Obey my voice, and I will be your God, and you shall be my people; and walk in all the way that I command you, that it may be well with you.' They did not obey, but walked in their own counsels, and went backward and not forward. From the day your fathers came out of Egypt to this day, I have persistently sent the prophets to this people; yet they did not incline their ear, but stiffened their neck. They did worse than their fathers.

"So you shall speak all these words to them, but they will not listen. You shall say to them, 'This is the nation that did not obey the voice of their God, and did not accept discipline; truth has perished; it is cut off from their lips. Raise a lamentation on the heights, for the LORD has rejected and forsaken the generation of his wrath.' "

MY GRIEF IS beyond healing, my heart is sick within me. Hark, the cry of the daughter of my people from the length and breadth of the land: "Is the LORD not in Zion? Is her King not in her? The harvest is past, the summer is ended, and we are not saved." For the wound of the daughter of my people is my heart wounded, I mourn, and dismay has taken hold on me.

Is there no balm in Gilead? Is there no physician there? Why then has the health of the daughter of my people not been restored? O that my head were waters, and my eyes a fountain of tears, that I might weep day and night for the slain of the daughter of my people!

O THAT I had in the desert a wayfarers' lodging place, that I might go away from my people! For they are treacherous men. They bend their tongue like a bow; falsehood has grown strong in the land; they proceed from evil to evil, says the LORD. Let every one beware of his neighbor, and put no trust in any brother; for every brother is a supplanter, and every neighbor a slanderer, and no one speaks the truth; they commit iniquity and are too weary to repent. Heaping deceit upon deceit, they refuse to know me.

Therefore thus says the LORD of hosts: "Behold, I will refine and test them, for what else can I do? Their tongue is a deadly arrow; with his mouth each speaks peaceably to his neighbor, but in his heart he plans an ambush for him. Shall I not punish them for these things?

"Take up weeping and wailing for the

mountains, and a lamentation for the pastures because they are laid waste; the lowing of cattle is not heard; the birds and the
beasts have fled. I will make Jerusalem a
lair of jackals, and the cities of Judah a
desolation."

Who is the man so wise that he can
understand this? To whom has the mouth
of the LORD spoken, that he may declare
it? Why is the land ruined, so that no one
passes through? And the LORD says: "Because they have forsaken my law and have
not obeyed my voice, but have gone after
the Baals. Therefore I will feed this people
with wormwood. I will scatter them
among nations whom neither they nor
their fathers have known; and I will send
the sword after them, until I have consumed them.

"Hear, O women, the word of the
LORD; teach to your daughters a lament,
and each to her neighbor a dirge. For
death has come up into our windows, it
has entered our palaces, cutting off the
children from the streets and the young
men from the squares."

Thus says the LORD: "Let not the wise

man glory in his wisdom, let not the mighty man glory in his might, let not the rich man glory in his riches; but let him who glories glory in this, that he understands and knows me, that I am the LORD who practice steadfast love, justice, and righteousness in the earth; for in these things I delight."

THE WORD THAT came to Jeremiah from the LORD: "Hear the words of this covenant, and speak to the men of Judah and the inhabitants of Jerusalem. You shall say to them, Thus says the LORD, the God of Israel: Cursed be the man who does not heed the words of this covenant which I commanded your fathers when I brought them out of the land of Egypt, saying, Listen to my voice, and do all that I command you. So shall you be my people, and I will be your God, that I may perform the oath which I swore to your fathers, to give them a land flowing with milk and honey, as at this day." Then I answered, "So be it, LORD."

And the LORD said to me, "I solemnly warned your fathers, warning them persistently even to this day, saying, Obey my voice. Yet they did not, but every one walked in the stubbornness of his evil heart. Therefore I brought upon them all the words of this covenant, which I commanded them to do, but they did not."

Again the LORD said to me, "There is revolt among the men of Judah. They have turned back to the iniquities of their forefathers, who refused to hear my words; they have gone after other gods; the houses of Israel and Judah have broken my covenant which I made with their fathers. Therefore, thus says the LORD, Behold, I am bringing evil upon them which they cannot escape; though they cry to me, I will not listen to them. Then they will go and cry to the gods to whom they burn incense, but they cannot save them in time of trouble. For as many as the streets of Jerusalem, O Judah, are the altars you have set up to Baal.

"Therefore do not pray for this people, or lift up a cry on their behalf, for I will not listen when they call. What right has my beloved in my house, when she has done vile deeds? Can vows and sacrificial flesh avert your doom? The LORD once called you, 'A green olive tree, fair with goodly fruit'; but with the roar of a great tempest he will set fire to it, and its branches will be consumed. The LORD of hosts, who planted you, has pronounced evil against you, because of the evil which you have done, provoking me to anger by burning incense to Baal."

THE LORD MADE known to me the evil deeds of my neighbors of Anathoth. But I was like a gentle lamb led to the slaughter. I did not know it was against me they devised schemes, saying, "Let us cut him off from the land of the living, that his name be remembered no more." O LORD of hosts, who judgest righteously, let me see thy vengeance upon them, for to thee have I committed my cause.

Concerning the men of Anathoth, who say, "Do not prophesy in the name of the LORD or you will die by our hand," thus says the LORD: "Behold, I will bring evil upon the men of Anathoth."

Righteous art thou, O LORD, when I complain to thee; yet I would plead my

case before thee. Why does the way of the
wicked prosper? Why do all who are
treacherous thrive? Thou plantest them,
and they bring forth fruit; thou art near in
their mouth and far from their heart. But
thou knowest me, and triest my mind toward thee. Pull them out like sheep for the
slaughter.

"If you have raced with men on foot
and they have wearied you, how will you
compete with horses? And if in a safe
land you fall down, how will you do in
the jungle of the Jordan? For even your
brothers and the house of your father
have dealt treacherously with you; even
they are in full cry after you; believe
them not, though they speak fair words
to you."

"I HAVE FORSAKEN my house, I have given
the beloved of my soul into the hands of
her enemies. My heritage has become to
me like a lion in the forest, she has lifted
up her voice against me; therefore I hate
her. Is my heritage to me like a speckled
bird of prey, with other birds of prey
against her round about? Go, assemble all

the wild beasts; bring them to devour.

"Many shepherds have destroyed my vineyard, they have made my pleasant portion a wilderness. Desolate, it mourns to me, but no man lays it to heart. Upon the heights in the desert destroyers have come; the sword of the LORD devours from one end of the land to the other; no flesh has peace. They have sown wheat and reaped thorns, they have tired themselves out but profit nothing. They shall be ashamed of their harvests because of the fierce anger of the LORD."

Thus says the LORD concerning all my evil neighbors who touch the heritage given my people Israel: "Behold, I will pluck them up from their land, and Judah from among them. After I have plucked them up, I will again have compassion on them, and bring them again each to his heritage. This shall come to pass, if they will diligently learn the ways of my people: to swear by my name, 'As the LORD lives,' even as they taught my people to swear by Baal. But if any nation will not listen, then I will utterly pluck it up and destroy it, says the LORD."

THE LORD SAID to me, "Go and buy a linen waistcloth, and put it on your loins, and do not dip it in water." So I bought a waistcloth and put it on my loins. The word of the LORD came to me a second time, "Take the waistcloth which is upon your loins, go to the Euphrates, and hide it there in a cleft of the rock." So I went, and hid it by the Euphrates, as the LORD commanded. After many days the LORD said to me, "Arise, take the waistcloth I commanded you to hide." Then I went to the Euphrates, and dug, and I took the waistcloth from where I had hidden it. And behold, it was spoiled, good for nothing.

Then the word of the LORD came to me: "Even so will I spoil the pride of Judah and the great pride of Jerusalem. This stubborn people who follow their own heart and have gone after other gods shall be like this waistcloth, which is good for nothing. For as the waistcloth clings to the loins of a man, so I made the houses of Israel and Judah cling to me, says the LORD, that they might be for me a people, a name, a praise, and a glory, but they would not listen.

"You shall speak to them this word: 'Thus says the LORD, the God of Israel: Every jar shall be filled with wine.' They will say, 'Do we not indeed know that?' Then you shall say, 'Thus says the LORD: Behold, I will fill with drunkenness all the inhabitants of this land: the kings who sit on David's throne, the priests, the prophets, and all the inhabitants of Jerusalem. And I will dash them one against another, fathers and sons together, says the LORD.'

"Can the Ethiopian change his skin or the leopard his spots? Then also you can do good who are accustomed to do evil. I will scatter you like chaff driven by the wind from the desert. This is the portion I have measured out to you, says the LORD, because you have trusted in lies. I have seen your abominations on the hills in the field. Woe to you, O Jerusalem! How long will it be before you are made clean?"

THE WORD OF the LORD which came to Jeremiah concerning the drought:

"Judah mourns and her gates languish; her people lament on the ground, and the cry of Jerusalem goes up. Her nobles send their servants for water; they come to the cisterns, find no water, return with their vessels empty; confounded, they cover their heads. Because of the ground which is dismayed since there is no rain, the farmers are ashamed and cover their heads. The hind in the field forsakes her newborn calf because there is no grass. The wild asses stand on the bare heights, they pant for air like jackals.

"Though our iniquities testify against us, act, O LORD, for thy name's sake; for our backslidings are many. O thou hope of Israel, why shouldst thou be like a stranger in the land, like a man confused, like a mighty man who cannot save? Yet thou, O LORD, art in the midst of us, and we are called by thy name; leave us not."

Thus says the LORD concerning this people: "They have loved to wander, they have not restrained their feet; therefore the LORD does not accept them, now he will remember their iniquity."

The LORD said to me: "Do not pray for the welfare of this people. Though they fast, I will not hear their cry; but I will consume them by the sword, by famine, and by pestilence." Then I said: "Ah, Lord GOD, behold, the prophets say to them, 'You shall not see the sword or famine, but I will give you assured peace in this place.' " And the LORD said: "Those prophets are prophesying lies in my name: I did not send them or speak to them. They are prophesying the deceit of their own minds. Therefore thus says the LORD: By sword and famine those prophets shall be consumed. The people to whom they prophesy shall be cast out in the streets of Jerusalem, victims of famine and sword, with none to bury them, their wives, sons, and daughters. For I will pour out their wickedness upon them."

"WHO WILL HAVE pity on you, O Jerusalem? Who will turn aside to ask about your welfare? You have rejected me, says the LORD; so I have stretched out my hand against you—I am weary of relenting. I have winnowed my people with a winnowing fork, I have destroyed them; they did not turn from their ways. I have made their widows more in number than the sand of the seas; I have brought against the mothers of young men a destroyer at noonday; I have made terror fall upon them suddenly. She who bore seven has swooned away, her sun went down while it was yet day. And the rest of them I will give to the sword before their enemies, says the LORD."

WOE IS ME, my mother, that you bore me, a man of strife and contention to the whole land! I have not lent, nor have I borrowed, yet all of them curse me. So let it be, O LORD, if I have not entreated thee for their good, if I have not pleaded with thee on behalf of the enemy in the time of distress! Can one break iron, iron from the north, and bronze?

O LORD, thou knowest; remember me and visit me, and take vengeance for me on my persecutors. Know that for thy sake I bear reproach. Thy words were found, and I ate them, and thy words became to me the delight of my heart; for I am called by thy name, O LORD, God of hosts. I did not sit in the company of merrymakers; I sat alone, because thy hand was upon me, for thou hadst filled me with indignation.

Why is my pain unceasing, my wound incurable, refusing to be healed? Wilt thou be to me like a deceitful brook, like waters that fail?

Therefore thus says the LORD: "If you return, I will restore you. If you utter what is precious, and not what is worthless, you shall be as my mouth. They shall turn to you, but you shall not turn to them. And I will make you to this people a fortified wall of bronze; they will fight against you, but they shall not prevail, for I am with you, says the LORD. I will deliver you out of the hand of the wicked."

THE WORD OF the LORD came to me: "You shall not take a wife, nor shall you have sons or daughters in this place. For thus says the LORD concerning the sons and daughters born in this place, and the mothers who bore them and the fathers who begot them: They shall die of deadly diseases. They shall perish by sword and famine, and their bodies be food for the beasts.

"Do not enter the house of mourning to bemoan them; for I have taken away my peace from this people, my steadfast love and mercy. Both great and small shall die and not be buried, and no one shall lament for them. No one shall break bread for the mourner, to comfort him; nor shall any give him the cup of consolation. You shall not go into the house of feasting to sit with them. For behold, I will make to cease from this place in your days the voice of mirth and the voice of gladness, the voice of the bridegroom and the voice of the bride.

"And when you tell this people these words, and they say to you, 'Why has the LORD pronounced all this great evil against us? What is the sin that we have committed against the LORD our God?' then you shall say to them: 'Because your fathers have forsaken me and gone after other gods, says the LORD, and have not kept my law; and because you have done worse than your fathers, every one of you following his stubborn evil will, refusing to listen to me; therefore I will hurl you into a land which neither you nor your fathers have known, and there you shall serve other gods day and night, for I will show you no favor.'

"Behold, I am sending for many fishers, says the LORD, and they shall catch them; and afterwards I will send for many hunters, and they shall hunt them from every mountain, and out of the clefts of the rocks. For my eyes are upon all their ways; their iniquity is not hid from me. And I will doubly recompense their sin, because they have polluted my land with the carcasses of their detestable idols.

"The sin of Judah is written with a pen of iron; with a point of diamond it is engraved on the tablet of their heart, and on the horns of their altars, while their children remember their altars beside every green tree. Your wealth and all your treasures I will give for spoil as the price of your sin. You shall loosen your hand from your heritage which I gave to you, and I will make you serve your enemies in a land which you do not know, for in my anger a fire is kindled which shall burn for ever."

THUS SAYS THE LORD: "Cursed is the man who trusts in man and whose heart turns away from the LORD. He is like a shrub in the desert; he shall dwell in parched places, in an uninhabited salt land.

"Blessed is the man who trusts in the LORD. He is like a tree planted by water, that sends out its roots by the stream, and does not fear when heat comes, for its leaves remain green, and is not anxious in the year of drought, for it does not cease to bear fruit."

The heart is deceitful above all things; who can understand it? "I the LORD search the mind and try the heart, to give to every man according to the fruit of his doings."

Like the partridge that gathers a brood which she did not hatch, so is he who gets riches but not by right; in the midst of his days they will leave him, and at his end he will be a fool.

A glorious throne set on high from the beginning is the place of our sanctuary. O LORD, the hope of Israel, all who turn away from thee shall be written in the earth, for they have forsaken the LORD, the fountain of living water.

HEAL ME, O LORD, and I shall be healed; save me, and I shall be saved; for thou art my praise. Behold, they say to me, "Where is the word of the LORD? Let it come!"

I have not pressed thee to send evil, thou knowest; that which came out of my lips was before thy face. Be not a terror to me; thou art my refuge in the day of evil. Let those be put to shame who persecute me, but let me not be put to shame; let them be dismayed; bring upon them the day of evil!

THE LORD SAID to me: "Go and stand in the Benjamin Gate, by which the kings of Judah enter and go out, and say: 'Hear the word of the LORD, you kings of Judah, and all Judah, and all who enter by these gates: Take heed for the sake of your lives, and do not bear a burden on the sabbath day or do any work, but keep the sabbath holy, as I commanded your fathers. Yet they did not incline their ear, but stiffened their neck, that they might not receive instruction. If you listen to me, says the LORD, and keep the sabbath holy, then there shall enter by the gates of this city kings who sit on the throne of David, riding in chariots and on horses, they and their princes, the

men of Judah and the inhabitants of Jerusalem; and this city shall be inhabited for
ever. And people shall come from the cities of Judah round about, bringing thank
offerings to the house of the LORD. But if
you do not listen to me, to keep the sabbath day holy, then I will kindle a fire in
these gates, and it shall devour the palaces
of Jerusalem and shall not be quenched.' "

THE WORD THAT came to Jeremiah from the
LORD: "Arise, and go down to the potter's
house, and there I will let you hear my
words." So I went to the potter's house,
and there he was working at his wheel.
And the vessel he was making of clay was
spoiled in his hand, and he reworked it
into another vessel, as it seemed good to
him to do.

Then the word of the LORD came to me:
"O house of Israel, can I not do with you
as this potter has done? Like the clay in
the potter's hand, so are you in my hand.
If at any time I declare concerning a nation
that I will pluck up and destroy it, and if
that nation then turns from its evil, I will
repent of the evil I intended to do to it.

And if I declare concerning a nation that I will build and plant it, and it does evil in my sight, then I will repent of the good I had intended to do to it. Now therefore say to the men of Judah: 'Thus says the LORD, Behold, I am devising a plan against you. Return, every one from his evil way.'

"But they say, 'That is in vain! We will follow our own plans, and will every one act according to the stubbornness of his heart.' "

Thus said the LORD, "Go, buy a potter's earthen flask, and take some of the elders of the people and senior priests, and go out to Topheth in the valley of the son of Hinnom at the entry of the Potsherd Gate, and proclaim there these words that I tell you: 'Hear the word of the LORD, O kings of Judah and inhabitants of Jerusalem. Behold, I am bringing such evil upon this place that the ears of every one who hears of it will tingle. Because the people have profaned this place by burning incense in it to other gods, and have filled it with the blood of innocents, and built the high places to burn their sons as offerings to Baal, which I did not command or decree, nor did it come into my mind; therefore days are coming, says the LORD, when this place shall no more be called Topheth, or the valley of the son of Hinnom, but the valley of Slaughter. In this place I will make void the plans of Judah and Jerusalem, and will cause their people to fall by the sword before their enemies, and I will give their dead bodies for food to the birds of the air and to the beasts of the earth. I will make this city a horror, a thing to be hissed at. I will make them eat the flesh of their sons and their daughters, and every one shall eat the flesh of his neighbor in the siege, and in the distress with which those who seek their life afflict them.'

"Then you shall break the earthen flask in the sight of the men who go with you, and say to them, 'Thus says the LORD of hosts: So will I break this city, as one breaks a potter's vessel, so it can never be mended. Men shall bury in Topheth because there will be no place else to bury. Thus will I do to this place, making this city like Topheth. The houses of Jerusalem and the houses of the kings of Judah—all the houses upon whose roofs incense has been burned and drink offerings poured out to other gods—shall be defiled like the place of Topheth.' "

Then Jeremiah came from Topheth, where the LORD had sent him to prophesy, and he stood in the court of the LORD's house, and said to all the people: "Thus says the LORD of hosts, Behold, I am bringing upon this city all the evil I have pronounced against it, because they have refused to hear my words."

Now PASHHUR THE priest, who was chief officer in the house of the LORD, heard Jeremiah prophesying these things. Then Pashhur beat Jeremiah, and put him in the stocks that were in the upper Benjamin Gate of the house of the LORD.

On the morrow, when Pashhur released him from the stocks, Jeremiah said, "The LORD does not call your name Pashhur, but Terror on every side. For thus says the LORD: I will make you a terror to yourself and to all your friends. They shall fall by the sword of their enemies while you look on. And I will give all Judah into the hand of the king of Babylon; he shall carry them

captive to Babylon and slay them with the
sword. Moreover, I will give all the treasures of the city and of the kings of Judah
into the hand of their enemies. And you,
Pashhur, shall go into captivity; to Babylon
you shall go; there you shall die and be
buried, you and all your friends, to whom
you have prophesied falsely."

O LORD, THOU hast deceived me, and I was
deceived; thou art stronger than I, and
thou hast prevailed. Every one mocks me.
For whenever I speak, I shout, "Violence
and destruction!" The word of the LORD
has become for me a reproach and derision all day long. If I say, "I will not speak
any more in his name," there is in my
heart as it were a burning fire shut up in
my bones, and I am weary with holding it
in, and I cannot. Terror is on every side!
"Denounce him! Let us denounce him!"
say all my familiar friends, watching for
my fall. "Perhaps he will be deceived, and
then we can overcome him and take our
revenge."
   But the LORD is with me as a dread
warrior. Therefore my persecutors will

stumble. They will be greatly shamed, for they will not succeed. O LORD of hosts, who triest the righteous, who seest the heart and the mind, to thee have I committed my cause.

Sing to the LORD; praise the LORD! For he has delivered the life of the needy from the hand of evildoers.

THIS IS THE word which came to Jeremiah from the LORD, when Zedekiah king of Judah sent to him Zephaniah the priest and another, saying, "Inquire of the LORD for us, for Nebuchadrezzar king of Babylon is making war against us; perhaps the LORD will deal with us according to all his wonderful deeds, and will make him withdraw from us."

Jeremiah said: "Say to Zedekiah, 'Thus says the LORD: Behold, I will turn back the weapons of war with which you are fighting against the king of Babylon and the Chaldeans besieging your walls; and I will bring them together into this city. I myself will fight against you with outstretched hand and strong arm in great wrath, and I will smite the inhabitants of this city, both man and beast; they shall die of a great pestilence. Afterward I will give Zedekiah, and his servants, and the people in this city who survive the pestilence and sword, into the hand of Nebuchadrezzar king of Babylon. He shall not pity or spare them.'

"And to this people you shall say: 'Thus says the LORD: Behold, I set before you the way of life and the way of death. He who stays in this city shall die; but he who goes out and surrenders to the Chaldeans shall have his life as a prize of war. For I have set my face against this city for evil and not for good, says the LORD; it shall be given into the hand of the king of Babylon, and he shall burn it with fire.' "

THUS SAYS THE LORD: "Go down to the house of the king, and say, Hear the word of the LORD, O King of Judah, who sit on the throne of David, you, and your servants, and your people: Do justice and righteousness, and deliver from the hand of the oppressor him who has been robbed. And do no wrong or violence to the alien, the fatherless, and the widow, nor shed innocent blood in this place. For if you will indeed obey this word, then there shall enter these gates kings who sit on the throne of David. But if you will not heed these words, I swear by myself, says the LORD, that this house shall become a desolation. For you are as Gilead to me, as the summit of Lebanon, yet surely I will make you a desert. I will prepare destroyers against you and they shall cut down your choicest cedars and cast them into the fire. Many nations will pass by, and every man will say to his neighbor, 'Why has the LORD dealt thus with this great city?' And they will answer, 'Because they forsook the covenant of the LORD their God, and worshiped other gods.' "

WEEP NOT FOR him who is dead; but weep bitterly for him who goes away, for he shall return no more to see his native land. Thus says the LORD concerning Jehoahaz the son of Josiah, king of Judah, who reigned instead of his father, and went away from this place: "He shall return here no more, but in the place where they have carried him captive, there shall he die."

"WOE TO HIM who builds his house by unrighteousness, who makes his neighbor serve him and does not give him his wages; who says, 'I will build myself a great house with spacious upper rooms,' and cuts out windows for it, paneling it with cedar, and painting it with vermilion. Do you think you are a king because you compete in cedar? Did not your father eat and drink and do justice and righteousness? He judged the cause of the poor and needy; then it was well with him. Is not this to know me? says the LORD. But you have eyes and heart only for your dishonest gain, and for practicing oppression and violence."

Therefore thus says the LORD concerning Jehoiakim the son of Josiah, king of Judah: "They shall not lament for him, saying, 'Ah my brother!' or 'Ah his majesty!' With the burial of an ass he shall be buried, dragged, and cast forth beyond the gates of Jerusalem."

"GO UP TO Lebanon, and cry out, for all your lovers are destroyed. I spoke to you in your prosperity, but you said, 'I will not listen.' This has been your way from your youth. The wind shall shepherd all your shepherds, and your lovers shall go into captivity; then you will be confounded because of your wickedness. How you will groan when pangs come upon you, pain as of a woman in travail!"

"As I live, says the LORD, though Jehoiachin the son of Jehoiakim, king of Judah, were the signet ring on my right hand, yet I would tear you off and give you into the hand of those of whom you are afraid, even Nebuchadrezzar king of Babylon and the Chaldeans. I will hurl you and the mother who bore you into another country, where you were not born, and there you shall die."

Is this man Jehoiachin a despised, broken pot, a vessel no one cares for? Why are he and his children hurled into a land which they do not know? O land, land, land, hear the word of the LORD: Write this man down as childless, a man who shall not succeed in his days; for none of his offspring shall succeed in sitting on the throne of David, and ruling again in Judah.

"WOE TO THE shepherds who destroy and scatter the sheep of my pasture!" says the LORD. "You have driven my flock away, and you have not attended to them. Behold, I will attend to you for your evil doings. Then I will gather the remnant of my flock out of all the countries and bring them back to their fold, and they shall be fruitful and multiply. I will set shepherds over them who will care for them, and they shall fear no more, nor be dismayed, neither shall any be missing.

"Behold, the days are coming, says the LORD, when I will raise up for David a righteous Branch, and he shall reign as king and deal wisely, and shall execute justice and righteousness in the land. In his days Judah will be saved, and Israel will dwell securely. And this is the name by which he will be called: 'The LORD is our righteousness.' Men shall no longer say, 'As the LORD lives who brought up the people of Israel out of Egypt,' but 'As the LORD lives who brought the descendants of the house of Israel out of the north country and all the countries where he had driven them.' Then they shall dwell in their own land."

THUS SAYS THE LORD of hosts: "Do not listen to the words of the prophets who fill you with vain hopes; they speak visions of their own minds, not from the LORD. They say continually to those who despise the word of the LORD, 'It shall be well with you'; and to every one who stubbornly follows his own heart, they say, 'No evil shall come upon you.' "

For who among them has stood in the council of the LORD or given heed to his word? "I did not send the prophets, yet they ran; I did not speak to them, yet they prophesied. But if they had stood in my council, they would have proclaimed my words to my people, and they would have turned them from their evil way.

"Am I a God at hand, says the LORD, and not a God afar off? Can a man hide himself so I cannot see him? Do I not fill heaven and earth? I have heard what the prophets say who prophesy lies in my name: 'I have dreamed, I have dreamed!' How long shall prophets prophesy the deceit of their own heart, who think to make my people forget my name by their dreams which they tell one another, even as their fathers forgot my name for Baal? Let the prophet who has a dream tell the dream, but let him who has my word speak my word faithfully. What has straw in common with wheat? says the LORD. Is not my word like fire, and like a hammer which breaks the rock in pieces? Therefore, behold, I am against the prophets who steal my words from one another. I am against the prophets who use their tongues and say, 'Says the LORD.' I am against those who lead my people astray by their lies and recklessness when I did not send them or charge them. They do not profit this people at all, says the LORD.

"When one of this people, or a prophet, or a priest asks you, 'What is the burden of the LORD?' you shall say to them, 'You are the burden, and I will cast you off, says the LORD.' "

AFTER NEBUCHADREZZAR KING of Babylon had taken into exile from Jerusalem Jehoiachin the son of Jehoiakim, king of Judah, together with the princes, the craftsmen, and the smiths, and had brought them to Babylon, the LORD showed me this vision: Behold, two baskets of figs placed before the temple of the LORD. One basket had very good figs, like first-ripe figs, but the other basket had very bad figs. And the LORD said to me, "What do you see, Jeremiah?" I said, "Figs, the good figs very good, and the bad figs so bad that they cannot be eaten."

The LORD said, "Like these good figs, so I will regard as good the exiles from Judah, whom I have sent to the land of the Chaldeans. I will set my eyes upon them for good, and bring them back to this land; I will plant them, and not uproot them. I will give them a heart to know that I am the LORD; and they shall be my people and I will be their God, for they shall return to me with their whole heart.

"But like the bad figs which are so bad they cannot be eaten, so will I treat Zedekiah the king of Judah, his princes, the remnant of Jerusalem in this land, and those who dwell in Egypt. I will make them a horror to all the kingdoms of the earth, a reproach, a byword, and a curse in all the places where I shall drive them. And they shall be utterly destroyed from the land which I gave to them and their fathers."

THE WORD THAT came to Jeremiah concerning all the people of Judah, in the fourth year of Jehoiakim the son of Josiah, king of Judah (that was the first year of Nebuchadrezzar king of Babylon), which Jeremiah the prophet spoke: "For twenty-three years, from the thirteenth year of Josiah to this day, the word of the LORD has come to me, and I have spoken to you. But you have not inclined your ears to hear, although the LORD persistently sent you all his servants the prophets, saying, 'Turn now, every one of you, from his wrong doings, and dwell upon the land which the LORD has given you; do not go after other gods, or provoke me to anger with the work of your hands. Then I will do you no harm.' Yet you have not listened to me, says the LORD, that you might provoke me to anger.

"Therefore thus says the LORD of hosts: Behold, I will send for all the tribes of the north, and for Nebuchadrezzar the king of Babylon, my servant, and I will bring them against this land and all these nations round about. I will banish from these nations the voice of mirth and gladness, the voice of the bridegroom and the bride, the grinding of the millstones and the light of the lamp. And they shall serve the king of Babylon seventy years. Then, after seventy years, I will punish the king of Babylon and the Chaldeans for their iniquity, says the LORD. I will bring upon that land all the words I have uttered against it, everything written in this book, which Jeremiah prophesied against all the nations. For many nations and great kings shall make slaves even of them; for I will recompense them according to their deeds."

Thus the LORD, the God of Israel, said to me: "Take from my hand this cup of the wine of wrath, and make all the nations to whom I send you drink it. They shall drink and stagger and be crazed because of the sword which I am sending among them."

So I took the cup from the LORD's hand, and made all the nations to whom the

LORD sent me drink it: Judah, its kings and princes; Pharaoh of Egypt, all his people, and all the foreign folk among them; all the kings of the north, far and near; all the kingdoms on the face of the earth. And after them the king of Babylon shall drink.

"Then you shall say, 'Thus says the God of Israel: Drink, fall, rise no more, because of the sword I am sending among you.'

"And if they refuse to accept the cup from your hand, then you shall say, 'Thus says the LORD of hosts: You must drink! For behold, I begin to work evil at the city which is called by my name, and shall you go unpunished? You shall not go unpunished, for I am summoning a sword against all the inhabitants of the earth.'"

IN THE BEGINNING of the reign of Jehoiakim this word came from the LORD: "Stand in the court of the LORD's house, and speak there all the words that I command you; do not hold back a word. It may be they will listen, and that I may repent of the evil I intend to do them. You shall say, 'Thus says the LORD: If you will not walk in my law and heed the words of my servants the prophets whom I send you urgently, then I will make this house like Shiloh, and this city a curse for all the nations of the earth.' "

The priests and the prophets and all the people heard Jeremiah speaking these words in the house of the LORD. And when he had finished, they laid hold of him, saying, "You shall die! Why have you prophesied in the name of the LORD, saying, 'This house shall be like Shiloh, and this city without inhabitant'?" And all the people gathered about Jeremiah. When the princes of Judah heard these things, they came up from the king's house and took their seat in the entry of the New Gate of the house of the LORD. The priests and prophets said to the princes and to all the people, "This man deserves the sentence of death, because he has prophesied against this city, as you have heard with your own ears."

Then Jeremiah spoke to all the princes and all the people, saying, "The LORD sent me to prophesy against this house and this city. Now therefore amend your ways, and obey the voice of the LORD your God, and the LORD will repent of the evil he has pronounced against you. But as for me, behold, I am in your hands. Do with me as seems right to you. Only know for certain that if you put me to death, you will bring innocent blood upon yourselves and upon this city, for in truth the LORD sent me to you to speak all these words in your ears."

Then the princes and all the people said to the priests, "This man does not deserve death, for he has spoken to us in the name of the LORD our God." And certain of the elders arose and spoke to the assembled people, saying, "Micah prophesied in the days of King Hezekiah to the people of Judah: 'Thus says the LORD, Zion shall be plowed as a field; Jerusalem shall become a heap of ruins, and the mountain of the house a wooded height.' Did Hezekiah put him to death? Did he not fear the LORD, and did not the LORD repent of the evil he had pronounced against them? But we are about to bring great evil upon ourselves."

The hand of Ahikam the son of Shaphan was with Jeremiah, so that he was not given over to the people to be put to death.

IN THE BEGINNING of the reign of Zedekiah the son of Josiah, king of Judah, the LORD said to me: "Make yourself thongs and yoke-bars, and put them on your neck. Send word to the kings of Edom, Moab, and Ammon, and the kings of Tyre and Sidon by the hand of the envoys who have come to Jerusalem to Zedekiah. Give them this charge: 'Thus says the LORD of hosts, the God of Israel, to your masters: It is I who by my great power have made the earth, with the men and animals that are on it, and I give it to whomever it seems right to me. Now I have given all these lands into the hand of Nebuchadrezzar, the king of Babylon, my servant, and I have given him also the beasts of the field to serve him. All the nations shall serve him and his son and his grandson, until the time of his own land comes.' "

To Zedekiah king of Judah I spoke thus: "Bring your necks under the yoke of the king of Babylon, serve him, and live. Why will you die, as the LORD has spoken concerning any nation which will not serve the king of Babylon? Do not listen to prophets who say, 'You shall not serve Nebuchad-

rezzar,' for I have not sent them, says the
LORD. They prophesy falsely in my name,
says the LORD, with the result that I will
drive you out and you will perish, you and
those prophets."

Then I spoke to the priests and to all
this people: "Do not listen to prophets
who say, 'Behold, the vessels of the LORD's
house will now shortly be brought back
from Babylon,' for it is a lie. Do not listen
to them; serve the king of Babylon and
live. If they are prophets and the word of
the LORD is with them, then let them intercede with him, that the vessels which are
still in the house of the LORD, in the house
of the king of Judah, and in Jerusalem may
not go to Babylon. For thus says the LORD
concerning the pillars, the sea, the stands,
and the rest of the vessels which Nebuchadrezzar did not take when he took into
exile Jehoiachin king of Judah: They shall
be carried to Babylon and remain there
until the day when I give attention to
them. Then I will restore them to this
place."

In that same year, at the beginning of
the reign of Zedekiah, Hananiah the

prophet from Gibeon spoke to me in the house of the LORD, saying, "Thus says the LORD of hosts: I have broken the yoke of the king of Babylon. Within two years I will bring back to this place all the vessels of the LORD's house which Nebuchadrezzar carried to Babylon. I will also bring back Jehoiachin the son of Jehoiakim, and all the exiles from Judah, says the LORD."

Then Jeremiah spoke to Hananiah in the presence of all the people: "Amen! May the LORD make your words come true and bring back from Babylon all the vessels and all the exiles. Yet hear now this word. The prophets who preceded you and me from ancient times prophesied war, famine, and pestilence against many countries. As for the prophet who prophesies peace, when the word of that prophet comes to pass, then it will be known that the LORD has truly sent the prophet."

Then Hananiah took the yoke-bars from the neck of Jeremiah and broke them. And he spoke, saying, "Thus says the LORD: Even so will I break the yoke of Nebuchadrezzar king of Babylon from the neck of all the nations within two years."

But Jeremiah the prophet went his way.

Sometime after this, the word of the LORD came to Jeremiah: "Go, tell Hananiah, 'Thus says the LORD: You have broken wooden bars, but I will make in their place bars of iron. For I have put upon the neck of all these nations an iron yoke of servitude to the king of Babylon, for I have given to him even the beasts of the field.' " Jeremiah said, "Listen, Hananiah, the LORD has not sent you, and you have made this people trust in a lie. Therefore thus says the LORD: 'Behold, I will remove you from the face of the earth. This very year you shall die, because you have uttered rebellion against the LORD.' "

In that same year, in the seventh month, the prophet Hananiah died.

THE WORD THAT came to Jeremiah from the LORD: "Write in a book all the words I have spoken to you. For behold, days are coming when I will restore the fortunes of my people and bring them back to the land I gave to their fathers."

These are the words the LORD spoke concerning Israel and Judah: "We have heard a cry of panic, and no peace. Ask now, can a man bear a child? Why then do I see every man with his hands on his loins like a woman in labor? Why has every face turned pale? Alas! that day is so great there is none like it; it is a time of distress for Jacob; yet he shall be saved out of it. And it shall come to pass in that day that I will break the yoke from off their neck, and I will burst their bonds, and strangers shall no more make servants of them. But they shall serve the LORD their God and David their king, whom I will raise up for them.

"Then fear not, O Jacob my servant, says the LORD, for lo, I will save you from afar, and your offspring from captivity. Jacob shall return, and none shall make him afraid. For I am with you to save you, says the LORD; I will make a full end of all the nations among whom I scattered you, but of you I will not make a full end. I will chasten you in just measure.

"Your wound is grievous. There is none to uphold your cause, no healing for you. All your lovers have forgotten you; for I have dealt you the blow of an enemy, because your guilt is great. Why do you cry out over your hurt? Your pain is incurable. Because your sins are flagrant, I have done this to you.

"Yet all who devour you shall be devoured, and your foes, every one of them, shall go into captivity; all who prey on you I will make a prey. For I will restore health to you, and your wounds I will heal, says the LORD. Behold, I will restore the fortunes of the tents of Jacob; the city shall be rebuilt upon its mound, and the palace shall stand where it used to be. Out of them shall come songs of thanksgiving, and the voices of those who make merry. I will multiply them, and make them honored. Their children shall be as they were of old, their congregation established before me. Their prince, their ruler, shall come forth from their midst; I will make him draw near, and he shall approach me, for who would dare of himself to approach me? says the LORD. You shall be my people, and I will be your God."

Behold the storm of the LORD! A whirling tempest will burst upon the head of the wicked. The fierce anger of the LORD will not turn back until he has accomplished the intents of his mind. In the latter days you will understand this.

"At that time, says the LORD, I will be the God of all the families of Israel, and they shall be my people."

Thus says the LORD: "The people who survived the sword found grace in the wilderness; when Israel sought for rest, the LORD appeared to him from afar. I have loved you with an everlasting love; therefore I have continued my faithfulness to you. Again I will build you, O virgin Israel! Again you shall adorn yourself with timbrels and go forth in the dance of the merrymakers. Again you shall plant vineyards upon the mountains of Samaria and enjoy the fruit. For there shall be a day when watchmen will call in the hill country of Ephraim: 'Arise, and let us go up to Zion, to the LORD our God.' "

For thus says the LORD: "Sing aloud with gladness for Jacob, give praise, and say, 'The LORD has saved his people, the remnant of Israel.' Behold, I will gather them from the farthest parts of the earth, among them the blind and the lame, the woman with child and her who is in travail; a great company, they shall return. With consolations I will lead them back, I will make them walk by brooks of water, in a path in which they shall not stumble; for I am a father to Israel, and Ephraim is my first-born.

"Hear the word of the LORD, O nations, and declare in the coastlands afar off: 'He who scattered Israel will gather him, and will keep him as a shepherd keeps his flock.' For the LORD has ransomed Jacob from hands too strong for him. They shall come and sing aloud on the height of Zion, they shall be radiant over the goodness of the LORD, over the grain, the wine, and the oil, and over the young of the flock and the herd; their life shall be like a watered garden. Then shall the maidens rejoice in the dance, and young men and old shall be merry. I will give them gladness for sorrow. I will feast the soul of the priests with abundance, and my people shall be satisfied with my goodness."

Thus says the LORD: "A voice is heard in Ramah, lamentation and bitter weeping. Rachel is weeping for her children; she refuses to be comforted, because they are not.

"Keep your eyes from tears. There is hope for your future, and your children shall come back to their own country, says the LORD. I have heard Ephraim bemoaning, 'Thou hast chastened me like an untrained calf; bring me back, that I may be restored. For after I had turned away, I repented; and after I was instructed, I smote upon my thigh; I was confounded, because I bore the disgrace of my youth.' Is Ephraim my dear son? Is he my darling child? For as often as I speak against him, I do remember him still. Therefore my heart yearns for him; I will surely have mercy on him, says the LORD.

"Set up waymarks for yourself, make yourself guideposts; consider well the highway, the road by which you went. Return, O virgin Israel, return to these your cities. How long will you waver, O faithless daughter? For the LORD has created a new thing on the earth: a woman protects a man.

"Once more they shall use these words in the land of Judah and in its cities, when

I restore their fortunes: 'The LORD bless you, O habitation of righteousness, O holy hill!' And Judah and all its cities shall dwell there together, and the farmers and those who wander with their flocks. For I will satisfy the weary soul, and every languishing soul I will replenish."

Thereupon I awoke and looked, and my sleep was pleasant to me.

"Behold, the days are coming, says the LORD, when I will sow the house of Israel and the house of Judah with the seed of man and the seed of beast. And it shall come to pass that as I have watched over them to pluck up and break down, to destroy, and bring evil, so I will watch over them to build and to plant. In those days they shall no longer say: 'The fathers have eaten sour grapes, and the children's teeth are set on edge.' But every one shall die for his own sin; each man who eats sour grapes, his teeth shall be set on edge.

"Behold, the days are coming when I will make a new covenant with Israel and Judah, not like the covenant which I made with their fathers when I took them by the hand to bring them out of Egypt, my covenant which they broke, though I was their husband, says the LORD. But this is the covenant which I will make with Israel: I will put my law within them, and I will write it upon their hearts; and I will be their God, and they shall be my people. And no longer shall each man teach his neighbor and each his brother, saying, 'Know the LORD,' for they shall all know me, from the least of them to the greatest; for I will forgive their iniquity, and I will remember their sin no more."

Thus says the LORD, who gives the sun for light by day and the fixed order of the moon and the stars for light by night, who stirs up the sea so that its waves roar—the LORD of hosts is his name: "If this fixed order departs from before me, then shall the descendants of Israel cease from being a nation for ever. If the heavens above can be measured, and the foundations of the earth below explored, then I will cast off all the descendants of Israel."

IN THE TENTH year of Zedekiah king of Judah, which was the eighteenth year of Nebuchadrezzar, when the army of the

king of Babylon was besieging Jerusalem,
Jeremiah the prophet was shut up in the
court of the guard in the palace of the
king. For Zedekiah had imprisoned him,
saying, "Why do you prophesy, 'Thus says
the LORD: I am giving this city into the
hand of the king of Babylon; and Zedekiah
shall surely not escape the Chaldeans, but
shall speak with the king of Babylon face
to face, and eye to eye; and he shall take
Zedekiah to Babylon'?"

Jeremiah said, "The word of the LORD
came to me: Behold, Hanamel the son of
your uncle will come to you and say, 'Buy
my field which is at Anathoth, for the right
of purchase is yours.' Then my cousin
came to me in the court of the guard and
said, 'Buy my field which is at Anathoth in
the land of Benjamin, for the right of possession is yours; buy it for yourself.' And I
knew that this was the word of the LORD.

"I bought the field from Hanamel my
cousin, and weighed out the money to
him, seventeen shekels of silver. I signed
the deed, sealed it, got witnesses, and
weighed the money on scales. Then I took
the sealed deed of purchase, containing the

terms and conditions, and the open copy; and I gave the deed of purchase to Baruch the son of Neriah, in the presence of Hanamel my cousin and the witnesses who signed the deed, and in the presence of all the Jews who were sitting in the court of the guard. I charged Baruch, saying: 'Take these deeds, both this sealed deed of purchase and this open deed, and put them in an earthenware vessel, that they may last for a long time. For thus says the LORD: Houses and fields and vineyards shall again be bought in this land.'

"After I had given the deed to Baruch, I prayed to the LORD: 'Ah, Lord GOD! It is thou who hast made the heavens and the earth by thy outstretched arm! Nothing is too hard for thee, who showest steadfast love to thousands, but dost requite the guilt of fathers to their children after them, O great and mighty God whose name is the LORD of hosts. Thou didst bring thy people Israel out of Egypt with signs and wonders, and thou gavest them this land, a land flowing with milk and honey; and they took possession of it. But they did nothing of all thou didst command them to

do. Therefore thou hast made all this evil
come upon them. Behold, the siege
mounds have come up to the city to take
it. What thou didst speak has come to
pass, and thou seest it. Yet thou, O Lord
GOD, hast said to me, "Buy the field for
money and get witnesses"—though the
city is given into the hands of the
Chaldeans.' "

The word of the LORD came to Jeremiah: "I am the LORD, the God of all
flesh; is anything too hard for me? Behold,
I am giving this city into the hand of Nebuchadrezzar king of Babylon. The Chaldeans shall set this city on fire, and burn the
houses on whose roofs incense has been
offered to Baal and drink offerings poured
out to other gods. This city has aroused my
anger from the day it was built. I will
remove it from my sight because of all
the evil the sons of Israel and of Judah
did to provoke me. They have turned to
me their back and not their face; they
have not listened to instruction. They set
up their abominations in the house which
is called by my name, to defile it. They
built the high places of Baal to offer

up their sons and daughters to Molech.

"Now thus says the LORD: Behold, I will gather them from all the countries to which I drove them in my great indignation; I will bring them back to this place, and I will make them dwell in safety. They shall be my people, and I will be their God. I will give them one heart and one way, that they may fear me for ever, for their own good and the good of their children after them. I will make with them an everlasting covenant, that I will not turn away from doing good to them; and I will put the fear of me in their hearts, that they may not turn from me. I will rejoice in doing them good, and I will plant them in this land in faithfulness, with all my heart and all my soul.

"For thus says the LORD: Just as I have brought all this great evil upon this people, so I will bring upon them all the good that I promise them. Fields shall be bought in this land of which you are saying, It is a desolation, without man or beast; it is given into the hands of the Chaldeans. Deeds shall be signed and sealed and witnessed, in the land of Benjamin, in the places about Jerusalem, and in the cities of Judah, in the cities of the hill country, in the Shephelah, and the Negeb; for I will restore their fortunes."

THE WORD WHICH came to Jeremiah from the LORD in the days of Jehoiakim the son of Josiah, king of Judah: "Go to the house of the Rechabites, and bring them to the house of the LORD, into one of the chambers; then offer them wine to drink." So I took Jaazaniah, and his brothers, and all his sons, and the whole house of the Rechabites. I brought them to the house of the LORD and into a chamber near the chamber of the princes.

Then I set before the Rechabites pitchers full of wine, and cups; and I said to them, "Drink." But they answered, "We will drink no wine, for our father, Jonadab the son of Rechab, commanded us, 'You shall not drink wine, neither you nor your sons for ever; you shall not build a house; you shall not sow seed; you shall not plant a vineyard; but you shall live in tents, that you may live many days in the land where you sojourn.' We have obeyed the voice of

Jonadab our father in all that he commanded us. We have no vineyard or field or
seed; and we have lived in tents. But when
Nebuchadrezzar king of Babylon came up
against the land, we said, 'Come, let us go
to Jerusalem for fear of the army of the
Chaldeans.' So we are living in Jerusalem."

Then the word of the LORD came to
Jeremiah: "Go and say to the inhabitants
of Jerusalem, Will you not receive instruction? says the LORD. The command which
Jonadab the son of Rechab gave to his
sons, to drink no wine, has been kept; and
they drink none to this day. I have spoken
to you persistently, but you have not
obeyed me. Therefore, behold, I am bringing on Judah and all the inhabitants of
Jerusalem all the evil I have pronounced
against them; because I have called to
them and they have not answered."

But Jeremiah said to the Rechabites,
"Because you have obeyed the command
of your father, and kept all his precepts,
therefore thus says the LORD of hosts, the
God of Israel: Jonadab the son of Rechab
shall never lack a man to stand before
me."

IN THE FOURTH year of Jehoiakim, king of
Judah, this word came to Jeremiah from
the LORD: "Take a scroll and write on it
all the words I have spoken to you
against Israel and Judah from the days of
Josiah until today. It may be that the
house of Judah will hear the evil I intend to do them, so that every one may
turn from his evil way and I may
forgive."

Then Jeremiah called Baruch the son of
Neriah, and Baruch wrote upon a scroll at
the dictation of Jeremiah all the words the
LORD had spoken to him. And Jeremiah
ordered Baruch, saying, "I am debarred
from going to the house of the LORD; so
you are to go, and on a fast day in the
hearing of all the people you shall read the
words of the LORD from this scroll. You
shall read them also in the hearing of all
the men of Judah who come out of their
cities. It may be that their supplication will
come before the LORD, and that every one
will turn from his evil way, for great is the
wrath that the LORD has pronounced
against them." And Baruch did as Jeremiah
ordered him.

The next year, in the ninth month, all the people in Jerusalem and all the people who came to Jerusalem from the cities of Judah proclaimed a fast before the LORD. Then, in the hearing of the people, Baruch read the words of Jeremiah from the scroll in the house of the LORD, in the chamber of Gemariah the son of Shaphan the secretary, which was in the upper court, at the entry of the New Gate of the LORD's house.

When Micaiah the son of Gemariah heard all the words from the scroll, he went down to the king's house, into the secretary's chamber, where all the princes were sitting. And Micaiah told them all he had heard Baruch read. Then the princes sent Jehudi the son of Nethaniah to say to Baruch, "Take in your hand that scroll, and come." So Baruch took it and came. "Sit down and read it," they said. So he read them all the words of the LORD from the scroll, and they turned one to another in fear, and said, "We must report this to the king." Then they asked Baruch, "Tell us, how did you write these words? Was it at his dictation?" Baruch answered them,

"He dictated the words to me, while I wrote them with ink on the scroll." Then they said to Baruch, "Go and hide, you and Jeremiah, and let no one know where you are."

So the princes went into the court to King Jehoiakim, having put the scroll in the chamber of Elishama the secretary, and reported all the words to him. Then the king sent Jehudi to get the scroll, and Jehudi read it to the king and all the princes. It was the ninth month, and the king was sitting in the winter house and there was a fire burning in the brazier before him. As Jehudi read three or four columns, the king would cut them off with a penknife and throw them into the brazier, until the entire scroll was consumed in the fire. Yet neither the king, nor any of his servants who heard all these words, was afraid. Even when some urged the king not to burn the scroll, he would not listen. And the king commanded Jerahmeel his son and two others of his court to seize Baruch and Jeremiah the prophet; but the LORD hid them.

Now, after the king had burned the

scroll, the word of the LORD came to Jeremiah: "Take another scroll and write on it all the words that were in the first scroll. And concerning Jehoiakim king of Judah you shall say, 'Thus says the LORD, You have burned this scroll, saying, "Why have you written in it that the king of Babylon will certainly destroy this land, and will cut off from it man and beast?" Therefore thus says the LORD concerning Jehoiakim, He shall have none to sit upon the throne of David, and his dead body shall be cast out to the heat by day and the frost by night. And I will punish him and his offspring and his servants; I will bring upon them, upon Jerusalem, and upon Judah, all the evil that I have pronounced against them, but they would not hear.' "

Then Jeremiah took another scroll and gave it to Baruch, who wrote on it at his dictation all the words of the scroll which Jehoiakim had burned; and many similar words were added to them.

ZEDEKIAH THE SON of Josiah, whom Nebuchadrezzar king of Babylon made king in the land of Judah, reigned instead of Jehoiachin the son of Jehoiakim. But neither he nor the people listened to the words of the LORD which he spoke through Jeremiah the prophet.

King Zedekiah sent Jehucal the son of Shelemiah, and Zephaniah the priest, to Jeremiah, saying, "Pray for us to the LORD our God." Now Jeremiah was still going in and out among the people, for he had not yet been put in prison. At that time the army of Pharaoh had come out of Egypt; and when the Chaldeans besieging Jerusalem heard news of them, they withdrew from the city.

Then the word of the LORD came to Jeremiah: "Say to the king, 'Behold, Pharaoh's army which came to help you is about to return to Egypt. And the Chaldeans shall come back and take this city. Do not deceive yourselves, saying, "The Chaldeans will surely stay away from us," for they will not. For even if you should defeat their whole army, and there remained of them only wounded men, every man in his tent, they would rise up and burn this city.' "

Now when the Chaldean army had withdrawn at the approach of Pharaoh's army, Jeremiah set out from Jerusalem to go to the land of Benjamin to receive his portion there. When he was at the Benjamin Gate, a sentry there named Irijah the son of Shelemiah seized him, saying, "You are deserting to the Chaldeans." And Jeremiah said, "It is false; I am not deserting to the Chaldeans." But the sentry would not listen, and brought him to the princes. And the princes were enraged at Jeremiah, and they beat him and imprisoned him in the house of Jonathan the secretary, for it had been made a prison.

When Jeremiah had remained in the dungeon cells many days, King Zedekiah sent for him, and questioned him secretly: "Is there any word from the LORD?" Jeremiah said, "There is. You shall be delivered into the hand of the king of Babylon."

Jeremiah then said to King Zedekiah, "What wrong have I done to you or this people, that you have put me in prison? Where are your prophets who said to you, 'The king of Babylon will not come against this land'? Now hear, I pray you, O my lord the king: do not send me back to the house of Jonathan the secretary, lest I die there." So King Zedekiah gave orders, and they committed Jeremiah to the court of the guard; and a loaf of bread was given him daily from the bakers' street, until all the bread of the city was gone. So Jeremiah remained in the court of the guard.

Now Jehucal the son of Shelemiah, and three others, heard the words that Jeremiah was saying to all the people, "Thus says the Lord, He who stays in this city shall die by the sword, by famine, and by pestilence; but he who goes out to the Chaldeans shall live. This city shall surely be taken." Then the princes went to the king and said, "Let this man be put to death, for he is weakening the hands of the soldiers who are left in this city, and of all the people. He is not seeking their welfare, but their harm." King Zedekiah said, "Behold, he is in your hands; for the king can do nothing against you." So they took Jeremiah and cast him into the cistern in the court of the guard, letting him down by ropes. There was no water in the cistern, but only mire, and Jeremiah sank in the mire.

When Ebed-melech the Ethiopian, a eunuch in the king's house, heard that they had put Jeremiah into the cistern, he went to the king and said, "My lord, these men have done evil in that they cast Jeremiah the prophet into the cistern; he will die there." Then the king commanded Ebed-melech, "Take three men with you from here, and lift Jeremiah out of the cistern before he dies." So Ebed-melech took the men and went to the house of the king, to a wardrobe of the storehouse, and took from there old rags and worn-out clothes, which he let down to Jeremiah in the cistern by ropes. Ebed-melech said to Jeremiah, "Put the rags and clothes between your armpits and the ropes." Jeremiah did so, and they drew him up out of the cistern. And Jeremiah remained in the court of the guard.

King Zedekiah sent for Jeremiah the prophet and received him at the third entrance of the temple of the LORD. The king said, "I will ask you a question; hide nothing from me." Jeremiah said, "If I tell you, will you not be sure to put me to death? And if I give you counsel, you will not listen to me." Then Zedekiah swore secretly, "As the LORD lives, I will not put you to death or deliver you into the hand of these men who seek your life."

Then Jeremiah said, "Thus says the LORD, If you will surrender to the king of Babylon, this city shall not be burned with fire, and you and your house shall live. But if you do not, the Chaldeans shall take the city and burn it, and you shall not escape from their hand." But Zedekiah said, "I am afraid of the Jews who have deserted to the Chaldeans, lest I be handed over to them and they abuse me." Jeremiah said, "You shall not be given to them. Obey now the voice of the LORD, and it shall be well with you. But if you refuse, this is the vision which the LORD has shown to me: Behold, all the women left in the house of the king of Judah were being led out to the princes of the king of Babylon and were saying, 'Your trusted friends have deceived you; now that your feet are sunk in the mire, they turn away from you.' Your wives and sons shall be led out to the Chaldeans, and you yourself shall be seized by the king of Babylon."

Then Zedekiah said, "Let no one know of these words and you shall not die. If the princes hear that I have spoken with you and come to you and say, 'Tell us what you said to the king and he to you; hide nothing and we will not put you to death,' then you shall say to them, 'I made a humble plea to the king that he would not send me back to the dungeon to die there.' " All the princes did ask, and Jeremiah answered as the king had instructed. So they left him, for the conversation had not been overheard. And Jeremiah remained in the court of the guard until the day that Jerusalem was taken.

In the eleventh year of Zedekiah, in the fourth month, on the ninth day of the month, a breach was made in the city. When Jerusalem was taken, all the princes and officers of the king of Babylon came and sat in the middle gate. When Zedekiah and his soldiers saw them, they fled at night by way of the king's garden through the gate between the two walls; and they went toward the Arabah. But the army of the Chaldeans pursued them, and overtook Zedekiah in the plains of Jericho; and they

brought him up to Nebuchadrezzar king of
Babylon, at Riblah; and he passed sentence upon him. The king of Babylon slew
the sons of Zedekiah at Riblah before his
eyes, and he also slew all the nobles of
Judah. He put out the eyes of Zedekiah,
and bound him in fetters to take him to
Babylon.

The Chaldeans burned the king's house
and the house of the people, and broke
down the walls of Jerusalem. Then the captain of the guard carried into exile the rest
of the people who were left in the city, and
those who had deserted to him. But he left
in Judah some of the poor people who
owned nothing, and gave them vineyards
and fields at the same time.

Nebuchadrezzar gave command concerning Jeremiah through the captain of
the guard, saying, "Look after him well
and do him no harm, but deal with him as
he tells you." So the chief officers of the
king of Babylon took Jeremiah from the
court of the guard. They entrusted him to
the governor whom Nebuchadrezzar had
appointed in Judah, Gedaliah the son of
Ahikam, son of Shaphan, that he should

take him home. So he dwelt among the people.

Now the word of the LORD had come to Jeremiah while he was shut up in the court of the guard: "Go, and say to Ebed-melech the Ethiopian, 'Thus says the LORD of hosts: Behold, I will fulfil my words against this city for evil and not for good. But I will deliver you on that day, and you shall not be given into the hand of the men of whom you are afraid. For I will surely save you; you shall not fall by the sword, but shall have your life as a prize of war, because you have put your trust in me, says the LORD.' "

WHEN ALL THE captains of the forces in the open country and their men heard that the king of Babylon had appointed Gedaliah governor of Judah, they went to him at Mizpah. Among these were Ishmael the son of Nethaniah of the royal family, and Johanan the son of Kareah. Gedaliah swore to them and their men, saying, "Do not be afraid to serve the king of Babylon, and it shall be well with you. I will dwell at Mizpah, to stand for you before the Chaldeans who will come to us; but as for you, gather wine and summer fruits and oil, and store them in your vessels, and dwell in your cities that you have taken." Likewise, when all the Jews who were in Moab or among the Ammonites or in other lands heard that the king of Babylon had left a remnant in Judah, they also returned to Gedaliah at Mizpah; and they gathered wine and summer fruits in great abundance.

Now Johanan and other leaders came and said to Gedaliah, "Do you know that the king of the Ammonites has sent Ishmael the son of Nethaniah to take your life?" Gedaliah would not believe them. Then Johanan spoke to him secretly, "Let me go and slay Ishmael, and no one will know it. Why should he take your life, so that all the Jews who are gathered about you would be scattered, and the remnant of Judah would perish?" But Gedaliah said, "You shall not do this thing, for you are speaking falsely of Ishmael."

In the seventh month, Ishmael came with ten men to Gedaliah. As they ate bread together there at Mizpah, Ishmael and the men with him rose up and struck down Gedaliah with the sword. Then Ishmael took away captive the king's daughters and all those whom Nebuchadrezzar had committed to Gedaliah, and set out to cross over to the Ammonites.

When Johanan and the captains with him heard of the evil Ishmael had done, they took their men and went to fight against him. They came upon him at the great pool in Gibeon. And all the people Ishmael had carried away captive saw Johanan, and rejoiced and went to him. But Ishmael escaped with eight men to the Ammonites. Then Johanan took all the rest of the people back from Gibeon. And they stayed at Geruth Chimham near Bethlehem, intending to go to Egypt because of the Chaldeans; for they were afraid of them, because Ishmael had slain Gedaliah, whom the king of Babylon had made governor.

THEN JOHANAN AND Azariah the son of Hoshaiah, and all the commanders of the forces, and all the people from the least to the greatest, came to Jeremiah the prophet.

"Pray to the LORD for us," they said, "for all this remnant (for we are left but a few of many), that the LORD may show us the way we should go, and the thing that we should do." Jeremiah said to them, "I will pray to the LORD according to your request, and whatever he answers I will tell you." They said, "May the LORD be a true and faithful witness against us if we do not act according to all the word the LORD sends to us. Whether it is good or evil, we will obey the voice of the LORD our God, that it may be well with us."

At the end of ten days the word of the LORD came to Jeremiah. Then he summoned Johanan and all the people, and said, "Thus says the LORD, to whom you sent me to present your supplication: If you will remain in this land, then I will build you up and not pull you down; I will plant you, and not pluck you up; for I repent of the evil which I did to you. Do not fear the king of Babylon, for I am with you. I will grant you mercy, that he may have mercy on you and let you remain in your own land.

"But if you disobey, saying, 'No, we will

go to Egypt, where we shall not see war or be hungry for bread,' then hear the word of the LORD, O remnant of Judah: If you set your faces to enter Egypt, then the sword which you fear shall overtake you there, and the famine shall follow hard after you. All who go to Egypt to live shall die; they shall have no survivor from the evil I will bring upon them.

"For thus says the LORD to you, O remnant of Judah: 'Do not go to Egypt.' Know that I have warned you this day that you go astray at the cost of your lives. For you sent me to the LORD, saying, 'Whatever the LORD says, we will do it.' And I have this day declared it to you. Now therefore know for a certainty that you shall die by the sword, by famine, and by pestilence in the place you desire to go to live."

When Jeremiah finished speaking, Azariah and Johanan and all the insolent men said to him, "You are telling a lie. The LORD did not send you to say, 'Do not go to Egypt to live'; but Baruch the son of Neriah has set you against us, to deliver us to the Chaldeans, that they may kill us or take us into exile in Babylon."

So Johanan and all the commanders of the forces took all the remnant who had returned to Judah from the nations to which they had been driven—the men, the women, the children, the princesses—and every person whom Nebuchadrezzar's captain of the guard had left with Gedaliah, also Jeremiah the prophet and Baruch the son of Neriah. And they came into Egypt, for they did not obey the voice of the LORD. And they arrived at Tahpanhes.

There the word of the LORD came to Jeremiah: "Take in your hands large stones, and hide them in the mortar in the pavement at the entrance to Pharaoh's palace in Tahpanhes, in the sight of the men of Judah, and say to them, 'Thus says the LORD of hosts, the God of Israel: Behold, I will send Nebuchadrezzar the king of Babylon, my servant, and he will set his throne above these stones and spread his royal canopy over them. He shall come and smite Egypt, giving to the pestilence those who are doomed to the pestilence, to captivity those who are doomed to captivity, and to the sword those who are doomed to the sword. He shall kindle a fire in the temples of the gods of Egypt; he shall clean the land of Egypt, as a shepherd cleans his cloak of vermin; and he shall go away from there in peace. He shall break the obelisks of Heliopolis; and the temples of the gods of Egypt he shall burn.' "

THE WORD THAT came to Jeremiah concerning all the Jews that dwelt in the land of Egypt, at Migdol, at Tahpanhes, at Memphis, and in the land of Pathros, "Thus says the LORD of hosts, the God of Israel: You have seen all the evil that I brought upon Jerusalem and the cities of Judah. Behold, this day they are a desolation, because they went to burn incense and serve gods that they knew not, neither they, nor you, nor your fathers. Yet I persistently sent to you all my servants the prophets, saying, 'Oh, do not do this abominable thing that I hate!' But they did not listen. Therefore my wrath was kindled and the cities of Judah became a waste, as at this day.

"And now thus says the LORD God of hosts: Why do you commit this great evil against yourselves, to cut off man and

woman, infant and child, from the midst
of Judah, leaving you no remnant? Why do
you provoke me to anger, burning incense
to other gods in Egypt, that you may become a curse among all the nations of the
earth? Have you forgotten the wickedness
of your fathers, of the kings of Judah and
their wives, your own wickedness, and the
wickedness of your wives, which they committed in the streets of Jerusalem? They
have not humbled themselves even to this
day, nor walked in my law which I set
before you and your fathers.

"Therefore, behold, I will set my face
against you for evil, to cut off all Judah.
The remnant who have come to Egypt to
live shall not return to Judah, except some
fugitives."

Then all the men who knew that their
wives had offered incense to other gods,
and all the women who stood by, a great
assembly, answered Jeremiah: "As for the
word which you have spoken to us in the
name of the LORD, we will not listen. We
will burn incense to the queen of heaven
and pour out libations to her, as we did,
both we and our fathers, our kings and our

princes, in the streets of Jerusalem; for then we had plenty of food, and prospered. But since we left off, we have lacked everything and have been consumed by sword and famine." And the women said, "Was it without our husbands' approval that we made cakes for the queen of heaven bearing her image and poured out libations to her?"

Then Jeremiah said to all the men and women who had given him this answer: "As for the incense that you burned in Judah, did not the LORD remember it? The LORD could no longer bear the abominations which you committed. It is because you sinned against the LORD and did not walk in his law that evil has befallen you, as at this day. Hear now the word of the LORD, all you of Judah who dwell in Egypt: You have declared, 'We will surely perform our vows to the queen of heaven and pour out libations to her.' Confirm your vows and perform your vows! Therefore, behold, I have sworn by my great name, says the LORD, that my name shall no more be invoked by the mouth of any man of Judah in all

Egypt, saying, 'As the Lord GOD lives.'

"Behold, I am watching over them for evil and not for good; all the men of Judah in Egypt shall be consumed until there is an end of them. Those who do escape shall return to Judah, few in number; and all the remnant shall know whose word will stand, mine or theirs. This shall be the sign to you, says the LORD, that I will punish you in this place, in order that you may know that my words will surely stand against you for evil: Behold, I will give Pharaoh Hophra king of Egypt into the hand of his enemies, as I gave Zedekiah king of Judah into the hand of Nebuchad-rezzar king of Babylon, who sought his life."

THE WORD THAT Jeremiah the prophet spoke to Baruch the son of Neriah, when he wrote these words in a book at the dictation of Jeremiah, in the fourth year of Jehoiakim the son of Josiah, king of Judah: "Thus says the LORD, the God of Israel, to you, O Baruch: You said, 'Woe is me! for the LORD has added sorrow to my pain; I am weary with my groaning, and I find no rest.' Thus says the LORD: Behold, what I have built I am breaking down, and what I have planted I am plucking up—that is, the whole land. And do you seek great things for yourself? Seek them not; for behold, I am bringing evil upon all flesh, says the LORD; but I will give you your life as a prize of war in all places to which you may go."

THE WORD OF the LORD which came to Jeremiah the prophet concerning the nations.

About Egypt. Concerning the army of Pharaoh Neco, king of Egypt, which was by the river Euphrates at Carchemish and which Nebuchadrezzar king of Babylon defeated in the fourth year of Jehoiakim, king of Judah:

"Prepare buckler and shield, and advance for battle! Harness the horses; mount, O horsemen! Take your stations, polish your spears, put on your coats of mail!

"Why have I seen it? They have turned backward. Their warriors have fled; they look not back—terror on every side! says the LORD. In the north by the river Euphrates they have stumbled and fallen.

"Who is this, rising like the Nile, like rivers whose waters surge? Egypt rises like the Nile. He said, I will cover the earth, destroy its cities. Advance, O horses! Let the warriors go forth!

"That day is the day of the Lord GOD, to avenge himself on his foes. The sword shall devour, and drink its fill of their blood. For the Lord GOD holds a sacrifice by the river Euphrates. Go up to Gilead, and take balm, O daughter of Egypt! In vain you have used many medicines; there is no healing for you. The nations have heard of your shame, and the earth is full of your cry; for warrior has stumbled against warrior; they have both fallen together."

THE WORD WHICH the LORD spoke to Jeremiah about the coming of Nebuchadrezzar king of Babylon to smite the land of Egypt:

"Declare in Egypt, in Migdol, Memphis, and Tahpanhes; say, 'Be prepared, for the sword shall devour round about you.' Why has Apis fled, why did your bull not stand?

Because the LORD thrust him down. Your multitude stumbled and fell, and said one to another, 'Arise! Let us go back to our own land, because of the sword of the oppressor.' Call the name of Pharaoh, king of Egypt, 'Noisy one who lets the hour go by.'

"As I live, says the King, whose name is the LORD of hosts, like Tabor among the mountains shall one come! Prepare your baggage for exile, O inhabitants of Egypt! For Memphis shall become a waste, a ruin. A beautiful heifer is Egypt, but a gadfly has come upon her. Even her hired soldiers, in her midst like fatted calves, have turned and fled; they did not stand; the day of their calamity has come.

"She makes a sound like a serpent gliding away, for her enemies march against her with axes. They shall cut down her forest, says the LORD, impenetrable though it is; for they are more numerous than locusts. The daughter of Egypt shall be put to shame.

"Behold, I am bringing punishment upon Egypt and her gods and her kings, upon Pharaoh and those who trust in him.

I will deliver them into the hand of Nebuchadrezzar king of Babylon. Afterward Egypt shall be inhabited as in the days of old, says the LORD.

"But fear not, O Israel my servant, for I am with you. I will make a full end of all the nations to which I have driven you. But of you I will not make a full end. I will chasten you in just measure."

THE WORD OF the LORD that came to Jeremiah concerning the Philistines, before Pharaoh smote Gaza.

"Thus says the LORD: Behold, waters are rising out of the north, and they shall overflow the land and all who dwell in it, and every inhabitant shall wail. At the noise of the stamping of stallions and the rumbling of chariot wheels, the fathers look not back to their children, so feeble are their hands. For the LORD is destroying the Philistines. Baldness has come upon Gaza, Ashkelon has perished.

"Ah, sword of the LORD! How long till you are quiet? Put yourself into your scabbard, rest and be still!

"How can it be quiet, when the LORD

has given it a charge? Against Ashkelon and against the seashore he has appointed it."

CONCERNING MOAB. THUS says the LORD of hosts, the God of Israel: "Woe to Nebo, for it is laid waste! Kiriathaim is put to shame, it is taken; the fortress is broken down; the renown of Moab is no more. Hark! a cry from Horonaim. Moab is destroyed.

"Flee! Save yourselves! Be like a wild ass in the desert! Because you trusted in strongholds and treasures, you shall be taken; Chemosh shall go into exile with his priests. No city shall escape, and the valley shall perish, as the LORD has spoken.

"Cursed is he who does the work of the LORD with slackness; and cursed is he who keeps back his sword from bloodshed. Moab has been at ease from his youth and has settled on his lees; he has not been emptied from vessel to vessel, nor has he gone into exile; so his taste remains in him. Therefore the days are coming, says the LORD, when I shall send to him tilters who will tilt him, and empty his vessels, and break his jars in pieces. Then Moab shall be ashamed of Chemosh.

"Make Moab drunk, because he magnified himself against the LORD; so he shall wallow in his vomit, and he too shall be held in derision. Was not Israel a derision to you? Was he found among thieves, that whenever you spoke of him you wagged your head? Dwell in the rock, O inhabitants of Moab, like the dove that nests in the sides of a gorge.

"We have heard of the pride of Moab— he is very proud—and of the haughtiness of his heart. I know his insolence, says the LORD; his boasts are false. Therefore I wail for all Moab. Upon your summer fruits and your vintage the destroyer has fallen. Gladness and joy have been taken away from the fruitful land; I have made the wine cease from the wine presses; no one treads them with shouts of joy; the shouting is not the shout of joy. On housetops, in the squares, there is nothing but lamentation; for I have broken Moab like a vessel for which no one cares.

"Woe to you, O Moab! The people of Chemosh is undone; your sons have been taken captive, and your daughters. Yet I will restore the fortunes of Moab in the latter days, says the LORD." Thus far is the judgment on Moab.

CONCERNING THE AMMONITES. Thus says the LORD: "Behold, the days are coming when I will cause the battle cry to be heard against Rabbah of the Ammonites; it shall become a desolate mound; then Israel shall dispossess those who dispossessed him. Wail, O Heshbon! Cry, O daughters of Rabbah! Gird yourselves with sackcloth, and run to and fro among the hedges! For Milcom shall go into exile, with his priests and his princes. You shall be driven out, every man straight before him, with none to gather the fugitives. But afterward I will restore the fortunes of the Ammonites, says the LORD."

CONCERNING EDOM. THUS says the LORD of hosts: "Is wisdom no more in Teman? Has counsel perished from the prudent? Dwell in the depths, O inhabitants of Dedan! For I will bring the calamity of Esau upon him when I punish him. If thieves came by night, would they not destroy only enough for themselves? But I have stripped Esau bare, I have uncovered his hiding places. His brothers are destroyed, and his neighbors; and he is no more.

"Leave your fatherless children, I will keep them alive; and let your widows trust in me."

For thus says the LORD: "If those who did not deserve to drink the cup must drink it, will you go unpunished? You shall not; you must drink. For I have sworn by myself, says the LORD, that Bozrah shall become a taunt, a waste, and a curse. Every one who passes by Edom will be horrified, and no man shall sojourn in her.

"Behold, one shall mount up and fly swiftly like an eagle, and spread his wings against Bozrah, and the heart of the warriors of Edom shall be in that day like the heart of a woman in her pangs."

CONCERNING DAMASCUS. "DAMASCUS has become feeble, she turned to flee, and panic seized her. How the famous city is forsaken, the joyful city! All her soldiers shall be destroyed in that day, says the LORD of hosts."

CONCERNING KEDAR AND the kingdoms of Hazor which Nebuchadrezzar king of Babylon smote. Thus says the LORD: "Rise up, advance against Kedar! Destroy the people of the east! Their tents, their camels, and their flocks shall be taken, and all their goods, and men shall cry to them: 'Terror on every side!' Flee, wander far away, O inhabitants of Hazor! says the LORD. For Nebuchadrezzar king of Babylon has made a plan against you.

"Rise up, advance against a nation at ease, that dwells securely, that has no gates or bars, that dwells alone. Their camels shall become booty, their cattle a spoil. I will scatter to every wind those who cut short their hair, and I will bring calamity on them from every side, says the LORD. Hazor shall become a haunt of jackals."

CONCERNING ELAM. THUS says the LORD of hosts: "Behold, I will break the bow of Elam, the mainstay of their might; and I will bring upon Elam the four winds from the four quarters of heaven; and I will scatter them to all those winds, and there shall be no nation to which those driven out of Elam shall not come. But in the latter days I will restore the fortunes of Elam."

THE WORD WHICH the LORD spoke concerning Babylon, by Jeremiah the prophet:

"Declare among the nations, set up a banner and proclaim: 'Babylon is taken! Her idols are put to shame.' For out of the north a nation has come up against her which shall make her land a desolation. In those days, says the LORD, the people of Israel and the people of Judah shall come together, weeping as they come; and they shall seek the LORD their God. They shall ask the way to Zion, with faces turned toward it, saying, 'Come, let us join ourselves to the LORD in an everlasting covenant.' Because of the sword of the oppressor, every one shall turn to his own people, and every one shall flee to his own land.

"Israel is a hunted sheep driven away by lions. First the king of Assyria devoured him, and now the king of Babylon has gnawed his bones. Therefore thus says the LORD: Behold, I am bringing punishment on Babylon, as I punished Assyria. I will restore Israel to his pasture, and he shall feed on Carmel, and be satisfied on the hills of Ephraim. In those days, says the LORD, iniquity shall be sought in Israel and Judah, and none shall be found; for I will pardon those whom I leave as a remnant.

"Hark! they escape from Babylon, to declare in Zion the vengeance of the LORD our God, vengeance for his temple.

"Thus says the LORD of hosts: The people of Israel are oppressed, and the people of Judah with them; all who took them captive have held them fast, they refuse to let them go. Their Redeemer is strong; the LORD of hosts is his name. He will surely plead their cause, that he may give rest to the earth, but unrest to the inhabitants of Babylon.

"A sword upon the Chaldeans, says the LORD, upon the inhabitants of Babylon, upon her princes and her wise men! A sword upon the diviners, that they may become fools! A sword upon her warriors, that they may be destroyed! A sword upon her horses and upon her chariots, and upon all the foreign troops in her midst, that they may become women! A sword upon all her treasures, that they may be plundered!

"Behold, like a lion coming up against a strong sheepfold, I will suddenly make them run away from her; and I will appoint over her whomever I choose. For who is like me? Who will summon me? What shepherd can stand before me? Therefore hear the plan which the LORD has made against Babylon. Babylon was a golden cup in the LORD's hand; the nations drank of her wine, therefore the nations went mad. Suddenly she has fallen and been broken; wail for her! We would have healed Babylon, but she was not healed. Forsake her, and let us go each to his own country; for her judgment has reached up to heaven. The LORD has brought forth our vindication; come, let us declare in Zion the work of the LORD our God.

"The LORD has stirred up the spirit of the kings of the Medes, because his purpose is to destroy Babylon, for that is the vengeance of the LORD for his temple. O you who dwell by many waters, rich in treasures, your end has come, the thread of your life is cut. The LORD of hosts has sworn by himself: Surely I will fill you with men, as many as locusts, and they shall raise the shout of victory over you.

"You are my hammer and weapon of war: with you I break nations in pieces; with you I break the horse and his rider, the chariot and the charioteer; with you I break in pieces man and woman, the young man and the maiden; with you I break in pieces the shepherd and his flock, the farmer and his team; with you I break in pieces governors and commanders.

"But now I will requite Babylon and all the inhabitants of Chaldea before your very eyes for all the evil they have done in Zion. Behold, I am against you, O destroying mountain, which destroys the whole earth; I will stretch out my hand and roll you down from the crags, and make you a burnt mountain. No stone shall be taken from you for a corner and no stone for a foundation, but you shall be a perpetual waste, says the LORD."

Let Jerusalem say, "Nebuchadrezzar the king of Babylon has crushed me; he has made me an empty vessel, he has swallowed me like a monster; he has filled his belly with my delicacies, he has rinsed me out. The violence done to me and to my kinsmen be upon Babylon."

Therefore thus says the LORD: "Behold, I will plead your cause and take vengeance for you. They shall roar together like lions; they shall growl like lions' whelps. While they are inflamed I will prepare them a feast and make them drunk, till they swoon away and sleep a perpetual sleep.

"How Babylon is taken, the praise of the whole earth seized! I will punish Baal in Babylon, and take out of his mouth what he has swallowed. The nations shall flow to him no longer.

"Go out of the midst of her, my people! Let every man save his life from the fierce anger of the LORD! Babylon must fall for the slain of Israel, as for Babylon have fallen the slain of all the earth. You that have escaped from the sword, go, stand not still! Remember the LORD, let Jerusalem come into your mind: 'Dishonor has covered our face, for aliens have come into the holy places of the LORD's house.' Therefore, behold, the days are coming, says the LORD, when I will execute judgment upon her images. Though Babylon should mount up to heaven and fortify her strong height, yet destroyers would come from me upon her, says the LORD.

"Hark! a cry from Babylon! For the LORD is laying Babylon waste and will still her mighty voice; a destroyer has come upon her, upon Babylon. The LORD is a God of recompense, he will surely requite."

THE WORD WHICH Jeremiah the prophet commanded Seraiah the son of Neriah, when he went with Zedekiah king of Judah to Babylon, in the fourth year of his reign. Seraiah was the quartermaster. Jeremiah wrote in a book all the evil that should come upon Babylon, all these words that are written concerning Babylon. And Jeremiah said to Seraiah: "When you come to Babylon, see that you read all these words, and say, 'O LORD, thou hast said concerning this place that thou wilt cut it off, so that nothing shall dwell in it, neither man nor beast, and it shall be desolate for ever.' When you finish reading this book, bind a stone to it, and cast it into the midst of the Euphrates, and say, 'Thus shall Babylon sink, to rise no more, because of the evil that I am bringing upon her.' "

Thus far are the words of Jeremiah.

LAMENTATIONS

The Book of Lamentations is a collection of five laments, communal and personal, over the sack of Jerusalem in 586 B.C., and for other sufferings inflicted on the Jews by their Babylonian conquerors. The common theme is the agony of the people, their apparent desertion by God, and the hope that God will yet restore a humbled and repentant Israel to its former glory. The name of the author is uncertain. Tradition assigns the book to Jeremiah, but in many ways it is quite unlike his acknowledged work. The writing of Lamentations can probably be dated in about the year 538 B.C., when the Jews were allowed to return from their exile in Babylon to a Jerusalem in ruins.

———

How LONELY SITS the city that was full of people! How like a widow is she that was great among the nations! A princess among cities has become a vassal. She weeps in the night, tears on her cheeks; among all her lovers she has none to comfort her; her friends have become her enemies.

Judah has gone into exile; she finds no resting place; her pursuers have overtaken her in her distress.

The roads to Zion mourn, for none come to appointed feasts; all her gates are desolate; her priests groan; her maidens have been dragged away; her foes prosper. The LORD has made her suffer for the multitude of her transgressions. From the daughter of Zion has departed all majesty. Her princes have become like stags that find no pasture; they have fled without strength before the pursuer.

Jerusalem remembers in the days of her bitterness the precious things that were hers of old. When her people fell and there was none to help her, the foe gloated, mocking at her downfall. Jerusalem sinned grievously, therefore she became filthy; all who honored her despise her, for they have seen her nakedness; yea, she herself turns her face away. She took no thought of her doom, therefore her fall is terrible. "O LORD, behold my affliction, for the enemy has triumphed!"

The enemy has stretched out his hands over all her precious things; she has seen the nations invade her sanctuary, those whom thou didst forbid to enter thy congregation. All her people groan as they search for bread; they trade their treasures for food. "Look, O LORD, behold, I am despised."

"Is it nothing to you, all you who pass by? Look, see if there is any sorrow like the sorrow the LORD inflicted upon me on the day of his anger. From on high he sent fire into my bones; he spread a net for my feet. My transgressions were bound into a yoke, and by his hand they were set upon my neck; he caused my strength to fail.

"The Lord flouted my mighty men in the midst of me; he summoned an assembly against me to crush my young men; the Lord has trodden as in a wine press the virgin daughter of Judah. For these things I weep."

Zion stretches out her hands, but there is none to comfort her; the LORD has commanded against Jacob that his neighbors should be his foes.

"The LORD is in the right, for I have rebelled against his word; but behold my suffering, all you peoples; my maidens and young men have gone into captivity. I called to my lovers but they deceived me; my priests and elders perished in the city while seeking food.

"Behold, O LORD, my soul is in tumult, my heart is wrung within me, because I have been rebellious. In the street the sword bereaves; in the house it is like death.

"All my enemies have heard of my trouble; they are glad that thou hast done it. Bring thou the day thou hast announced, and let them be as I am. Let all their evildoing come before thee; and deal with them as thou hast dealt with me because of all my transgressions; for my groans are many and my heart is faint."

How THE LORD in his anger has set the daughter of Zion under a cloud! He has cast down from heaven the splendor of Israel. He has destroyed without mercy the habitations of Jacob, and brought to dishonor the kingdom and its rulers. He has bent his bow like an enemy, and has slain the pride of Zion; he has poured out his fury like fire. The Lord has destroyed Israel, all its palaces and strongholds, and has multiplied in Judah lamentation and mourning.

The Lord has laid in ruins the place of his worship; he has ended in Zion sabbath and feast. The Lord has scorned his altar, disowned his sanctuary, and delivered them into the enemy's hand.

He determined to lay in ruins the wall of Jerusalem; he restrained not his hand, causing rampart and wall to languish together. Her gates have sunk into the ground; her princes are exiled; the law is no more, and her prophets obtain no vision from the LORD. The elders sit silent in sackcloth; the maidens bow their heads to the ground.

My eyes are spent with weeping, because of the destruction of my people, because infants and babes faint in the streets.

"Where is bread?" they cry, as their life is poured out on their mothers' bosom. What can I say, O daughter of Zion, to comfort you? Vast as the sea is your ruin; who can restore you? Your prophets have seen for you false and deceptive visions; they have not exposed your iniquity to restore your fortunes.

All who pass by wag their heads at Jerusalem. "Is this the city once called the perfection of beauty, the joy of all the earth?" Your enemies rail against you; they cry: "We have destroyed her! This is the day we longed for; now we see it!" The LORD has done what he purposed long ago.

Cry aloud to the Lord, O daughter of Zion! Let tears stream down without respite! Arise, cry out in the night! Pour out your heart like water before the Lord! Lift your hands to him for the lives of your children, who hunger.

O LORD, with whom hast thou dealt thus? Should women eat the children of their tender care? Should priest and prophet be slain in thy sanctuary? In the dust lie the young and the old; in the day of thy anger thou hast slain them without mercy. Thou didst invite as to an appointed feast my terrors on every side; none escaped or survived that day; those I pampered and reared my enemy destroyed.

I AM THE man afflicted by the rod of his wrath; he turns his hand against me the whole day long. He has made my flesh waste away and broken my bones; he has made me dwell in darkness like the dead of long ago. He has walled me about so I cannot escape; though I cry for help, he shuts out my prayer; he has blocked my ways with hewn stones, he has made my paths crooked.

He is to me like a bear lying in wait; he led me off my way and tore me to pieces. His bow drove into my heart the arrows of his quiver; I have become the laughing-stock of all peoples, the burden of their songs. He has made my teeth grind on gravel, and made me cower in ashes; my soul is bereft of peace, I have forgotten what happiness is; so I say, "Gone is my glory, my expectation from the LORD."

Remember my affliction and my bitterness, the wormwood and the gall! My soul is bowed down within me. But this I call to mind, and therefore I have hope: the steadfast love of the LORD never ceases, his mercies never come to an end; they are new every morning; great is thy faithfulness. "The LORD is my portion," says my soul, "therefore I will hope in him."

The LORD is good to those who wait for him, to the soul that seeks him. It is good to wait quietly for his salvation. It is good for a man to bear the yoke in his youth. Then let him sit alone in silence; let him put his mouth in the dust—there may yet be hope.

For the Lord will not cast off for ever, but, though he cause grief, he will have compassion according to the abundance of his steadfast love; for he does not willingly afflict or grieve the sons of men. To crush under foot the prisoners of the earth, to turn aside the right of a man in the presence of the Most High, to subvert a man in his cause, the Lord does not approve.

Whose command has come to pass, unless the Lord has ordained it? Is it not from the mouth of the Most High that good and evil come? Why should a living man complain about the punishment of his sins?

Let us examine our ways, and return to the LORD! Lift hearts and hands to God in heaven: "We have rebelled, and thou hast not forgiven. Thou hast wrapped thyself with anger and pursued us; thou hast wrapped thyself with a cloud no prayer can pass through. Thou hast made us as refuse among the peoples. Panic has come upon us; my eyes will flow with tears unceasing because of the destruction of my people, until the LORD from heaven looks down and sees.

"I have been hunted like a bird by those who were my enemies without cause; they flung me into the pit and cast stones on me; water closed over my head; I said, 'I am lost.' I called on thy name, O LORD, from the depths; thou didst hear my plea and didst come near, saying, 'Do not fear!'

"Thou hast redeemed my life, O LORD. Thou hast seen the wrong done me; judge thou my cause. Thou hast heard their taunts; their lips and thoughts are against me all day. I am the burden of their songs.

"Thou wilt requite them, O LORD, according to the work of their hands. Thou wilt give them dullness of heart; thy curse will be on them. Thou wilt pursue them in anger and destroy them."

How THE GOLD has grown dim, how the pure gold is changed! The holy stones lie scattered at the head of every street. The precious sons of Zion, worth their weight in fine gold, how they are reckoned as earthen pots, the work of a potter's hands! Even the jackals give the breast to their young, but the daughter of my people has become cruel. The tongue of the nursling cleaves to the roof of its mouth for thirst; the children beg for food. Those who feasted on dainties perish in the streets; those brought up in purple lie on ash heaps. For the chastisement of the daughter of my people has been greater than the punishment of Sodom, which was overthrown in a moment. Her princes were whiter than milk, their bodies more ruddy than coral. Now blacker than soot, they are not recognized in the streets; their skin has shriveled dry as wood. Happier were the victims of the sword than the victims of hunger, stricken by want. The hands of compassionate women have boiled their own children for food.

The LORD gave full vent to his wrath. He poured out hot anger, and kindled a fire in Zion which consumed its foundations. The kings of the earth did not believe, nor any inhabitants of the world, that foe or enemy could enter Jerusalem's gates. It happened because of the sins of her prophets and priests, who shed in her midst the blood of the righteous. They wandered, blind, through the streets, so defiled with blood that none could touch their garments. "Away! Unclean!" men cried. "Touch not!" So they became fugitives, wanderers; men said among the nations, "They shall stay with us no longer." The LORD himself has scattered them; no honor was shown to the priests, no favor to the elders.

Our eyes failed, ever watching for help; we watched for a nation which could not save. Men dogged our steps, we could not walk in our streets; our days were numbered, for our end had come. Our pursuers were swifter than vultures; they chased us on the mountains, they lay in wait for us in the wilderness. He who was the breath of our nostrils, the LORD'S anointed, was taken in their traps; he of whom we said, "Under his shadow we shall live among the nations."

Rejoice, O daughter of Edom, dweller in the land of Uz; but to you also the cup shall pass; you shall be drunk and strip yourself naked. The punishment of your iniquity, O daughter of Zion, is accomplished; he will keep you in exile no longer. But you, O daughter of Edom, he will punish; your sins he will bare.

REMEMBER, O LORD, what has befallen us; behold our disgrace! Our inheritance has been turned over to strangers; we have become orphans. We must pay for the water we drink, the wood we get. With a yoke on our necks we are driven hard. We have held out our hands to Egypt, and to Assyria, to get enough bread.

Our fathers sinned, and are no more; we bear their iniquities. Slaves rule over us; there is none to deliver us. We get our bread at peril of our lives because of the sword in the wilderness. Our skin is hot as an oven with the burning heat of famine.

Women are ravished, princes hung up by their hands; no respect is shown to the elders. Young men are compelled to grind at the mill; boys stagger under loads of wood. The old men have quit the city gate, the young men their music. Our dancing has been turned to mourning.

The crown has fallen from our head; woe to us, we have sinned! Our heart has become sick, our eyes have grown dim, Mount Zion lies desolate.

But thou, O LORD, dost reign for ever; thy throne endures to all generations. Why dost thou so long forsake us? Restore us to thyself, O LORD! Renew our days as of old! Or hast thou in thine anger rejected us utterly?

EZEKIEL

Eleven years before the fall of Jerusalem (586 B.C.), Ezekiel was deported, with other Jewish captives, to a settlement in Babylon. Here he received visions and was called to preach to his fellow exiles, a task he pursued faithfully for at least twenty-five years. He was a man of stern and inflexible energy of will and character, and his work consisted not only in sermons but also in prophetic behavior, such as sleeping on one side, not mourning over the sudden death of his wife, and eating a book. His prophecy falls into three main divisions: a warning to his people to repent or perish; judgments of doom directed against seven surrounding nations; and, after the fall of Jerusalem, prophecies of restoration and return, as in the vision of the valley of dry bones. Unlike other prophets of Israel, Ezekiel was also a priest, which accounts for his special interest in how the temple in Jerusalem should be restored after the Exile ended. His book explicitly revokes the principle that the sins of the fathers are visited on the children, and stresses the idea of personal responsibility before God.

―――――

IN THE THIRTIETH year, in the fourth month, on the fifth day of the month, as I was among the exiles by the river Chebar, the heavens were opened, and I saw visions of God. On the fifth day of the month (it was the fifth year of the exile of King Jehoiachin), the word of the LORD came to Ezekiel the priest, the son of Buzi, in the land of the Chaldeans by the river Chebar; and the hand of the LORD was upon him there.

As I looked, behold, a stormy wind came out of the north, and a great cloud, with brightness round about it, and fire flashing forth continually, and in the midst of the fire, as it were gleaming bronze. From the midst of it came the likeness of four living creatures. They had the form of men, but each had four faces and four wings. Their legs were straight, and the soles of their feet were like the sole of a calf's foot; they sparkled like burnished bronze. Under their wings on their four sides they had human hands. As for the likeness of their faces, each had the face of a man in front, the face of a lion on the right side, the face of an ox on the left side, and the face of an eagle at the back. Such were their faces. And each creature had two wings spread out above, each of which touched the wing of another, while two covered their bodies. And each went straight forward; wherever the spirit would go, they went, without turning. In the midst of the living creatures there was something that looked like burning coals of fire, like torches moving to and fro among the living creatures; the fire was bright, and out of it went forth lightning. And the living creatures darted to and fro, like a flash of lightning.

Now as I looked, I saw a wheel upon the

earth beside the living creatures, one for each of the four of them. As for the wheels, their appearance was like the gleaming of a chrysolite; and the four had the same likeness, their construction being as it were a wheel within a wheel. When they went, they went in any of their four directions without turning. The wheels had rims and spokes; and their rims were full of eyes round about. When the living creatures went, the wheels went beside them; and when the living creatures rose from the earth, the wheels rose. Wherever the spirit would go, they went, and the wheels rose along with them; for the spirit of the living creatures was in the wheels. When those went, these went; and when those stood, these stood; and when those rose from the earth, the wheels rose along with them; for the spirit of the living creatures was in the wheels.

Over the heads of the living creatures there was the likeness of a firmament, shining like crystal, spread out above their heads. Under the firmament their wings were stretched out straight, one toward another; and each creature had two wings

covering its body. When they went, I heard
the sound of their wings like the sound of
many waters, like the thunder of the Almighty, a sound of tumult like the sound
of a host; when they stood still, they let
down their wings. And there came a voice
from above the firmament over their
heads.

And above the firmament over their
heads there was the likeness of a throne, in
appearance like sapphire; seated above it
was a likeness as it were of a human form.
Upward from what had the appearance of
his loins I saw gleaming bronze, like the
appearance of fire enclosed round about;
and downward I saw as it were the appearance of fire. There was brightness round
about him. Like the bow that is in the
cloud on the day of rain, so was the brightness round about.

Such was the appearance of the likeness
of the glory of the LORD. When I saw it, I
fell upon my face, and I heard a voice:
"Son of man, stand upon your feet, and I
will speak with you." When he spoke, the
Spirit entered into me and set me upon my
feet. "Son of man," he said, "I send you to

the people of Israel, to a nation of rebels; they and their fathers have transgressed against me to this very day. The people also are impudent and stubborn. You shall say to them, 'Thus says the Lord GOD.' And whether they hear or refuse to hear, they will know there has been a prophet among them. Be not afraid of them, though briers and thorns are with you and you sit upon scorpions; be not afraid of their words, nor dismayed at their looks. Speak my words to them, whether they hear or refuse to hear; for they are a rebellious house.

"But you, son of man, hear what I say to you; be not rebellious. Open your mouth, and eat what I give you." And behold, a hand was stretched out to me, and a scroll was in it. He spread it before me, and written on the front and on the back were words of lamentation and woe. "Son of man," he said, "eat what is offered to you; eat this scroll, and go, speak to the house of Israel." So I opened my mouth, and he gave me the scroll to eat. It was in my mouth as sweet as honey. "Son of man, go," he said. "Speak with my words to the

house of Israel. For you are not sent to a
people of foreign speech and a hard language, whose words you cannot understand. Surely, if I sent you to such, they
would listen to you. But the house of Israel
will not listen, for they are not willing to
listen to me; they are of a hard forehead
and a stubborn heart. But I have made
your face hard against their faces, and your
forehead hard against their foreheads.
Harder than flint have I made your forehead; fear them not. All my words that I
shall speak to you receive in your heart.
Get you to the exiles, your people, and say
to them, 'Thus says the Lord GOD,' whether
they hear or refuse to hear."

Then the Spirit lifted me up, and as the
glory of the LORD arose from its place, I
heard behind me the sound of a great
earthquake; it was the sound of the wings
of the living creatures as they touched one
another, and the sound of the wheels beside them. The Spirit lifted me up and took
me away, and I went in the heat of my
spirit, the hand of the LORD being strong
upon me; and I came to the exiles at Tel-
abib, who dwelt by the river Chebar. I sat

there overwhelmed among them seven days.

At the end of seven days the word of the LORD came to me: "Son of man, I have made you a watchman for the house of Israel; whenever you hear a word from my mouth, you shall give them warning from me. If I say to the wicked, 'You shall surely die,' and you give him no warning to turn from his wicked way in order to save his life, that man shall die in his iniquity; but his blood I will require at your hand. But if you warn him, and he does not turn from his wickedness, he shall die in his iniquity; but you will have saved your life. Again, if a righteous man turns from his righteousness and commits iniquity, and you do not warn him, he shall die for his sin, and his righteous deeds shall not be remembered; but his blood I will require at your hand. Nevertheless if you warn the righteous man not to sin, and he does not sin, he shall surely live, because he took warning; and you will have saved your life."

The hand of the LORD was there upon me. "Arise," he said, "go forth into the

plain, and there I will speak with you." So
I went into the plain; and lo, the glory of
the LORD stood there, like the glory which
I had seen by the river Chebar; and I fell
on my face. But the Spirit entered into me,
and set me upon my feet. "Go," he said,
"shut yourself within your house. And behold, O son of man, cords will be placed
upon you, and you shall be bound with
them, so that you cannot go out among the
people; and I will make your tongue cleave
to the roof of your mouth, so that you shall
be dumb and unable to reprove them; for
they are a rebellious house. But when I
speak with you, I will open your mouth,
and you shall say to them, 'Thus says the
Lord GOD'; he that will hear, let him hear,
and he that will refuse to hear, let him
refuse.

"And you, O son of man, take a brick
and lay it before you, and portray upon it a
city, even Jerusalem. Build a siege wall
against it, and cast up a mound; set camps
also against it, and plant battering rams
round about. Take an iron plate, and place
it as a wall between you and the city; set
your face toward it, and press the siege

against it. This is a sign for the house of Israel. Then lie on your left side, and I will lay the punishment of the house of Israel upon you; for three hundred and ninety days, the number of the years of their punishment, you shall bear the punishment of the house of Israel. When you have completed these, you shall lie on your right side and bear the punishment of the house of Judah; forty days I assign you, a day for each year. And you shall set your face toward the siege of Jerusalem and prophesy against the city. And behold, I will put cords upon you, so that you cannot turn from one side to the other, till you have completed the days of your siege.

"Take wheat and barley, beans and lentils, millet and spelt, and make bread of them. During the days that you lie on your side you shall eat it by weight, eight ounces a day. Water you shall drink by measure, a quart a day; once a day you shall eat and drink. And you shall bake your bread in the people's sight on human dung. Thus shall the people of Israel eat their bread unclean, among the nations whither I will drive them."

"Ah Lord God!" I said. "I have never
defiled myself; from my youth up till now I
have never eaten what died of itself or was
torn by beasts, nor has foul flesh come into
my mouth." Then he said, "See, I will let
you have cow's dung instead of human
dung, on which to prepare your bread. But
I will break the staff of bread in Jerusalem;
they shall eat bread by weight and with
fearfulness, and drink water by measure
and in dismay. I will do this that they may
lack bread and water, and waste away under their punishment.

"And you, O son of man, take a sharp
sword; use it as a barber's razor over your
head and beard; then take balances for
weighing, and divide the hair. A third you
shall burn in the fire in the midst of the
city when the days of the siege are completed; a third you shall take and strike
with the sword round about the city; and a
third you shall scatter to the wind, and I
will unsheathe the sword after them. You
shall take from these a small number, and
bind them in the skirts of your robe. Of
these again you shall take some, and burn
them in the fire; from there a fire will

come forth into all the house of Israel.

"This is Jerusalem; I have set her in the center of the nations, with countries round about her, and she has wickedly rebelled against my ordinances more than the other nations.

"Therefore thus says the Lord GOD: Because you are more turbulent than the nations round about you, and have not walked in my statutes, therefore I, even I, am against you; and I will execute judgments in the midst of you in the sight of the nations. Because of all your abominations I will do with you what I have never yet done, and the like of which I will never do again. Fathers shall eat their sons in the midst of you, and sons shall eat their fathers; any of you who survive I will scatter to all the winds. Wherefore, as I live, says the Lord GOD, surely, because you have defiled my sanctuary with your detestable things, therefore I will cut you down; my eye will not spare. A third of you shall die of pestilence and be consumed with famine in the midst of you; a third shall fall by the sword; and a third I will scatter to all the winds and will unsheathe the sword

after them. Thus shall my anger spend itself; and they shall know that I the LORD
have spoken in my jealousy.

"Yet I will leave some of you alive.
Those of you who escape will remember
me among the nations where they are carried captive, and they will be loathsome in
their own sight for evils they have committed. They shall know that I am the LORD; I
have not said in vain that I would do this
evil to them."

IN THE SIXTH year, in the sixth month, on
the fifth day of the month, as I sat in my
house, with the elders of Judah sitting before me, the hand of the Lord GOD fell
upon me. And lo, I beheld a form that had
the appearance of a man; below what appeared to be his loins it was fire, and
above, it was like the appearance of brightness, like gleaming bronze. He put forth
the form of a hand, and took me by a lock
of my head. The Spirit lifted me up between earth and heaven, and brought me
in visions of God to Jerusalem, to the entrance of the gateway of the inner court
that faces north, where was the seat of the

image of jealousy, which provokes to jealousy. And behold, the glory of the God of Israel was there, like the vision that I saw in the plain. "Son of man," he said, "lift up your eyes now in the direction of the north." So I lifted up my eyes, and behold, north of the altar gate, in the entrance, was this image of jealousy. "Son of man," he said, "do you see the great abominations that the house of Israel are committing here, to drive me from my sanctuary? You will see still greater abominations."

He brought me to the door of the court; and behold, there was a hole in the wall. "Son of man," he said, "dig in the wall"; and when I dug, lo, there was a door. "Go in," he said, "and see the vile abominations they are committing here." So I went in, and there, portrayed upon the wall round about, were all kinds of creeping things, and loathsome beasts, and all the idols of the house of Israel. Before them stood seventy elders, each with his censer in his hand, and the smoke of the cloud of incense went up. "Son of man," he said, "have you seen what the elders of the house of Israel are doing in the dark, every

man in his room of pictures? For they say,
'The LORD does not see us, the LORD has
forsaken the land.' You will see still greater
abominations which they commit."

Then he brought me to the entrance of
the north gate of the house of the LORD;
and behold, there sat women weeping for
an alien god. "Have you seen this, O son
of man?" he said. "You will see still greater
abominations." He brought me into the
inner court of the house of the LORD; and
behold, at the door, between the porch
and the altar, were about twenty-five men,
with their backs to the temple of the LORD
and their faces toward the east, worshiping
the sun. "Have you seen this, O son of
man?" he said. "Is it too slight a thing for
the house of Judah to commit these abominations, that they should fill the land with
violence, and provoke me further to anger? Therefore I will deal in wrath; my eye
will not spare, nor will I have pity; and
though they cry in my ears, I will not hear
them."

Then he cried with a loud voice, saying,
"Draw near, you executioners of the city,
each with his destroying weapon." And lo,

six men came from the direction of the upper gate, which faces north, every man with his weapon in his hand, and with them was a man clothed in linen, a writing case at his side. They went in and stood beside the bronze altar.

Now the glory of the God of Israel had gone up from the cherubim on which it rested to the threshold of the house; and he called to the man clothed in linen, and said, "Go through Jerusalem, and put a mark upon the foreheads of the men who sigh and groan over all the abominations that are committed in it." To the others he said, "Pass through the city after him, and smite; your eye shall not spare, and you shall show no pity; slay old men outright, young men and maidens, little children and women, but touch no one upon whom is the mark. Begin at my sanctuary." So they began with the elders who were before the house. Then he said to them, "Defile the house, and fill the courts with the slain. Go forth." So they went forth, and smote in the city. While they were smiting, and I was left alone, I fell on my face and cried, "Ah Lord GOD! wilt thou destroy all that remains of Israel in the outpouring of thy wrath upon Jerusalem?" He said, "The guilt of the house of Israel and Judah is exceedingly great; the land is full of blood, and the city full of injustice; for they say, 'The LORD has forsaken the land, and the LORD does not see.' As for me, my eye will not spare, nor will I have pity, but I will requite their deeds upon their heads."

And lo, the man clothed in linen, with the writing case at his side, brought back word, saying, "I have done as thou didst command me."

THE WORD OF the LORD came to me: "Son of man, how does the wood of the vine surpass any which is among the trees of the forest? Is wood taken from it to make anything? Do men take a peg from it to hang any vessel on? Lo, it is given to the fire for fuel; when the fire has consumed both ends of it, and the middle is charred, is it useful for anything? When it was whole, it was used for nothing; how much less, when the fire has charred it, can it ever be used for anything! Therefore thus says the Lord GOD: Like the wood of the vine which I have given to the fire for fuel, so will I give up the inhabitants of Jerusalem. I will set my face against them, and you will know that I am the LORD. I will make the land desolate, because they have acted faithlessly."

Again the word of the LORD came to me: "Son of man, make known to Jerusalem her abominations. Say to her, Thus says the Lord GOD: Your origin is of the land of the Canaanites; your father was an Amorite, and your mother a Hittite. As for your birth, on the day you were born your navel string was not cut, nor were you washed with water, nor rubbed with salt, nor swathed with bands. No eye pitied you, to do any of these things for you. You were cast out on the open field, for you were abhorred. When I passed by, and saw you weltering in your blood, I said to you, 'Live, and grow up like a plant of the field.' And you grew up and arrived at full maidenhood; your breasts were formed, and your hair had grown; yet you were naked and bare.

"When I passed by you again, behold, you were at the age for love; and I spread

my skirt over you, and covered your nakedness: yea, I plighted my troth to you
and entered into a covenant with you, and
you became mine. I bathed you with water
and anointed you with oil. I shod you with
leather, swathed you in fine linen, and covered you with silk. I decked you with gold
and silver, putting bracelets on your arms,
a chain on your neck, earrings in your ears,
and a beautiful crown upon your head.
You ate fine flour and honey and oil. You
came to regal estate, and your renown
went forth among the nations because of
your beauty, for it was perfect through the
splendor which I had bestowed upon you.

"But you trusted in your beauty, and
played the harlot because of your renown.
You took some of your garments, and
made for yourself gaily decked shrines, and
on them played the harlot; the like has
never been, nor ever shall be. You also
took your jewels of my gold and my silver
and made images of men, setting before
them my oil, my incense, and my bread,
made with fine flour and oil and honey.
And you took the sons and daughters you
had borne to me, and these you sacrificed

to them. Were your harlotries so small a matter that you delivered my children up as an offering by fire to them? In all your abominations you did not remember the days of your youth, when you were naked and bare, weltering in your blood.

"After all your wickedness (woe, woe to you! says the Lord GOD), you built yourself a vaulted chamber, and a lofty place at the head of every street, offering yourself to any passer-by. You played the harlot with the Egyptians, your lustful neighbors, to provoke me to anger. Therefore I stretched out my hand against you, and delivered you to your enemies, the daughters of the Philistines, who were ashamed of your lewd behavior. You played the harlot also with the Assyrians, because you were insatiable; yea, you multiplied your harlotry with the trading land of Chaldea, and even with this you were not satisfied.

"Wherefore, O Jerusalem, thus says the Lord GOD: Because your shame was laid bare, and because of all your idols, and the blood of your children that you gave to them, therefore, behold, I will gather all your lovers against you from every side, and will uncover your nakedness to them, that they may see it. I will judge you as women who break wedlock and shed blood are judged, and bring upon you the blood of wrath and jealousy. I will give you into the hand of your lovers, and they shall break down your lofty places; they shall strip you bare. They shall bring up a host against you, and stone you, and cut you to pieces with their swords. They shall execute judgments upon you in the sight of many women; I will make you stop playing the harlot. So will I satisfy my fury on you, and my jealousy shall depart from you; I will no more be angry. But because you have not remembered the days of your youth, and have enraged me, therefore I will requite your deeds upon your head, says the Lord GOD.

"Behold, every one who uses proverbs will use this proverb about you, 'Like mother, like daughter,' for you are the true daughter of your mother, who loathed her husband and children; and you are the true sister of your sisters, who loathed their husbands and children. Your elder sister is Samaria, to the north of you; and your younger sister, to the south, is Sodom. Yet you were not content to do according to their abominations; within a very little time you were more corrupt than they. As I live, says the Lord GOD, Sodom and her daughters have not done as you and your daughters have done. Behold, this was the guilt of Sodom: she and her daughters had pride, surfeit of food, and prosperous ease, but did not aid the poor and needy. They were haughty, and did abominable things; therefore I removed them. Samaria also has not committed half your sins. You have made your sisters appear righteous by all the abominations you have committed. So be ashamed, and bear your disgrace. I will restore the fortunes of Sodom and of Samaria, and I will restore your fortunes in the midst of them, that you may be ashamed of all that you have done, becoming a consolation to them. Was not your sister Sodom a byword in your mouth in the day of your pride, before your wickedness was uncovered? Now you have become like her an object of reproach for those round about who despise you. You bear the penalty of your lewdness, says the LORD.

"Yet I will remember my covenant with you in the days of your youth, and I will establish with you an everlasting covenant. Then you will remember your ways, and be ashamed when I take your sisters and give them to you as daughters. I will establish my covenant with you, and you shall know that I am the LORD, that you may be confounded, and never open your mouth again because of your shame, when I forgive you all that you have done, says the Lord GOD."

THE WORD OF the LORD came to me: "Son of man, propound a riddle, and speak an allegory to the house of Israel; say, Thus says the Lord GOD: A great eagle with great wings and long pinions, rich in plumage of many colors, came to Lebanon and broke off the topmost young twig of the cedar. Carrying it to a land of trade, he set it in a city of merchants. Then he took of the seed of the land and planted it in fertile soil beside abundant waters. It sprouted and became a low spreading vine, and its branches turned toward him. But there was another great eagle with great wings and much plumage; and behold, this vine now shot forth its branches toward him, that he might water it. From its bed he transplanted it, that it might bear fruit and become a noble vine. Behold, when it is transplanted, will it thrive? Will it not utterly wither when the east wind strikes it— wither away on the bed where it grew?"

Then the word of the LORD came to me: "Say now to the rebellious house, Do you not know what these things mean? Tell them, Behold, the king of Babylon came to Jerusalem, and took her king and princes and brought them to Babylon. He took one of the seed royal and made a covenant with him, putting him under oath. But the prince rebelled against the king of Babylon by sending ambassadors to Egypt, that they might give him horses and a large army. Will he succeed? Can he break the covenant and yet escape? As I live, says the Lord GOD, surely in the place where the king dwells who made him king, whose oath he despised, and whose covenant with him he broke, in Babylon he shall die. Pharaoh with his mighty army

will not help him in war, when mounds
are cast up and siege walls built. Because
he despised the oath, because he gave his
hand and yet did all these things, he shall
not escape. My covenant which he broke I
will requite upon his head. I will enter into
judgment with him for the treason he has
committed. The pick of his troops shall fall
by the sword, and the survivors shall be
scattered to every wind; you shall know
that I, the LORD, have spoken."

Thus says the Lord GOD: "I myself will
take a sprig from the lofty top of the cedar,
and on the mountain height of Israel will I
plant it, that it may bring forth boughs and
bear fruit, and become a noble cedar. Under it will dwell all kinds of beasts; in the
shade of its branches birds of every sort
will nest. And all the trees of the field shall
know that I the LORD bring low the high
tree, and make high the low tree, dry up the
green tree, and make the dry tree flourish. I
the LORD have spoken, and I will do it."

THE WORD OF the LORD came to me again:
"What do you mean by repeating this
proverb concerning the land of Israel, 'The

fathers have eaten sour grapes, and the children's teeth are set on edge'? As I live, says the Lord God, this proverb shall no more be used by you in Israel. Behold, all souls are mine; the soul of the father as well as the soul of the son: the soul that sins shall die.

"If a man does what is lawful and right—if he does not lift up his eyes to idols, does not defile his neighbor's wife, does not oppress any one, but restores to the debtor his pledge, commits no robbery, gives his bread to the hungry and covers the naked, does not lend at interest, withholds his hand from iniquity, executes true justice between man and man, walks in my statutes, and is careful to observe my ordinances—he is righteous, he shall surely live, says the Lord God.

"If he begets a son who is a robber, a shedder of blood, who does none of these duties, but commits abomination; shall this son then live? He shall not. He has done abominable things; his blood shall be upon himself. But if this son begets a son who sees all the sins which his father has done, and fears, and does not do likewise, but observes my ordinances, and walks in my statutes, the son shall not die for his father's iniquity; he shall live.

"Yet you say, 'Why should not the son suffer for the iniquity of the father?' When the son has done what is lawful and right, he shall surely live. The soul that sins shall die. The son shall not suffer for the iniquity of the father, nor the father for the iniquity of the son; the righteousness of the righteous shall be upon himself, and the wickedness of the wicked shall be upon himself. But if a wicked man turns away from all his sins, he shall not die. None of his transgressions shall be remembered against him; for the righteousness he has done he shall live. Have I any pleasure in the death of the wicked, says the Lord GOD, and not prefer that he should turn from his way and live? But when a righteous man turns away from his righteousness and does the same abominable things that the wicked man does, shall he live? None of his righteous deeds shall be remembered; for the treachery of which he is guilty and the sin he has committed, he shall die.

"Yet you say, 'The way of the Lord is not just.' Hear now, O house of Israel: Is my way not just? Is it not your ways that are not just? When a righteous man turns away from his righteousness and commits iniquity, he shall die. Again, when a wicked man turns away from the wickedness he has committed and does what is right, he shall save his life. Yet the house of Israel says, 'The way of the Lord is not just.' O house of Israel, are my ways not just? Is it not your ways that are not just?

"Therefore I will judge you, O house of Israel, every one according to his ways. Repent, lest iniquity be your ruin. Cast away all the transgressions which you have committed against me, and get yourselves a new heart and a new spirit! Why will you die, O Israel? For I have no pleasure in the death of any one, says the Lord GOD; so turn, and live."

IN THE SEVENTH year, in the fifth month, on the tenth day of the month, certain of the elders of Israel came to inquire of the LORD, and sat before me. And the word of

the LORD came to me: "Son of man, speak
to the elders, and say, Thus says the Lord
GOD: Is it to inquire of me that you come?
As I live, says the Lord GOD, I will not be
inquired of by you. Will you judge them,
son of man, will you judge them? Then let
them know the abominations of their fathers. Say to them, On the day when I
chose Israel, I swore to the seed of the
house of Jacob, making myself known to
them in the land of Egypt, saying, I am the
LORD your God. I swore that I would bring
them into a land flowing with milk and
honey, the most glorious of all lands. I said
to them, Cast away the detestable things
your eyes feast on, every one of you, and
do not defile yourselves with the idols of
Egypt; I am the LORD your God. But they
would not listen.

"Then I thought I would spend my anger against them in the midst of the land of
Egypt. But I acted for the sake of my
name, that it should not be profaned in the
sight of the nations among whom they
dwelt. I led them into the wilderness, and
gave them my statutes and ordinances, by
whose observance man shall live. More-

over I gave them my sabbaths, as a sign between me and them, that they might know that I the LORD sanctify them. But the house of Israel rebelled against me; they rejected my ordinances, and profaned my sabbaths; their heart went after idols.

"Wherefore, son of man, say to the house of Israel, After the manner of your fathers, you defile yourselves with all your idols to this day. Shall I be inquired of by you, O Israel? As I live, says the Lord GOD, I will not. With a mighty hand and an outstretched arm, and with wrath poured out, I will be king over you. I will gather you out of the countries where you are scattered, and bring you into the wilderness of the peoples. There I will enter into judgment with you face to face. I will purge the rebels from among you; they shall not enter the land of Israel. Then you will know that I am the LORD. Go serve your idols, now and hereafter, if you will not listen to me; but my holy name you shall no more profane.

"For on my holy mountain, the mountain height of Israel, says the Lord GOD, all the house of Israel, all of them, shall serve me; there I will accept you, and there I will require the choicest of your gifts, with all your sacred offerings. I will manifest my holiness among you in the sight of the nations. And you shall know that I am the LORD, when I bring you into the land which I swore to give to your fathers. There you shall remember all the doings with which you have polluted yourselves, and you shall loathe yourselves. You shall know that I am the LORD, when I deal with you for my name's sake, not according to your evil ways, O house of Israel, says the Lord GOD."

THE WORD OF the LORD came to me: "Son of man, preach against the south, and say, Thus says the Lord GOD: Behold, I will kindle a fire in you, and it shall devour every green tree and every dry tree; the blazing flame shall not be quenched. All faces from south to north shall be scorched by it, and all flesh shall see that I the LORD have kindled it." Then I said, "Ah Lord GOD! they are saying of me, 'Is he not a maker of allegories?' "

The word of the LORD came to me:

"Son of man, set your face toward Jerusalem and preach against the sanctuaries; say to the land of Israel, Thus says the LORD: Behold, I am against you, and will draw forth my sword out of its sheath, and cut off both righteous and wicked. All flesh shall know that I the LORD have drawn my sword; it shall not be sheathed again. Sigh therefore, son of man; sigh with breaking heart and bitter grief before their eyes. And when they say, 'Why do you sigh?' you shall say, 'Because of the tidings. When it comes, every heart will melt and all hands will be feeble, every spirit will faint and all knees will be weak as water. Behold, it comes and it will be fulfilled.' A sword is sharpened and polished, sharpened for slaughter, polished to flash like lightning! You have despised the rod, my son, so the sword is sharpened to be given into the hand of the slayer. Cry and wail, son of man, for it is against my people. I will satisfy my fury; I the LORD have spoken."

The word of the LORD came to me again: "Son of man, mark two ways for the sword of the king of Babylon to come.

Mark a way for the sword to come to Rabbah of the Ammonites, and to Judah, to Jerusalem the fortified. For the king of Babylon stands at the head of the two ways, to use divination; he shakes arrows, he consults idols, he looks at the liver. Into his right hand comes the lot for Jerusalem, where he is to set battering rams against the gates, cast up mounds, and build siege towers. To them it will seem like a false divination; but he brings their guilt to remembrance, that they may be captured. For thus says the Lord GOD: Because you have made your guilt to be remembered, so that in all your doings your sins appear, you shall be taken in them. And you, O unhallowed wicked one, prince of Israel, whose day has come, thus says the Lord GOD: Take off the crown; things shall not remain as they are; exalt that which is low, and abase that which is high. A ruin, ruin, ruin I will make it; there shall not be even a trace of it until he comes whose right it is; and to him I will give it."

THE WORD OF the LORD came to me: "Son of man, there were two women, the daughters of one mother; they played the harlot in Egypt in their youth; there their virgin breasts were handled. Oholah was the elder and Oholibah her sister. They became mine, and they bore sons and daughters. As for their names, Oholah is Samaria, and Oholibah is Jerusalem.

"Oholah played the harlot while she was mine; she doted on her lovers the Assyrians, warriors clothed in purple, governors and commanders, the choicest men of Assyria; and she defiled herself with all the idols of every one on whom she doted. Therefore I delivered her into the hands of her lovers the Assyrians. These uncovered her nakedness; they seized her sons and daughters; and her they slew with the sword; she became a byword among women when judgment had been executed upon her.

"Oholibah saw this, yet she was more corrupt than her sister. She also doted upon the Assyrians, but she carried her harlotry further than Oholah. She saw men portrayed upon the wall, girded with belts on their loins, with flowing turbans on their heads, images of Babylonians whose native land was Chaldea. She doted upon them, and sent messengers to them. The Babylonians came and defiled her with their lust; and after she was polluted by them, she turned from them in disgust. When she carried on her harlotry so openly, I turned in disgust from her, as I had turned from her sister. Yet she increased her harlotry, remembering her paramours in Egypt.

"Therefore, O Oholibah, I will bring your lovers against you from every side: the Babylonians and all the Assyrians. With chariots they shall come, and I will direct my indignation against you, that they may deal with you in fury. Thus I will put an end to your lewdness. For thus says the Lord GOD: Behold, I will deliver you into the hands of those whom you hate, and they shall deal with you in hatred. They shall take away the fruit of your labor and leave you naked. You have gone the way of your sister; therefore I will give her cup into your hand, a cup of horror and desolation. You shall drain it, and pluck out your hair and tear your breasts; for I have spoken. Because you have forgotten

me and cast me behind your back, therefore bear the consequences."

The LORD said to me: "Son of man, will
you judge Oholah and Oholibah? Then declare to them their abominable deeds. For
blood is upon their hands; with their idols
they have committed adultery; they have
even offered up to them for food the sons
they had borne to me. Moreover they have
defiled my sanctuary. For when they had
slaughtered their children in sacrifice to
their idols, on the same day they came into
my sanctuary to profane it. This is what
they did in my house. A messenger was
sent to summon men from far, and lo,
the men came. For them you bathed
yourself, painted your eyes, and decked
yourself with ornaments; you sat upon a
stately couch, with a table spread before
it on which you had placed my incense
and my oil. The sound of a carefree multitude was heard, and men of the common sort, drunkards, were brought from
the wilderness.

"Then I said, Do not men now commit
adultery when they practice harlotry with
them? For as men go in to a harlot, thus

they went in to Oholah and Oholibah. But righteous men shall pass judgment on them with the sentence of adulteresses; because they are adulteresses, and blood is upon their hands. Bring up a host against them, and make them an object of terror. The host shall stone them and dispatch them with swords; they shall slay their sons and daughters, and burn up their houses. Thus will I put an end to lewdness in the land, that all women may take warning. You shall bear the penalty for your sinful idolatry; and you shall know that I am the Lord GOD."

IN THE NINTH year, in the tenth month, on the tenth day of the month, the word of the LORD came to me: "Son of man, write down the name of this day. The king of Babylon has laid siege to Jerusalem this very day. Utter an allegory to the rebellious house and say, Thus says the Lord GOD: Set on the pot, pour in water; put in it the pieces of flesh, the good pieces, thigh and shoulder; fill it with choice bones, take the choicest of the flock. Pile the logs under it; boil its pieces, boil also its bones in it.

"Therefore thus says the Lord GOD: Woe to the bloody city, to the pot whose rust is in it, and whose rust has not gone out of it! Take out piece after piece, without making any choice. For the blood she has shed is still in the midst of her; she did not pour it on the ground to cover it with dust. To take vengeance, I have set on the bare rock the blood she has shed, that it may not be covered. Woe to the bloody city! I also will make the pile great: heap on the logs, kindle the fire, boil well the flesh, empty out the broth, let the bones be burned up. Then set the empty pot upon the coals, that it may become hot and its copper burn, that its filthiness may be melted in it, its rust consumed. In vain I have wearied myself; its thick rust does not go out of it by fire. This rust is your filthy lewdness. Because I would have cleansed you and you were not cleansed, you shall not be cleansed any more till I have satisfied my fury upon you. I the LORD have spoken; I will do it; I will not spare; according to your ways and your doings I will judge you."

Also the word of the LORD came to me:

"Son of man, behold, I am about to take the delight of your eyes away from you at a stroke; yet you shall not mourn, nor shall your tears run down. Sigh, but not aloud; make no mourning for the dead. Bind on your turban, and put your shoes on your feet; do not cover your lips, nor eat the bread of mourners."

So I spoke to the people in the morning, and at evening my wife died. On the next morning I did as I was commanded.

The people said to me, "Will you not tell us what these things mean for us, that you are acting thus?" I said, "The word of the LORD came to me: 'Say to the house of Israel, Thus says the Lord GOD: Behold, I will profane my sanctuary, the pride of your power, the delight of your eyes, and the desire of your soul; and your sons and daughters whom you left behind shall fall by the sword. And you shall do as I have done; you shall not cover your lips, nor eat the bread of mourners. Your turbans shall be on your heads and your shoes on your feet; you shall not mourn or weep, but you shall pine away in your iniquities and groan to one another. Thus shall Ezekiel be to you a sign; according to all that he has done, you shall do. When this comes, then you will know that I am the Lord GOD.'

"And you, son of man, on the day when I take from them their joy and glory, the delight of their eyes and their heart's desire, and also their sons and daughters, on that day a fugitive will come to you to report the news. The hand of the LORD will be upon you the evening before he comes, but in the morning your mouth will be opened to the fugitive, and you shall speak and be no longer dumb. So you will be a sign to them; and they will know that I am the LORD."

THE WORD OF the LORD came to me: "Son of man, prophesy against the Ammonites, and say, Thus says the Lord GOD: Because you said, 'Aha!' over my sanctuary when it was profaned, and over the land of Israel when it was made desolate; therefore I am handing you over to the people of the East for a possession, and they shall set their encampments among you; they shall eat your fruit and drink your milk. Because you have clapped your hands and stamped your feet and rejoiced with all the malice within you against the land of Israel, therefore, behold, I will cut you off from the peoples and make you perish out of the countries; I will destroy you. Then you will know that I am the LORD.

"Thus says the Lord GOD: Because Moab said, 'Behold, the house of Judah is like all the other nations,' therefore I will lay open the flank of Moab and give it along with the Ammonites to the people of the East as a possession, that it may be remembered no more among the nations. Then they will know that I am the LORD.

"Thus says the Lord GOD: Because Edom acted revengefully against the house of Judah, therefore I will stretch out my hand against Edom, and make it desolate. They shall know my vengeance.

"Thus says the Lord GOD: Because the Philistines took vengeance with malice of heart to destroy in never-ending enmity; therefore I will stretch out my hand against the Philistines, and execute great vengeance upon them with wrathful chastisements. Then they will know that I am the LORD."

Moreover the word of the LORD came to me: "Son of man, raise a lamentation over the king of Tyre, and say, Thus says the Lord GOD: You were the signet of perfection, full of wisdom and perfect in beauty. You were in Eden, the garden of God; every precious stone was your covering, and wrought in gold were your settings. On the day you were created they were prepared. With an anointed guardian cherub I placed you; you were on the holy mountain of God; in the midst of the stones of fire you walked.

"You were blameless in your ways from the day you were created, till iniquity was found in you. In the abundance of your trade you were filled with violence, and you sinned; so I cast you as a profane thing from the mountain of God, and the guardian cherub drove you out from the midst of the stones of fire. Your heart was proud because of your beauty; you corrupted your wisdom for the sake of your splendor. I cast you to the ground; I exposed you before kings, to feast their eyes on you. I brought forth fire from the midst of you; it consumed you, and I turned you to ashes upon the earth. All who know you are appalled at you; you have come to a dreadful end and shall be no more for ever."

The word of the LORD came to me: "Son of man, set your face toward Sidon; prophesy against her, and say, Thus says the Lord GOD: Behold, I am against you, O Sidon; I will manifest my glory in the midst of you. And they shall know that I am the LORD when I execute judgments and manifest my holiness in her; for I will send pestilence into her, and blood into her streets; and the slain shall fall in the midst of her, by the sword that is against her on every side.

"And for the house of Israel there shall be no more a brier to prick or a thorn to hurt them among all their neighbors who have treated them with contempt. When I gather them from the peoples among whom they are scattered, and manifest my holiness in them in the sight of the nations, then they shall dwell in their own land which I gave to my servant Jacob. They shall dwell securely in it, and build houses and plant vineyards. Then they will know that I am the LORD their God."

IN THE TENTH year, in the tenth month, on the twelfth day of the month, the word of the LORD came to me: "Son of man, set your face against Pharaoh and all Egypt; speak, and say, Thus says the Lord GOD: Behold, I am against you, Pharaoh king of Egypt, the great dragon that lies in the midst of his streams, that says, 'My Nile is my own; I made it.' I will put hooks in your jaws, and make the fish of your streams stick to your scales; and I will draw you up out of your streams, with the fish sticking to you. I will cast you forth into the wilderness, you and the fish; you shall fall upon the open field and not be buried. To the beasts and the birds I have given you as food. Then all the inhabitants of Egypt shall know that I am the LORD.

"Because you have been a staff of reed to the house of Israel—when they grasped you with the hand, you broke, and tore their shoulders; when they leaned upon you, you broke, and made their loins to shake—therefore, says the Lord GOD, I will bring a sword upon you and cut off from you man and beast. Because you said, 'The Nile is mine, and I made it,' therefore I am against you and your streams, and I will make the land of Egypt an utter waste and desolation. No foot of man or beast shall pass through it; it shall be uninhabited forty years, and I will scatter the Egyptians among the nations. At the end of forty years I will bring them back to the land of their origin; and there they shall be the most lowly of kingdoms. I will make them so small that they will never again rule over the nations. And Egypt shall never again be the reliance of the house of Israel, recalling their iniquity when they turn to them for aid.

"Nebuchadrezzar king of Babylon made his army labor hard against Tyre; every head was made bald and every shoulder rubbed bare; yet neither he nor his army got anything from Tyre to pay for the labor they had performed against it. Therefore thus says the Lord GOD: Behold, I will give the land of Egypt to Nebuchadrezzar as recompense, because he worked for me. He shall carry off its wealth and plunder it; and it shall be the wages for his army.

"On that day, son of man, I will cause a horn to spring forth to the house of Israel, and I will open your lips among them. Then they will know that I am the LORD."

IN THE ELEVENTH year, in the third month, on the first day of the month, the word of the LORD came to me: "Son of man, say to Pharaoh king of Egypt and to his multitude: Whom are you like in your greatness? Behold, I will liken you to a cedar in Lebanon, with fair branches and forest shade, and of great height, its top among the clouds. The waters nourished it, the deep made it grow tall, making its rivers flow round the place of its planting. So it towered high above all the trees of the forest. The birds made their nests in its boughs; under its branches the beasts brought forth their young; and under its shadow dwelt all great nations. No tree in the garden of God was like it in beauty, and all the trees of Eden envied it.

"Therefore thus says the Lord GOD: Because it towered high, and its heart was proud of its height, I will give it into the hand of a mighty one of the nations; he shall deal with it as it deserves. I have cast it out. Foreigners, the most terrible of the nations, will cut it down. On the mountains and in the valleys its branches will fall, and its boughs will lie broken in the watercourses of the land. All the peoples of the earth will go from its shadow and leave it. Upon its ruin will dwell the birds and the beasts. All this is in order that no trees by the waters may set their tops among the clouds; for they are all given over to death, to the nether world among mortal men, with those who go down to the Pit.

"Thus says the Lord GOD: When it goes down to Sheol, I will make the deep mourn for it and restrain its rivers; I will clothe Lebanon in gloom, and the trees of the field shall faint because of it. I will make the nations quake at the sound of its fall, and all the trees of Eden will be comforted in the nether world.

"Whom are you thus like in glory and in greatness among the trees of Eden? You shall be brought down with them; you shall lie among the uncircumcised, with those who are slain by the sword. This is Pharaoh, and all his multitude, says the Lord GOD."

IN THE TWELFTH year, in the first month, on the fifteenth day of the month, the word of the LORD came to me: "Son of man, wail over the multitude of Egypt, and send them with the daughters of majestic nations to those who have gone down to the Pit. Say to them, 'Whom do you surpass in beauty? Go down, and be laid with the uncircumcised.' They shall fall amid those who are slain by the sword, and the mighty chiefs shall speak of them out of the midst of Sheol: 'They have come down, they lie still, the uncircumcised, slain by the sword.'

"Assyria is there, and all her company, their graves round about her set in the uttermost parts of the Pit; all of them slain, fallen by the sword, who spread terror in the land of the living. Elam is there, and her multitude, and Meshech and Tubal; all of them slain by the sword; for they spread terror in the land of the living. They do not lie with the fallen mighty men of old who went down to Sheol with their weapons of war, whose swords were laid under their heads, and whose shields are upon their bones. So you, Pharaoh, with all your multitude, shall be broken and lie among the uncircumcised, with those slain by the sword."

IN THE TWELFTH year of our exile, in the tenth month, on the fifth day of the month, a man who had escaped from Jerusalem came to me and said, "The city has fallen." Now the hand of the LORD had been upon me the evening before the fugitive came, but he had opened my mouth by the time the man came to me, so I was no longer dumb.

The word of the LORD came to me: "Son of man, the inhabitants of these waste places in the land of Israel keep saying, 'Abraham was only one man, yet he got possession of the land; but we are many; the land is surely given us to possess.' Therefore say to them, Thus says the Lord GOD: You eat flesh with the blood, and lift up your eyes to your idols; you resort to the sword, and each of you defiles his neighbor's wife; shall you then possess the land? As I live, surely those who are in the waste places shall fall by the sword; him that is in the open field I will give to the beasts to be devoured; and those who are in strongholds and in caves shall die by pestilence. I will make the land a desolation, and her proud might shall come to an end. Then they will know that I am the LORD.

"As for you, son of man, your people who talk together about you by the walls and at the doors of the houses, say to one another, 'Come, and hear what the word is that comes forth from the LORD.' And they come to you and sit before you. They hear what you say but they will not do it; for with their lips they show much love, but their heart is set on their gain. And lo, you are to them like one who sings love songs with a beautiful voice, for they hear what you say, but they will not do it. But when this comes—and come it will!—then they will know that a prophet has been among them."

THE WORD OF the LORD came to me: "Son of man, prophesy against the shepherds of

Israel, and say, Thus says the Lord GOD:
Ho, shepherds of Israel who have been
feeding yourselves! Should not shepherds
feed the sheep? You eat the fat, you clothe
yourselves with the wool, you slaughter the
fatlings; but you do not feed the sheep.
The weak you have not strengthened, the
sick you have not healed, the crippled you
have not bound up, the strayed you have
not brought back, and with force and
harshness you have ruled them. So because there was no shepherd, they became
food for all the wild beasts. My sheep wandered over all the mountains, and were
scattered over the face of the earth, with
none to seek for them.

"Therefore, you shepherds, hear the
word of the LORD: Because my sheep have
become food for wild beasts, and because
my shepherds have fed themselves, and
have not fed my sheep, I am against the
shepherds. I will require my sheep at their
hand; I will rescue my sheep from their
mouths, that they may not be food for
them.

"For thus says the Lord GOD: Behold, I,
I myself will search for my sheep, as a

shepherd seeks out his flock. I will rescue them from all places where they have been scattered on a day of clouds and thick darkness. I will gather them from the countries and bring them into their own land; and I will feed them with good pasture upon the mountain heights of Israel. I myself will be the shepherd of my sheep. I will seek the lost and bring back the strayed; I will bind up the crippled; I will strengthen the weak, and the fat and the strong I will watch over; I will feed them in justice.

"As for you, my flock, thus says the Lord God: Behold, I judge between sheep and sheep, rams and he-goats. Is it not enough for you to feed on the good pasture, that you must tread down the rest of it; and to drink of clear water, that you must foul the rest with your feet? Must my sheep eat what you have trodden and drink what you have fouled with your feet? Therefore behold, I, I myself will judge between the fat sheep and the lean sheep. Because you push with side and shoulder, and thrust at all the weak with your horns, till you have scattered them abroad, I will save my flock. They shall no longer be a prey; and I will judge between sheep and sheep. I will set up over them one shepherd, my servant David, and he shall feed them. I the LORD will be their God, and my servant David shall be prince among them; I, the LORD, have spoken.

"I will make with them a covenant of peace and banish wild beasts from the land, so that they may dwell securely in the wilderness and sleep in the woods. I will make them and the places round about my hill a blessing; and I will send down the showers in their season; they shall be showers of blessing. The trees of the field shall yield their fruit, and the earth shall yield its increase, and they shall be secure in their land. I will provide for them prosperous plantations, so that they shall no more be consumed with hunger, and no longer suffer the reproach of the nations. They shall know that I, the LORD their God, am with them, and that they, the house of Israel, are my people. You are my sheep, the sheep of my pasture, and I am your God, says the Lord GOD."

The word of the LORD came to me:

"Son of man, when the house of Israel dwelt in their own land, they defiled it. So I poured out my wrath upon them; in accordance with their conduct and their deeds I judged them. But when they came to the nations to which I scattered them, they profaned my holy name, in that men said of them, 'These are the people of the LORD, and yet they had to go out of his land.'

"Therefore say to the house of Israel, Thus says the Lord GOD: It is not for your sake, O Israel, that I am about to act, but for the sake of my holy name, which you have profaned among the nations to which you came. Through you I will vindicate the holiness of my great name, and the nations will know that I am the LORD. For I will gather you from them and bring you into your own land. I will sprinkle clean water upon you; from all your idols I will cleanse you. A new heart I will give you, and a new spirit I will put within you; I will take out of your flesh the heart of stone and give you a heart of flesh. And I will put my spirit within you, and cause you to walk in my statutes. You shall dwell in the land which I gave to your fathers; and you shall be my people, and I will be your God. I will make the fruit of the tree and the increase of the field abundant, that you may never again suffer the disgrace of famine. Then you will remember your evil ways and loathe yourselves for your abominable deeds. It is not for your sake that I will act, says the Lord GOD; let that be known to you. Be ashamed and confounded for your ways, O house of Israel.

"Thus says the Lord GOD: On the day that I cleanse you from all your iniquities, I will cause the waste places to be rebuilt, and all who pass by will say, 'This land that was desolate has become like the garden of Eden; and the ruined cities are now inhabited and fortified.' Then the nations that are left round about you shall know that I the LORD have rebuilt the ruined places and replanted that which was desolate; I, the LORD, have spoken, and I will do it."

THE HAND OF the LORD was upon me, and he brought me out by the Spirit of the LORD, and set me down in the midst of the valley; it was full of bones. He led me round among them; and behold, there were very many upon the valley; and lo, they were very dry. "Son of man," he said, "can these bones live?" I answered, "O Lord GOD, thou knowest." Again he said, "Prophesy to these bones, and say, O dry bones, hear the word of the LORD. Thus says the Lord GOD to these bones: Behold, I will cause breath to enter you, and you shall live. I will lay sinews upon you, and cause flesh to come upon you, and cover you with skin; and you shall know that I am the LORD."

So I prophesied as I was commanded; and as I prophesied, there was a rattling; and the bones came together, bone to its bone. As I looked, there were sinews on them, and flesh had come upon them, and skin had covered them; but there was no breath in them. Then he said, "Prophesy to the breath, son of man, and say, Thus says the Lord GOD: Come from the four winds, O breath, and breathe upon these slain, that they may live." So I prophesied as he commanded, and the breath came into them. They lived, and stood upon their feet, an exceedingly great host.

Then he said, "Son of man, these bones are the whole house of Israel. They say, 'Our bones are dried up, and our hope is lost; we are clean cut off.' Therefore say to them, Thus says the Lord GOD: Behold, I will open your graves, and raise you from them, O my people; and I will bring you home into the land of Israel. I will put my Spirit within you, and you shall live, and I will place you in your own land; then you shall know that I, the LORD, have spoken, and I have done it."

The word of the LORD came to me: "Son of man, take a stick and write on it, 'For Judah, and the children of Israel associated with him'; then take another stick and write upon it, 'For Joseph (the stick of Ephraim) and all the house of Israel associated with him'; and join them together into one stick. When your people say to you, 'Will you not show us what you mean by these?' say to them, Thus says the Lord GOD: Behold, I am about to take the stick of Joseph and join with it the stick of Judah, and make them one. I will gather the people of Israel and bring them to their own land; I will make them one nation upon the mountains of Israel; one king shall be king over them all, and they shall be no longer divided into two kingdoms. They shall not defile themselves any more with their detestable things. I will save them from all the backslidings in which they have sinned, and will cleanse them; they shall be my people, and I will be their God.

"My servant David shall be king over them; and they shall all have one shepherd. They shall follow my ordinances and be careful to observe my statutes. They shall dwell where your fathers dwelt, in the land that I gave to my servant Jacob; they and their children and their children's children shall dwell there for ever; and David my servant shall be their prince for ever. I will make a covenant of peace with them, an everlasting covenant; and I will bless them and multiply them, and will set my sanctuary in the midst of them for evermore. My dwelling place shall be with them; I will be their God, and they shall be my people. Then the nations will know that I the LORD sanctify Israel, when my sanctuary is in the midst of them for evermore."

THE WORD OF the LORD came to me: "Son of man, set your face toward Gog, of the land of Magog, the chief prince of Meshech and Tubal; prophesy against him, and say, Thus says the Lord GOD: Behold, I am against you, O Gog, and I will put hooks into your jaws, and bring you forth with all your army, clothed in full armor, a great company, all wielding swords; Persia, Cush, and Put are with them; Gomer and all his hordes; Beth-togarmah from the uttermost parts of the north—many peoples are with you. Be ready, you and all the hosts assembled about you. In the latter years you will go against the land where people were gathered from many nations upon the mountains of Israel and now dwell securely. You will advance like a storm, you and all your hordes. On that day thoughts will come into your mind, and you will devise an evil scheme, and say, 'I will go up against the land of unwalled villages; I will fall upon the quiet people who dwell securely, without bars or gates.' Therefore, son of man, prophesy, and say to Gog, Thus says the Lord GOD: On that day, when my people Israel are dwelling securely, you will come from the uttermost parts of the north, you and a mighty army. I will bring you against my land, that the nations may know me, when through you, O Gog, I vindicate my holiness before their eyes.

"Thus says the Lord GOD: Are you he of whom I spoke in former days by my servants the prophets of Israel, who in those days prophesied that I would bring you against them? On that day, when Gog shall come against Israel, my wrath will be roused. There shall be a great shaking in the land of Israel; the fish of the sea, the birds of the air, the beasts of the field, all creeping things that creep on the ground, and all the men that are upon the face of the earth, shall quake at my presence; mountains shall be thrown down, cliffs shall fall, and every wall shall tumble to the ground. I will summon every kind of terror against Gog; every man's sword will be against his brother. With pestilence and bloodshed I will enter into judgment with him, and I will rain upon him and the many peoples with him, torrential rains and hailstones, fire and brimstone. So I will show my greatness and my holiness and make myself known in the eyes of many nations. Then they will know that I am the LORD."

IN THE TWENTY-FIFTH year of our exile, at the beginning of the year, on the tenth day of the month, in the fourteenth year after the city was conquered, on that very day, the hand of the LORD was upon me. In visions of God he brought me into the land of Israel, and set me down upon a very high mountain. A structure like a city was opposite me, and when he brought me there, behold, there was a man, whose appearance was like bronze, standing in the gateway. He had a line of flax and a measuring reed in his hand. And the man said to me, "Son of man, look with your eyes, and hear with your ears; set your mind upon all that I show you, for you were brought here that I might show it to you; declare all you see to the house of Israel."

And behold, there was a wall around the outside of the temple area. The man measured its thickness, ten and a half feet; and its height, ten and a half feet. Then he went into the gateway facing east. Going up its steps, he measured the threshold of the gate, ten and a half feet deep; and the three side rooms on either side of the gate, each ten and a half feet long and ten and a half feet broad. He measured the vestibule of the gateway, thirty-five feet in length and fourteen feet in breadth; all around the vestibule was the outer court. The gateway had windows round about, narrowing inwards into their jambs in the side rooms, and likewise the vestibule had windows round about, and on the jambs were carved palm trees.

He brought me into the outer court; and behold, there were thirty chambers fronting on a pavement round about the court; this was the lower pavement. He went before me to the gate of the outer court which faced north, and measured its length and breadth. Its side rooms and jambs, its windows, vestibule, and palm trees were of the same size as those of the gate facing east. He led me to the south gate, and measured its jambs and vestibule; they had the same size as the others. Then he brought me to the inner court, and measured the south gate; it was the same size as the others, but its vestibule faced the outer court. He measured the gates to the inner court on the east and north sides; they were the same size as the one on the south.

There was a chamber with its door in the vestibule of the gate, where the burnt offering was to be washed. Four tables were inside the vestibule, and four outside, on which the sacrifices were to be slaughtered. There were also four tables of hewn stone on which to lay the instruments with which the burnt offerings were to be slaughtered. Hooks, a handbreadth long, were fastened round about within.

There were two chambers in the inner court, one at the side of the north gate facing south, the other at the side of the south gate facing north. "This chamber which faces south," the man said, "is for the priests who have charge of the temple, and the chamber which faces north is for the priests who have charge of the altar; these are the sons of Zadok, who alone among the sons of Levi may come near to the LORD to minister to him." He brought me to the vestibule of the temple; ten steps led up to it, and then he brought me to the nave. He went alone into the inner room, beyond the nave. "This," he said, "is the most holy place."

When the man had finished measuring the interior of the temple area, he led me out to the gate facing east. And behold, the glory of the God of Israel came from the east; the sound of his coming was like the sound of many waters; and the earth shone with his glory. The vision I saw was like the vision I had seen by the river Chebar; and I fell upon my face. As the glory of the LORD entered the temple, the Spirit lifted me up, and brought me into the inner court; and behold, the glory of the LORD filled the temple.

While the man was standing beside me, I heard one speaking to me out of the temple. "Son of man," he said, "this is the place of my throne and the place of the soles of my feet, where I will dwell in the midst of the people of Israel for ever. The house of Israel shall no more defile my holy name, neither they, nor their kings. Describe to them the temple and its plan, that they may be ashamed of their iniquities. And if they are ashamed of all that they have done, portray the temple, its arrangement, its exits and entrances, and its whole form. Make known to them all its ordinances and laws, that they may observe and perform them. This is the law of the temple: the whole territory upon the top of the mountain shall be most holy."

Then the man brought me back to the outer gate of the sanctuary, which faces east; and it was shut. "This gate," he said, "shall not be opened; for the LORD, the God of Israel, has entered by it. Only the prince may sit in it to eat bread before the LORD."

He brought me by way of the north gate to the front of the temple; and behold, the glory of the LORD filled the temple of the LORD; and I fell upon my face. "Son of man," the LORD said, "mark well those who may be admitted to the temple and those who are to be excluded from the sanctuary. No foreigner, uncircumcised in heart and flesh, of all the foreigners who are among the people of Israel, shall enter my sanctuary. The Levites who went far from me, going after idols when Israel went astray, shall bear their punishment. They shall be ministers, having oversight at the gates of the temple, and serving in it; they shall slay the sacrifice for the people and attend on the people, to serve them; but they shall not come near me to serve me as priest, nor come near any of my sacred things.

"The Levitical priests, the sons of Zadok, who kept the charge of my sanctuary when the people of Israel went astray, shall come near me to minister to me; they shall enter my sanctuary, approach my table, and keep my charge. They shall teach my people the difference between the holy and the common, and show them how to distinguish between the unclean and the clean. In a controversy they shall act as judges, and judge it according to my judgments. They shall keep my laws in all my appointed feasts, and they shall keep my sabbaths holy, says the Lord God."

Then the man brought me back to the door of the temple; and behold, water was issuing from below the threshold of the temple toward the east (for the temple faced east); the water was flowing down from below the south end of the threshold of the temple, south of the altar. He brought me out by way of the north gate, and led me round on the outside to the outer gate, which faces east; and the water was coming out on the south side. Going on eastward with a line in his hand, the man measured fifteen hundred feet, and then led me through the water; it was ankle-deep. Again he measured fifteen hundred feet, and led me through the water; it was knee-deep. Again he measured fifteen hundred feet, and led me through the water; it was up to the loins. Again he measured fifteen hundred feet, and the water was deep enough to swim in, a river that could not be passed through. "Son of man," he said, "have you seen this?"

Then he led me back along the bank of the river, and I saw very many trees on both sides. "This water flows toward the eastern region," he said, "and goes down into the Arabah. When it enters the stagnant waters of the sea, the water will become fresh. Wherever the river goes every living creature which swarms will live. Fishermen will stand beside the sea, and it will be a place for the spreading of nets; its fish will be of very many kinds, like the fish of the Great Sea. But its swamps and marshes will not become fresh; they are to be left for salt. On the banks, on both sides of the river, there will grow all kinds of trees for food. Their leaves will not wither nor their fruit fail; they will bear fresh fruit every month, because the water for them flows from the sanctuary. Their fruit will be for food, and their leaves for healing."

THUS SAYS THE Lord GOD: "You shall divide the land for inheritance among you according to the tribes of Israel. You shall allot it as an inheritance for yourselves and for the aliens who reside among you and have begotten children among you. They shall be to you as native-born sons of Israel. In whatever tribe the alien resides, there you shall assign him his inheritance, says the Lord GOD.

"Adjoining the territory of Judah, from the east side to the west, shall be the portion which you shall set apart for the LORD, with the sanctuary in the midst of it. A special portion from the holy portion of the land shall belong to the consecrated priests, the sons of Zadok. Alongside the territory of the priests, the Levites shall have an allotment. They shall not sell or exchange any of it; they shall not alienate this choice portion of the land, for it is holy to the LORD.

"The remainder shall be for dwellings and for open country. In the midst of it shall be the city, one and a half miles square. The exits of the city shall be twelve, three on each of the four sides, the gates being named after the tribes of Israel. And the name of the city henceforth shall be, The LORD is there."

DANIEL

Two themes recur in the stories about Daniel and his friends during their exile in Babylon. First is the religious challenge arising from their hostile, foreign environment. Will they remain loyal to the Levitical laws on kosher diet? Will they pray to the king? Will they worship idols? Because they are faithful in these matters, defying their captors, they are sentenced to death, by fire or by being eaten alive. The second theme is Daniel's wisdom. As a sage and an interpreter of dreams, he proves far superior to all the wise men of Babylon, especially in the incident of "the handwriting on the wall." The book ends with a series of dream visions granted to Daniel, visions full of a dense symbolism (only the first is retained herein). Most scholars hold that the book was compiled during the persecutions (168–165 B.C.) of the Jewish people by Antiochus Epiphanes. It encourages the reader to be faithful to God and his law, and to trust that he is Lord of the secrets of world history.

————

IN THE THIRD year of the reign of Jehoiakim, king of Judah, Nebuchadnezzar, king of Babylon, besieged Jerusalem. And the Lord gave Jehoiakim into his hand, with some of the vessels of the house of God; and he brought the vessels to Babylon, where he placed them in the treasury of his god.

The king also brought some of the youths of Israel, of the royal family and the nobility, those without blemish, endowed with knowledge, and competent to serve in the king's palace. They were assigned a daily portion of rich food and wine, and they were to be educated for three years in the literature and language of Babylon.

Among these youths were Daniel, Hananiah, Mishael, and Azariah of the tribe of Judah. To them the chief eunuch gave new names: Daniel he called Belteshazzar, Hananiah he called Shadrach, Mishael he called Meshach, and Azariah he called Abednego. To all four God had given skill in letters and wisdom, and Daniel had understanding in all visions and dreams.

Now Daniel resolved that he would not defile himself with the king's rich food, so he asked the chief eunuch to allow him only vegetables and water. But the chief eunuch said, "I fear lest the king should see that you were in poorer condition than the other youths. You would endanger my head."

Then Daniel said to the steward whom the chief eunuch had appointed over them, "Test us for ten days on vegetables and water. Then let our appearance be observed, and according to what you see deal with us." So he tested them, and at the end of ten days it was seen that they were better in appearance and fatter in flesh than all the other youths. So the steward took away their rich food and gave them vegetables.

At the end of the appointed time the chief eunuch brought all the youths in before Nebuchadnezzar. The king spoke with them, and none was found like Daniel, Shadrach, Meshach, and Abednego; therefore they entered the king's service.

IN THE SECOND year of his reign, Nebuchadnezzar had dreams; his spirit was troubled, and his sleep left him. Then he commanded that the magicians and sorcerers be summoned. They came in and stood before the king, and he said to them, "I had a dream, and my spirit is troubled to understand it."

"O king, live for ever!" they said. "Tell your servants the dream, and we will show the interpretation."

"The word from me is sure," the king answered. "If you do not make known to me both the dream and its interpretation, you shall be torn limb from limb, and your houses shall be laid in ruins. But if you show the dream and its interpretation, you shall receive rewards and great honor."

"Let the king tell his servants the dream," they answered a second time, "and we will show its interpretation."

"I know that you are trying to gain

time," the king said, "because you see that the word from me is sure. You have agreed to speak lying words before me till the times change. Therefore tell me what the dream was, and I shall know that you can show me its interpretation."

"There is not a man on earth who can meet the king's demand," they answered, "for no great king ever asked such a thing. None can show it to the king except the gods, whose dwelling is not with flesh."

At this the king was furious, and he commanded that all the wise men of Babylon be destroyed. So the decree went forth, and they sought Daniel and his companions, to slay them. But Daniel spoke to Arioch, the captain of the king's guard, asking, "Why is the decree of the king so severe?" Arioch explained, and Daniel went to his house and made the matter known to Shadrach, Meshach, and Abednego. He told them to seek mercy of the God of heaven concerning this mystery, so that they might not perish with the rest of the wise men. Then, in a vision of the night, the mystery was revealed to Daniel, and he blessed the God of heaven in these words:

"Blessed be the name of God for ever and ever, to whom belong wisdom and might. He changes times and seasons; he removes kings and sets up kings; he gives wisdom to the wise and knowledge to those who have understanding; he reveals deep and mysterious things; he knows what is in the darkness, and the light dwells with him. To thee, O God of my fathers, I give thanks and praise."

After this, Daniel went again to Arioch. "Do not destroy the wise men of Babylon," he said; "bring me in before the king, and I will show the interpretation." Arioch brought him before the king and said, "I have found a man who can make known the interpretation."

"Are you able to make known to me both the dream and its interpretation?" the king asked Daniel.

"No wise men can show the mystery which the king has asked," Daniel answered, "but there is a God in heaven who reveals mysteries, and he has made known to King Nebuchadnezzar what will be in the latter days. This was the dream: You saw as you lay in bed, O king, a great image, mighty and of exceeding brightness. Its appearance was frightening. The head was of fine gold, its breast and arms of silver, its belly and thighs of bronze, its legs of iron, its feet partly of iron and partly of clay. As you looked, a stone was cut out from a mountain by no human hand, and it smote the image on its feet and broke them in pieces. Then the iron, the clay, the bronze, the silver, and the gold, all together were broken in pieces, and became like the chaff of the summer threshing floors. And the wind carried them away, so that not a trace of them could be found. But the stone that struck the image became a great mountain and filled the whole earth.

"That was the dream; now we will tell its interpretation. You, O king, to whom the God of heaven has given the kingdom, the power, the might, and the glory, you are the head of gold. After you shall arise another kingdom inferior to you, and yet a third kingdom, of bronze, which shall rule over all the earth. And there shall be a fourth kingdom, strong as iron, and it shall break and crush all these. And as you saw the feet and toes partly of clay and partly of iron, it shall be a divided kingdom. As the toes were partly iron and partly clay, so the kingdom shall be partly strong and partly brittle. As you saw the iron mixed with clay, so they will mix with one another in marriage, but they will not hold together, just as iron does not mix with clay.

"And in the days of those kings the God of heaven will set up a kingdom which shall never be destroyed, nor shall its sovereignty be left to another people. It shall break in pieces all these kingdoms and bring them to an end, and it shall stand for ever. A great God has made known to the king what shall be hereafter. The dream is certain, and its interpretation sure."

Then King Nebuchadnezzar fell upon his face, and did homage to Daniel. "Truly, your God is God of gods and Lord of kings," he said, "and a revealer of mysteries." He gave Daniel high honors and many great gifts, and made him ruler over the whole province of Babylon, and chief prefect over all the wise men. At Daniel's request he also appointed Shadrach, Meshach, and Abednego to administer the affairs of the province of Babylon.

KING NEBUCHADNEZZAR MADE an image of gold, ninety feet high and nine feet broad. He set it up on the plain of Dura, in Babylon. Then he assembled the satraps, governors, counselors, justices, and all the officials of the provinces for the dedication. They stood before the image, and the herald proclaimed, "You are commanded, that when you hear the sound of the horn, lyre, harp, bagpipe, and every kind of music, you are to fall down and worship the golden image. Whoever does not worship shall immediately be cast into a burning fiery furnace." As soon as the people heard the sound of the music, all fell down and worshiped the golden image.

At that time certain men came to King Nebuchadnezzar and maliciously accused the Jews. "O king, live for ever!" they said. "You, O king, have made a decree, that every man shall fall down and worship the golden image; and whoever does not worship shall be cast into a burning fiery furnace. There are certain Jews whom you have appointed over the affairs of the province of Babylon: Shadrach, Meshach, and Abednego. These men, O king, pay no heed to you; they do not serve your gods or worship the golden image."

In a furious rage, Nebuchadnezzar commanded that Shadrach, Meshach, and Abednego be brought before him. "Is it true that you do not serve my gods or worship the golden image?" he asked. "Now if you are ready, when you hear the sound of the music, fall down and worship. If you do not, you shall immediately be cast into a burning fiery furnace; and who is the god that will deliver you out of my hands?"

"O Nebuchadnezzar," the three said, "we have no need to answer you in this matter. If it be so, our God whom we serve is able to deliver us from the burning fiery furnace. But if he does not, be it known to you, O king, that we will not serve your gods or worship the golden image."

His face full of fury, Nebuchadnezzar ordered the furnace heated seven times more than its usual heat. And he ordered

Shadrach, Meshach, and Abednego to be bound and cast into it. Because the furnace was very hot, the flame of the fire slew those men who took up the three to cast them in.

Then King Nebuchadnezzar was astonished, and he rose up in haste. "Did we not cast three men bound into the fire?" he said to his counselors. "I see four men loose, walking in the midst of the fire, and they are not hurt; and the appearance of the fourth is like a son of the gods." He came near to the door of the furnace. "Shadrach, Meshach, and Abednego," he called, "servants of the Most High God, come forth!"

The three came out, and everyone saw that the fire had not had any power over their bodies; the hair of their heads was not singed, their clothes were not harmed, and no smell of fire had come upon them.

"Blessed be the God of Shadrach, Meshach, and Abednego," the king said, "who has sent his angel and delivered his servants, who trusted in him, and set at nought the king's command, and yielded up their bodies rather than serve and wor-

ship any god except their own God. Therefore I make a decree: Any people, nation,
or language that speaks anything against
the God of these men shall be torn limb
from limb, and their houses laid in ruins;
for there is no other god who is able to
deliver in this way." Then the king pro-
moted Shadrach, Meshach, and Abednego
in the province of Babylon.

A PROCLAMATION OF King Nebuchadnezzar
to all peoples and nations that dwell in the
earth: Peace be multiplied to you! It has
seemed good to me to show the signs and
wonders that the Most High God has
wrought toward me. How great are his
signs, how mighty his wonders! His kingdom is an everlasting kingdom, and his
dominion is from generation to generation.

I, Nebuchadnezzar, was at ease and
prospering in my palace. As I lay in bed I
had a dream which alarmed me. Therefore
I called all the wise men of Babylon that
they might interpret the dream, but they
could not. At last Daniel came before me,
and I told him the dream, saying, "I saw a
great tree in the midst of the earth; its top

reached to heaven, and it was visible to the end of the whole earth. Its leaves were fair and its fruit abundant, and in it was food for all. The beasts of the field found shade under it, and the birds of the air dwelt in its branches, and all flesh was fed from it. And behold, a watcher, a holy one, came down from heaven. He cried aloud and said thus, 'Hew down the tree and cut off its branches, strip off its leaves and scatter its fruit. But leave the stump of its roots in the earth, bound with a band of iron and bronze, amid the tender grass of the field. Let him be wet with the dew of heaven; let his lot be with the beasts in the grass of the earth; let his mind be changed from a man's, and let a beast's mind be given to him; and let seven years pass over him. The sentence is by the decree of the watchers, the decision by the word of the holy ones, so that the living may know that the Most High rules the kingdom of men, gives it to whom he will, and sets over it the lowliest of men.' "

Daniel was dismayed for a moment, and his thoughts alarmed him. "My lord," he said, "may the dream be for those who hate you and its interpretation for your enemies! The great tree you saw, O king, is you. Your greatness reaches to heaven, and your dominion to the ends of the earth. And this is the interpretation: It is a decree of the Most High that you shall be driven from among men, and your dwelling shall be with the beasts of the field. You shall be made to eat grass like an ox, and you shall be wet with the dew of heaven. Seven years shall pass over you, till you know that the Most High rules the kingdom of men, and gives it to whom he will. And as it was commanded to leave the stump of the tree, your kingdom shall be sure for you from the time that you know that Heaven rules. Therefore, O king, break off your iniquities by showing mercy to the oppressed, that there may perhaps be a lengthening of your tranquillity."

All this came upon me. At the end of twelve months I was walking on the roof of the royal palace. "Is not this great Babylon," I said, "which I have built by my mighty power?" While the words were still in my mouth, there fell a voice from heaven, "O King Nebuchadnezzar, to you it is spoken: The kingdom has departed from you." Immediately the word was fulfilled. I was driven from among men, and ate grass like an ox, and my body was wet with the dew of heaven till my hair grew as long as eagles' feathers, and my nails were like birds' claws.

At the end of the days I lifted my eyes to heaven, and my reason returned to me, and I blessed the Most High, and praised and honored him who lives for ever; for his dominion is an everlasting dominion, and his kingdom endures from generation to generation. He does according to his will in the host of heaven and among the inhabitants of the earth; and none can stay his hand or say to him, "What doest thou?"

At the same time my majesty and splendor returned to me. My counselors and my lords sought me, and I was established in my kingdom, and still more greatness was added to me. Now I, Nebuchadnezzar, praise and extol and honor the King of heaven; for all his works are right and his ways are just. Those who walk in pride he is able to abase.

KING BELSHAZZAR OF Babylon made a great feast for a thousand of his lords, and he commanded that the vessels of gold and of silver which had been taken out of the temple in Jerusalem be brought. Then the king and his lords, his wives, and his concubines drank from them, while they praised their gods of gold and silver, bronze, iron, wood, and stone.

Immediately the fingers of a man's hand appeared and wrote on the wall of the palace, opposite the lampstand; and the king saw the hand as it wrote. His color changed, his limbs gave way, and his knees knocked together. He cried aloud to bring in the wise men, and he said, "Whoever reads this writing, and shows me its interpretation, shall be clothed with purple, and have a chain of gold about his neck, and shall be the third ruler in the kingdom." But all the wise men could not read the writing or make known the interpretation. Then King Belshazzar was greatly alarmed, and his lords were perplexed.

The queen came into the banqueting hall, and she said, "O king, live for ever!

Let not your thoughts alarm you or your color change. There is in your kingdom a man in whom is the spirit of the holy gods. In the days of your father, understanding and wisdom were found in him. Now let this Daniel be called, and he will show the interpretation." When Daniel was brought in, the king said, "I have heard that the spirit of the holy gods is in you. Now the wise men could not show the interpretation of this matter. If you can do so, you shall be clothed with purple and a chain of gold, and shall be the third ruler in the kingdom."

"Let your gifts be for yourself," Daniel answered, "and give your rewards to another; nevertheless I will read the writing and make known the interpretation. O king, the Most High God gave Nebuchadnezzar your father kingship and majesty; and all peoples trembled before him. But when his spirit was hardened so that he dealt proudly, he was deposed, and his glory was taken from him, until he knew that the Most High God rules the kingdom of men. You, his son, though you knew all this, have not humbled your heart. The vessels of the Lord's house have been brought in, and you and your company have drunk wine from them. You have praised gods which do not see or hear or know, but the God in whose hand is your breath you have not honored. From his presence the hand was sent, and this is the writing: MENE, MENE, TEKEL, and PARSIN. This is the interpretation of the matter: MENE, God has numbered the days of your kingdom and brought it to an end; TEKEL, you have been weighed in the balances and found wanting; PERES, your kingdom is divided and given to the Medes and Persians."

Then Belshazzar clothed Daniel with purple, a chain of gold was put about his neck, and proclamation was made that he should be the third ruler in the kingdom. That very night Belshazzar was slain, and Darius the Mede received the kingdom.

IT PLEASED DARIUS to set over the kingdom a hundred and twenty satraps, and over them three presidents, of whom Daniel was one. Because an excellent spirit was in him, Daniel became distinguished above all, and the king planned to set him over the whole kingdom. When the presidents and the satraps heard this, they sought a ground for complaint against Daniel, but they could find no fault in him. Then they said, "We shall not find any complaint against this Daniel unless we find it in connection with the law of his God."

The presidents and satraps came by agreement to the king and said, "O King Darius, live for ever! We are all agreed that the king should establish an ordinance that whoever makes petition to any god or man for thirty days, except to you, O king, shall be cast into the den of lions. Now, O king, establish the interdict according to the law of the Medes and the Persians, which cannot be revoked." King Darius signed the document.

When Daniel heard of this, he went to his house, where he had windows in his upper chamber open toward Jerusalem; and three times a day he got down upon his knees and prayed, as he had done previously. Then these men found Daniel making supplication before his God, and they went to the king and said, "O king!

Daniel pays no heed to your interdict, but makes his petition three times a day."

At these words the king was much distressed for Daniel, and he set his mind to rescue him. But those men came back and said, "Know, O king, that it is a law of the Medes and Persians that no interdict which the king establishes can be changed."

Then the king commanded Daniel to be brought and cast into the den of lions. "May your God, whom you serve continually, deliver you!" he said. A stone was laid upon the mouth of the den, and sealed with the king's own signet, and with the signet of his lords. In his palace, the king spent the night fasting; no diversions were brought to him, and sleep fled from him.

At break of day the king arose and went in haste to the den of lions. "O Daniel," he cried in a tone of anguish, "has your God been able to deliver you?"

"O king, live for ever!" Daniel answered. "My God sent his angel and shut the lions' mouths, and they have not hurt me, because I was found blameless before him; and before you also, O king, I have done no wrong." The king was exceedingly glad, and he commanded that Daniel be taken up out of the den. No kind of hurt was found upon him, because he had trusted in his God. And the king commanded that those men who had accused Daniel be brought and cast among the lions—they, their children, and their wives; and before they reached the bottom of the den the lions overpowered them and broke all their bones in pieces.

Then King Darius wrote to all the peoples and nations that dwell in the earth: "Peace be multiplied to you. I make a decree, that in all my royal dominion men tremble before the God of Daniel, for he is the living God, enduring for ever. His kingdom shall never be destroyed and his dominion shall be to the end. He delivers and rescues, he works signs and wonders in heaven and on earth, he who has saved Daniel from the power of the lions."

So Daniel prospered during the reign of Darius and the reign of Cyrus the Persian.

IN THE FIRST year of Belshazzar king of Babylon, Daniel had a dream as he lay in bed. Then he wrote down the dream, and told the sum of the matter:

"Behold, the four winds of heaven were stirring up the great sea. And four great beasts came up out of the sea. The first was like a lion and had eagles' wings. Then its wings were plucked off, and it was made to stand upon two feet like a man; and the mind of a man was given to it. The second was like a bear. It was raised up on one side; it had three ribs between its teeth; and it was told, 'Arise, devour much flesh.' Another was like a leopard, with four wings on its back; and it had four heads, and dominion was given to it. The fourth beast was terrible and dreadful and exceedingly strong, and it had great iron teeth; it devoured and broke in pieces, and stamped the residue with its feet; and it had ten horns. I considered the horns, and behold, there came up among them another horn, a little one, before which three of the first horns were plucked up by the roots. In this horn were eyes like a man's, and a mouth speaking great things.

"As I looked, thrones were placed, and one that was ancient of days took his seat;

his raiment was white as snow, and the hair of his head like pure wool; his throne was fiery flames, its wheels were burning fire. A stream of fire came forth from before him; a thousand thousands served him, and ten thousand times ten thousand stood before him. The court sat in judgment, and the books were opened. I looked then because of the sound of the great words which the horn was speaking. And as I looked, the beast was slain, and its body given over to be burned. As for the rest of the beasts, their dominion was taken away, but their lives were prolonged for a season and a time.

"I saw in the night visions, and behold, with the clouds of heaven there came one like a son of man, and he came to the Ancient of Days and was presented before him. And to him was given dominion and glory and kingdom, that all peoples, nations, and languages should serve him; his dominion is an everlasting dominion, which shall not pass away, and his kingdom one that shall not be destroyed.

"As for me, Daniel, my spirit was anxious and the visions alarmed me. I ap-

proached one of those who stood there
and asked him the truth concerning all
this. So he made known to me the interpretation: 'These four great beasts are four
kings who shall arise out of the earth. But
the saints of the Most High shall receive
the kingdom, and possess the kingdom for
ever, for ever and ever.' Then I desired to
know the truth concerning the fourth
beast, which was exceedingly terrible, and
concerning the ten horns, and the other
horn which came up. As I looked, this
horn made war with the saints, and prevailed over them, until the Ancient of Days
came, and judgment was given for the
saints of the Most High, and the time came
when the saints received the kingdom.

"Thus he said: 'As for the fourth beast,
there shall be a fourth kingdom on earth,
different from all, and it shall devour the
whole earth. As for the ten horns, out of
this kingdom ten kings shall arise, and another shall arise after them; he shall be
different from the former ones, and shall
put down three kings. He shall speak
words against the Most High, and shall
wear out the saints of the Most High, and

shall think to change the times and the law; and they shall be given into his hand for a time, two times, and half a time. But the court shall sit in judgment, and his dominion shall be taken away, to be consumed to the end. And the kingdom and the dominion and the greatness of the kingdoms under the whole heaven shall be given to the people of the saints of the Most High; their kingdom shall be an everlasting kingdom, and all dominions shall serve and obey them.' "

HOSEA

Telling the story of his own tragic home life, Hosea interprets his experiences with his unfaithful wife, Gomer, as a parable of God's enduring love for the wayward nation of Israel. Concerned about idolatry among the people and their ruthless oppression of the poor, he develops the theme of Israel's apostasy and unfaithfulness, for which divine judgment rests upon the nation. The book closes with the promise that eventually Israel will be restored. A younger contemporary of Amos (eighth century B.C.), Hosea is the first Biblical writer to describe the relation between God and his people in terms of marriage. This symbolism is carried on in the New Testament with the imagery of the church as the bride of Christ.

———

THE WORD OF the LORD that came to Hosea the son of Beeri, in the days of Uzziah, Jotham, Ahaz, and Hezekiah, kings of Judah, and in the days of Jeroboam the son of Joash, king of Israel.

When he first spoke through Hosea, the LORD said to him, "Go, take to yourself a wife of harlotry, for the land commits great harlotry by forsaking the LORD. Love a woman who is an adulteress; even as the LORD loves the people of Israel, though they turn to other gods."

So Hosea took Gomer the daughter of Diblaim to be his wife, and she conceived and bore him a son. "Name him Jezreel," the LORD said, "for in a little while I will punish the house of Jehu for the blood which was shed at Jezreel, and I will put an end to the kingdom of Israel. On that day I will break the bow of Israel in the valley of Jezreel." Gomer conceived again and bore a daughter. "Name her Not pitied," the LORD said, "for I will no more have pity on the house of Israel." When she had weaned Not pitied, Gomer conceived and bore another son. "Name him Not my people," the LORD said, "for you are not my people, and I am not your God."

Yet in the place where it was said to the people of Israel, "You are not my people," it shall be said to them, "Sons of the living God." And the people of Judah and Israel shall be gathered together. They shall appoint for themselves one head, and they shall go up from the land, for great shall be the day of Jezreel. Then you shall say to your brother, "My people," and to your sister, "She has obtained pity."

Plead with your mother, plead—for she is not my wife, and I am not her husband—that she put away her harlotry, lest I strip her naked as in the day she was born and make her like a parched land, and slay her with thirst. Upon her children also I will have no pity, because they are children of harlotry. Their mother has acted shamefully. "I will go after my lovers," she has said, "who give me my bread and my water, my wool and my flax, my oil and my drink." Therefore I will hedge up her way with thorns, so that she cannot find her paths. She shall pursue her lovers, but not overtake them. Then she shall say,

"I will return to my husband, for it was better with me then than now."

She did not know that it was I who gave her the grain, the wine, and the oil, and who lavished upon her the silver and gold which she used for Baal. Therefore I will take back my grain in its time, and my wine in its season; I will take away my wool and my flax, which were to cover her nakedness. I will uncover her lewdness in the sight of her lovers, and I will put an end to all her mirth, her feasts, her new moons, and her sabbaths. I will lay waste her vines and her fig trees, of which she said, "These my lovers have given me." And I will punish her for the days when she decked herself with jewelry and burned incense to the Baals, and forgot me, says the LORD.

Then, behold, I will allure her, and bring her into the wilderness, and speak tenderly to her. There I will give her her vineyards, and make the valley of trouble a door of hope. And there she shall answer as in the days of her youth, when she came out of the land of Egypt.

In that day, says the LORD, you will call

me, "My husband," and no longer will you call me, "My Baal." For I will remove the names of the Baals from your mouth, and they shall be mentioned no more. I will make for you a covenant with the beasts of the field, the birds of the air, and the creeping things of the ground; I will abolish war from the land, and make you lie down in safety. I will betroth you to me for ever in righteousness and in justice, in steadfast love, and in mercy. I will betroth you to me in faithfulness; and you shall know the LORD. In that day I will answer the heavens and they shall answer the earth; and the earth shall answer the cry of Jezreel with grain, and wine, and oil. I will have pity on Not pitied, and I will say to Not my people, "You are my people"; and he shall say, "Thou art my God."

HEAR THE WORD of the LORD, O people of Israel; for the LORD has a controversy with the inhabitants of the land. There is no faithfulness or kindness, and no knowledge of God in the land; there is swearing, lying, killing, stealing, and committing adultery; they break all bounds and murder follows murder. Therefore the land mourns, and all who dwell in it languish. Like a stubborn heifer, Israel is stubborn. Can the LORD now feed them like a lamb in a broad pasture? Joined to idols, a band of drunkards, they love shame more than their glory. A wind shall wrap them in its wings, and they shall be ashamed because of their altars.

Hear this, O priests! Give heed, O Israel! Hearken, O house of the king! For I will chastise all of you. You have played the harlot; Israel is defiled. Their deeds do not permit them to return to their God. With their flocks and herds they shall seek the LORD, but they will not find him; he has withdrawn from them. They have dealt faithlessly with the LORD; for they have borne alien children. Now the new moon shall devour them with their fields.

Blow the horn in Gibeah; sound the alarm at Beth-aven; tremble, O Benjamin! Yet you shall become a desolation in the day of punishment. Among the tribes of Israel I declare what is sure. The princes of Judah have abused their power; Israel was determined to go after vanity. Therefore I am like a moth to Israel, and like dry rot to the house of Judah.

When Israel saw his sickness, and Judah his wound, Israel went to Assyria, and sent to the great king. But he is not able to cure them or heal their wound. For I will be like a lion to Israel, and like a young lion to the house of Judah. I will rend and go away. I will carry off, and none shall rescue. Then I will return again to my place, until they acknowledge their guilt and seek me in their distress, saying, "Let us return to the LORD; for he has torn, that he may heal us; he has stricken, and he will bind us up. After two days he will revive us; on the third day he will raise us up, that we may live before him. Let us press on to know the LORD; he will come to us as the spring rains that water the earth."

What shall I do with you, O Israel? What shall I do with you, O Judah? Your love is like a morning cloud, like the dew that goes early away. Therefore I have slain you by the words of my mouth. For I desire steadfast love, not sacrifice, the knowledge of God, rather than burnt offerings.

When I would restore the fortunes of

my people, when I would heal Israel, their corruption is revealed. They deal falsely but do not consider that I remember all their evil works. Now their deeds encompass them; they are before my face. By their wickedness they make the king glad, and the princes by their treachery. On the day of their king, the princes become sick with the heat of wine; and the king joins hands with mockers. Their hearts burn with intrigue. Hot as an oven, they devour their rulers. All their kings have fallen; and none of them calls upon me.

Israel mixes himself with the peoples; aliens devour his strength. Gray hairs are sprinkled upon him, and he knows it not. The pride of Israel witnesses against him; yet they do not return to the LORD, for all this.

Israel is like a dove, silly and without sense, calling upon Egypt, going to Assyria for help. As they go, I will spread my net over them and bring them down. I will chastise them for their wicked deeds. Woe to them, for they have strayed from me! Destruction to them, for they have rebelled against me! I would redeem them, but they speak lies against me. They do not cry to me from the heart but wail upon their beds. For grain and wine they gash themselves. Although I trained and strengthened their arms, they devise evil against me. They return to Baal.

Israel has multiplied altars, but they have become altars for sinning. Were I to write for them my laws by ten thousands, they would be regarded as a strange thing. They love sacrifice; they sacrifice flesh and eat it; but the LORD has no delight in them. Now he will remember their iniquity, and punish their sins. They shall return to Egypt.

REJOICE NOT, O Israel! You have loved a harlot's hire, forsaking your God. Threshing floor and winevat shall not feed them. They shall not remain in the land of the LORD. Behold, they are going to Assyria! Egypt shall gather them; Memphis shall bury them. The days of punishment have come; Israel shall know it. The prophet is a fool, made mad by your great iniquity. A snare is on all his paths, and hatred in the house of his God. They have deeply corrupted themselves; now the LORD will punish their sins.

LIKE GRAPES IN the wilderness, I found Israel. Like the first fruit on the fig tree, I saw your fathers. But they came to Baal-peor, and consecrated themselves to Baal, and became detestable like the thing they loved. Israel's glory shall fly away like a bird—no birth, no pregnancy, no conception! Even if they bring up children, I will bereave them till none is left. Woe to them when I depart from them! Give them, O LORD—what wilt thou give? Give them a miscarrying womb and dry breasts.

Every evil of theirs is in Gilgal; there I began to hate them. Because of the wickedness of their deeds I will drive them out of my house. I will love them no more. Israel is stricken, their root is dried up, they shall bear no fruit. Even though they bring forth, I will slay their beloved children.

My God will cast them off, because they have not hearkened to him; they shall be wanderers among the nations.

ISRAEL IS A luxuriant vine that yields its
fruit. The more his fruit increased, the
more altars he built; as his country improved, he improved his pillars. Their heart
is false; now they must bear their guilt. The
LORD will break down their altars and destroy their pillars. Then they will say: "We
have no king, for if we fear not the LORD,
what could a king do for us?" They utter
mere words; with empty oaths they make
covenants; so judgment springs up like poi-
sonous weeds in the furrows of the field.

The inhabitants of Samaria shall mourn
for the calf of Beth-aven. Its idolatrous
priests shall wail over its departed glory.
Yea, the thing itself shall be carried to
Assyria as tribute to the great king, and
Israel shall be ashamed of his idol. Samaria's king shall perish, like a chip of wood
on the face of the waters; the sin of Israel
shall be destroyed. Thorn and thistle shall
grow up on the altars; and the people shall
say to the mountains, "Cover us," and to
the hills, "Fall upon us."

FROM THE DAYS of Gibeah you have sinned,
O Israel. You were a trained heifer that

loved to thresh, and I spared your fair neck; but I will put you to the yoke. Sow for yourselves righteousness, reap the fruit of steadfast love; break up your fallow ground, for it is the time to seek the LORD, that he may come and rain salvation upon you.

But you have plowed iniquity, you have reaped injustice, you have eaten the fruit of lies. Because you have trusted in your chariots and in the multitude of your warriors, the tumult of war shall arise among you. As Beth-arbel was destroyed on the day of battle, and mothers were dashed in pieces with their children, thus it shall be done to you, O house of Israel.

When Israel was a child, I loved him, and out of Egypt I called my son. The more I called, the more they went from me. They kept sacrificing to the Baals, and burning incense to idols. Yet it was I who taught Israel to walk. I took them up in my arms; but they did not know that I healed them. I led them with cords of compassion, with bands of love.

How can I give you up, O Israel? How can I hand you over? My heart recoils within me; my compassion grows warm and tender. I will not execute my fierce anger. I will not again destroy Israel, for I am God and not man, the Holy One in your midst, and I will not come to destroy. My sons shall come trembling like birds from Egypt, and like doves from the land of Assyria; and I will return them to their homes, says the LORD.

WHEN ISRAEL SPOKE, men trembled; he was exalted. But he incurred guilt through Baal and died. And now they sin more and more, and make for themselves molten images, idols skilfully made of silver. "Sacrifice to these," they say. Therefore they shall be like the morning mist or like smoke from a window.

I AM THE LORD your God from the land of Egypt; you know no God but me, and besides me there is no savior. It was I who cared for you in the wilderness, in the land of drought. But when you had fed to the full, and your heart was lifted up, you forgot me. So I will lurk and fall upon you like a leopard, tearing open your breast as a wild beast would.

If I destroy you, O Israel, who can help you? Where now is your king, to save you? Where are all your princes, to defend you—those of whom you said, "Give me a king and princes"? I have given them to you in my anger, and I have taken them away in my wrath.

The iniquity of Israel is kept in store. The pangs of childbirth come for him, but he is an unwise son; for he does not present himself at the mouth of the womb. Shall I ransom him from the power of Sheol? Shall I redeem him from Death? O Death, where are your plagues? O Sheol, where is your destruction? Compassion is hid from my eyes. Though Israel may flourish as the reed plant, the wind of the LORD shall come, rising from the wilderness; and it shall strip his treasury of every precious thing. Samaria shall bear her guilt.

RETURN, O ISRAEL, to the LORD your God. Return and say to the LORD, "Take away all iniquity; accept that which is good and we will render the fruit of our lips. Assyria shall not save us. We will not ride upon horses. We will say no more, 'Our God,' to the work of our hands. In thee the orphan finds mercy."

I WILL HEAL their faithlessness; I will love them freely, for my anger has turned from them. They shall return and dwell beneath my shadow; they shall flourish as a garden. I will be as the dew to Israel; he shall strike root as the poplar. His beauty shall be like the olive, his fragrance like Lebanon. What more has Israel to do with idols? It is I who answer and look after you. I am like an evergreen cypress; from me comes your fruit.

WHOEVER IS WISE, let him understand these things; whoever is discerning, let him know them; for the ways of the LORD are right, and the upright walk in them, but transgressors stumble.

JOEL

When a vast plague of locusts descends on Israel, first swarming into the countryside and then descending on the capital, the prophet Joel sees it as a portent of the Day of Judgment. His urgent call to repentance, expressed in apocalyptic language, is followed by a vision of the future, in which the Lord will compensate his people for their sufferings, as well as punish their enemies. Of Joel personally nothing is known. Most scholars assign his book to a time after the Exile, about 400 to 350 B.C. The passage predicting the outpouring of God's spirit on all flesh is cited in the Book of Acts as foreshadowing the gift of the Holy Spirit at Pentecost.

_____

THE WORD OF the LORD that came to Joel, the son of Pethuel:

Hear this, you aged men, give ear, all inhabitants of the land! Has such a thing happened in your days, or in the days of your fathers? Tell your children of it, and let your children tell their children, and their children another generation.

What the cutting locust left, the swarming locust has eaten. What the swarming locust left, the hopping locust has eaten, and what the hopping locust left, the destroying locust has eaten. Awake, you drunkards, and weep; wail, all you drinkers of wine; the sweet wine is cut off from your mouth. An army has come up against my land, powerful and without number; its teeth are lions' teeth, and it has the fangs of a lioness. It has laid waste my vines, and splintered my fig trees. It has stripped off their bark; their branches are made white. The fields are laid waste; the ground mourns because the grain is destroyed.

Be confounded, O tillers of the soil, for the wheat and the barley have perished. Wail, O vinedressers. The vine withers.

Pomegranate, palm, and apple, all languish. Gladness fails from the sons of men.

Gird on sackcloth and lament, O priests. Wail, O ministers of the altar. Pass the night in sackcloth, O ministers of my God! Cereal offering and drink offering are withheld from the house of your God. Sanctify a fast; call a solemn assembly. Gather all the inhabitants of the land, and cry to the LORD your God. For the day of the LORD is near; as destruction from the Almighty it comes. Is not the food cut off before our eyes, joy and gladness from the house of our God?

The seed shrivels under the clods; the storehouses are desolate. How the beasts groan! The herds of cattle are perplexed because there is no pasture for them; the flocks of sheep are dismayed. Even the wild beasts, O LORD, cry unto thee because the water brooks are dried up, and fire has devoured the pastures of the wilderness.

Blow the trumpet in Zion; sound the alarm on my holy mountain! Let all the inhabitants of the land tremble, for the day of the LORD is near, a day of darkness and gloom! Like blackness there is spread upon the mountains a great and powerful host; their like has never been from of old, nor ever will be again.

Crackling fire devours before them, and after them a desolate wilderness. Their appearance is like the appearance of horses, and like war horses they run. As with the rumbling of chariots, they leap on the tops of the mountains. Before them peoples are in anguish; all faces grow pale. Like warriors they charge; like soldiers they scale the wall. They march each on his way; they do not swerve from their paths. They burst through weapons and are not halted. They leap upon the city; they climb into the houses; they enter through the windows like a thief.

The earth quakes before them; the heavens tremble. The sun and the moon are darkened, and the stars withdraw their shining. The LORD thunders at the head of his army; mighty are those who obey his command. The day of the LORD is terrible—who can endure it?

"YET EVEN NOW," says the LORD, "return to me with all your heart, with fasting,

with weeping, and with mourning." Return
to the LORD your God, for he is gracious
and merciful, slow to anger, abounding in
steadfast love. Who knows whether he will
not turn and repent?

Blow the trumpet in Zion; sanctify a
fast; assemble the elders; gather all the
people, even nursing infants. Let the
bridegroom leave his room, and the bride
her chamber. Between the vestibule and
the altar let the priests, the ministers of
the LORD, weep and say, "Spare thy people, O LORD, and make not thy heritage a
reproach, a byword among the nations.
Why should they say, 'Where is their
God?' "

Then the LORD had pity on his people.
He said to them, "Behold, I am sending
you grain, wine, and oil. You will be satisfied; and I will no more make you a reproach among the nations. I will remove
the destroyer far from you, and drive him
into a desolate land, his front into the eastern sea, his rear into the western sea. Fear
not, O land; be glad and rejoice, for the
LORD has done great things! Fear not, you
beasts of the field, for the pastures of the

wilderness are green; the tree bears its fruit; the fig tree and vine give their full yield. Be glad, O sons of Zion; the LORD has poured down for you abundant rain, both autumn and spring rains, as before.

"The threshing floors shall be full of grain; the vats shall overflow with wine and oil. I will restore to you the years which the swarming locust has eaten, the hopper, the destroyer, and the cutter, the great army which I sent among you. You shall praise the name of the LORD, who has dealt wondrously with you. You shall know that I am in the midst of Israel, that I am the LORD your God; and there is none else. My people shall never again be put to shame.

"It shall come to pass afterward that I will pour out my spirit on all flesh; your sons and your daughters shall prophesy; your old men shall dream dreams, and your young men shall see visions. And I will give portents in the heavens and on the earth; the sun shall be turned to darkness, and the moon to blood, before the great and terrible day of the LORD comes. And it shall come to pass that all who call upon the name of the LORD shall be delivered.

"Behold, at that time, when I restore the fortunes of Judah and Jerusalem, I will bring all the nations down to the valley of Jehoshaphat, and I will enter into judgment with them there, because they have scattered my people Israel among the nations, and have divided up my land; they have cast lots for my people, and have given a boy for a harlot, and have sold a girl for wine."

PROCLAIM THIS AMONG the nations: Prepare war, stir up the mighty men. Let all the men of war draw near. Beat your plowshares into swords, and your pruning hooks into spears; let the weak say, "I am a warrior." Hasten and come to the valley of Jehoshaphat; there I will sit to judge all the nations round about, for their wickedness is great.

Multitudes, multitudes, in the valley of decision! The day of the LORD is near. The sun and the moon are darkened, and the stars withdraw their shining. The LORD roars from Zion, and utters his voice from

Jerusalem; the heavens and the earth shake. But the LORD is a refuge and a stronghold to the people of Israel.

"YOU SHALL KNOW that I am the LORD your God, who dwell in Zion, my holy mountain. Jerusalem shall be holy, and strangers shall never again pass through it. And in that day the mountains shall drip sweet wine, and the hills shall flow with milk; all the streambeds of Judah shall flow with water; and a fountain shall come forth from the house of the LORD.

"Egypt shall become a desolation and Edom a wilderness for the violence done to the people of Judah, because they have shed innocent blood in their land. But Judah shall be inhabited for ever, and Jerusalem to all generations. I will avenge their blood, and I will not clear the guilty, for the LORD dwells in Zion."

AMOS

From a small Judean village, where he lived a shepherd's life, Amos was called to preach in the northern kingdom of Israel under Jeroboam II (786–746 B.C.). Israel was then at the peak of her political might and national prosperity, but was ridden with social injustices. Outraged at the hypocritical worship, oppression of the poor, and immorality, Amos denounced Israel uncompromisingly, and his forceful preaching soon brought him into conflict with the authorities of the day. He was expelled from the royal sanctuary at Bethel and commanded not to prophesy there again. It is thought that he returned to Judah, where he wrote down the essence of his public preaching, to become the first of a notable succession of writing prophets. His powerful book, which insists that social justice is inseparable from true piety, ends on a happier note, promising a glorious age to come.

———

THE WORDS OF Amos, who was among the shepherds of Tekoa, which he saw concerning Israel in the days of Uzziah king of Judah and in the days of Jeroboam the son of Joash, king of Israel, two years before the earthquake. And he said: "The LORD roars from Zion, and utters his voice from Jerusalem; the pastures of the shepherds mourn, and the top of Carmel withers."

Thus says the LORD: "For three transgressions of Damascus, and for four, I will not revoke the punishment. Because they have threshed Gilead with sledges of iron, I will break the bar of Damascus, and the people of Syria shall go into exile. For three transgressions of Gaza, and for four, I will not revoke the punishment. Because they carried into exile a whole people to deliver them up to Edom, I will send a fire upon the wall of Gaza, and it shall devour her strongholds. The remnant of the Philistines shall perish. For three transgressions of Tyre, and for four, I will not revoke the punishment. Because they delivered up a whole people to Edom, and did not remember the covenant of brotherhood, I will send a fire upon the wall of Tyre, and it shall devour her strongholds."

Thus says the LORD: "For three transgressions of Edom, and for four, I will not revoke the punishment. Because he pursued his brother with the sword, cast off all pity, and kept his wrath for ever, I will send a fire upon Teman, and it shall devour the strongholds of Bozrah. For three transgressions of the Ammonites, and for four, I will not revoke the punishment. Because they have ripped up women with child in Gilead, that they might enlarge their border, I will kindle a fire in the wall of Rabbah, and it shall devour her strongholds. Her king shall go into exile, he and his princes together. For three transgressions of Moab, and for four, I will not revoke the punishment. Because he burned to lime the bones of the king of Edom, I will send a fire upon Moab, and it shall devour the strongholds of Kerioth. Moab

shall die amid shouting and the sound of
the trumpet. For three transgressions of
Judah, and for four, I will not revoke the
punishment. Because they have rejected
the law of the LORD, and have not kept
his statutes, I will send a fire upon Judah,
and it shall devour the strongholds of
Jerusalem."

Thus says the LORD: "For three transgressions of Israel, and for four, I will not
revoke the punishment. Because they sell
the righteous for silver, and the needy for a
pair of shoes—they that trample the head
of the poor into the dust, and turn aside
the way of the afflicted; a man and his
father go in to the same maiden, so that
my holy name is profaned; they lay themselves down beside every altar upon garments taken in pledge; and in the house of
their God they drink the wine of those
who have been fined.

"Yet I destroyed the Amorite before
them, who was as strong as the oaks; I
destroyed his fruit above, and his roots
beneath. I brought you up out of Egypt,
and led you forty years in the wilderness,
to possess the land of the Amorite. I raised

up some of your sons for prophets, and some for Nazirites. Is it not indeed so, O people of Israel?" says the LORD. "But you made the Nazirites drink wine, and commanded the prophets, saying, 'You shall not prophesy.'

"Behold, I will press you down in your place, as a cart full of sheaves presses down. Flight shall perish from the swift, and the strong shall not retain his strength; he who handles the bow shall not stand, nor shall he who rides the horse save his life; and he who is stout of heart shall flee away naked in that day," says the LORD.

HEAR THIS WORD that the LORD has spoken against you, O Israel, against the whole family brought up out of Egypt: "You only have I known of all the families of the earth; therefore I will punish you for all your iniquities.

"Do two walk together, unless they have made an appointment? Does a lion roar in the forest, when he has no prey? Does a bird fall in a snare on the earth, when there is no trap for it? Does evil befall a city, unless the LORD has done it? Surely the Lord GOD does nothing without revealing his secret to his servants the prophets. The lion has roared; who will not fear? The Lord GOD has spoken; who can but prophesy?"

Proclaim to the strongholds in Assyria and in the land of Egypt, and say, "Assemble yourselves upon the mountains of Samaria, and see the great tumults within her, the oppressions in her midst."

"They do not know how to do right," says the LORD, "those who store up violence and robbery in their strongholds." Therefore thus says the Lord GOD: "An adversary shall surround the land, and bring down your defenses; your strongholds shall be plundered. As the shepherd rescues from the mouth of the lion two legs, or a piece of an ear, so shall the people of Israel who dwell in Samaria be rescued. Hear, and testify against the house of Jacob, that on the day I punish Israel for his transgressions, I will punish the altars of Bethel, and the horns of the altar shall be cut off and fall to the ground. I will smite the winter house with the summer house; the houses of ivory shall perish."

Hear this word which I take up over you in lamentation, O Israel: "Fallen, no more to rise, is the virgin Israel; forsaken on her land, with none to raise her up."

Thus says the LORD to the house of Israel: "Seek me and live; but do not seek Bethel, and do not enter into Gilgal or cross over to Beer-sheba; for Gilgal shall surely go into exile, and Bethel shall come to nought."

Seek the LORD and live, lest he break out like fire to devour the house of Joseph, O you who turn justice to wormwood, and cast down righteousness to the earth! You hate him who reproves in the gate, and abhor him who speaks the truth. Therefore, because you trample upon the poor, though you have built houses of hewn stone, you shall not dwell in them; though you have planted pleasant vineyards, you shall not drink their wine. For I know how great are your sins. Seek good, not evil, that you may live; and so the LORD, the God of hosts, will be with you. Hate evil, love good, and establish justice in the gate; it may be that the LORD will be gracious to the remnant of Joseph.

Therefore thus says the LORD, the God of hosts: "In all the squares there shall be wailing; and in all the streets they shall say, 'Alas! alas!' They shall call the farmers to mourning, and in all vineyards there shall be wailing, for I will pass through the midst of you."

Woe to you who desire the day of the LORD! It is darkness, not light; as if a man fled from a lion, and a bear met him; or went into the house and leaned with his hand against the wall, and a serpent bit him. Is not the day of the LORD gloom with no brightness in it?

"I hate, I despise your feasts," says the LORD, "and I take no delight in your solemn assemblies. Even though you offer me your burnt offerings, I will not accept them, and the peace offerings of your fatted beasts I will not look upon. Take away from me the noise of your songs; to the melody of your harps I will not listen. But let justice roll down like waters, and righteousness like an ever-flowing stream. Did you bring to me sacrifices and offerings the forty years in the wilderness, O Israel? You shall take up your images, which you made for yourselves; I will take you into exile beyond Damascus.

"Woe to those who are at ease in Zion, who feel secure on the mountain of Samaria, the notable men to whom the people of Israel come! Pass over to Calneh, and see; go to Hamath the great; then go down to Gath of the Philistines. Are you better than these kingdoms? Is your territory greater than their territory, O you who put far away the evil day, and bring near the seat of violence?

"Woe to those who lie upon beds of ivory, and eat lambs from the flock; who sing idle songs to the sound of the harp, and like David invent for themselves instruments of music; who drink wine in bowls, and anoint themselves with the finest oils, but are not grieved over the ruin of Joseph! They shall be the first to go into exile, and their revelry shall pass away." The Lord GOD has sworn by himself: "I abhor the pride of Jacob, and hate his strongholds; I will deliver up the city and all that is in it."

For behold, the LORD commands, and the great house shall be smitten into fragments, the little house into bits. Do horses run upon rocks? Does one plow the sea with oxen? But you have turned justice into poison and the fruit of righteousness into wormwood—you who say, "Have we not by our own strength taken Karnaim for ourselves?"

"Behold, I will raise up against you a nation, O Israel," says the LORD, "and they shall oppress you from the entrance of Hamath to the Brook of the Arabah."

THUS THE LORD GOD showed me: behold, he was forming locusts. When they had finished eating the grass of the land, I said, "O Lord GOD, forgive, I beseech thee! How can Jacob stand? He is so small!" The LORD repented concerning this, and said, "It shall not be."

Thus the Lord GOD showed me: behold, he was calling for a judgment by fire, and it devoured the great deep and was eating up the land. "O Lord GOD," I said, "cease, I beseech thee! How can Jacob stand? He is so small!" The LORD repented concerning this, and said, "This also shall not be."

He showed me: behold, the Lord was

standing beside a wall, with a plumb line in his hand. "Amos," the LORD said, "what do you see?" I said, "A plumb line." Then he said, "Behold, I am setting a plumb line in the midst of my people Israel; I will never again pass by them; the high places of Isaac shall be made desolate, the sanctuaries of Israel shall be laid waste, and I will rise against the house of Jeroboam with the sword."

Then Amaziah the priest of Bethel sent to Jeroboam king of Israel, saying, "Amos has conspired against you. He has said, 'Jeroboam shall die by the sword, and Israel must go into exile.' The land is not able to bear all his words." And Amaziah said to Amos, "O seer, go; flee to the land of Judah. Eat bread there, prophesy there. But never again prophesy at Bethel, for it is the king's sanctuary, a temple of the kingdom."

"I am no prophet," Amos answered, "nor a prophet's son; I am a herdsman, and a dresser of sycamore trees. The LORD took me from following the flock, and said, 'Go, prophesy to my people Israel.' You say, 'Do not prophesy against Israel,

or preach against the house of Isaac.'
Therefore thus says the LORD: 'Your wife
shall be a harlot in the city, your sons and
daughters shall fall by the sword, and your
land shall be parceled out by line; you
yourself shall die in an unclean land, and
Israel shall surely go into exile.' "

Thus the Lord GOD showed me: behold,
a basket of ripe summer fruit. "Amos," he
said, "what do you see?" I said, "A basket
of ripe summer fruit." Then the LORD said,
"The end has come upon my people Israel;
I will never again pass by them. The songs
of the temple shall become wailings in that
day; the dead bodies shall be many; in
every place they shall be cast out in
silence."

Hear this, you who trample upon the
needy, saying, "When will the sabbath be
over, that we may offer wheat for sale, and
deal deceitfully with false balances, that we
may buy the poor for silver and the needy
for a pair of sandals?" The LORD has
sworn: "Surely I will never forget any of
their deeds. Shall not the land tremble on
this account, and every one mourn who
dwells in it? On that day I will make the

sun go down at noon, and darken the earth in broad daylight. I will turn your feasts into mourning; I will bring sackcloth upon all loins, and baldness on every head; I will make it like the mourning for an only son.

"Behold, the days are coming," says the Lord GOD, "when I will send a famine on the land; not a famine of bread, nor a thirst for water, but of hearing the words of the LORD. They shall wander from sea to sea, and from north to east; they shall run to and fro, to seek the word of the LORD, but they shall not find it. In that day fair virgins and young men shall faint for thirst. Those who swear by the idols of Samaria shall fall, and never rise again."

I SAW THE LORD standing beside the altar, and he said: "Smite the capitals until the thresholds shake, and shatter them on the heads of all the people; what are left of them I will slay with the sword; not one shall escape. Though they dig into Sheol, from there shall my hand take them; though they climb up to heaven, from there I will bring them down. Though they hide on the top of Carmel, I will search them out; though they hide at the bottom of the sea, there I will command the serpent to bite them. And though they go into captivity, there I will command the sword to slay them; I will set my eyes upon them for evil and not for good."

The Lord, GOD of hosts, he who touches the earth and it melts, and all who dwell in it mourn; who builds his upper chambers in the heavens, and founds his vault upon the earth; who calls for the waters of the sea, and pours them out upon the surface of the earth—the LORD is his name.

"Are you not like the Ethiopians to me, O people of Israel?" says the LORD. "Did I not bring up Israel from Egypt, the Philistines from Caphtor and the Syrians from Kir? Behold, the eyes of the Lord GOD are upon the sinful kingdom, and I will destroy it; except that I will not utterly destroy the house of Jacob. For lo, I will shake the house of Israel among all the nations as one shakes with a sieve, but no pebble shall fall upon the earth. All the sinners of my people shall die by the sword, who say, 'Evil shall not overtake us.'

"In that day I will raise up the booth of David that is fallen and repair its breaches, and raise up its ruins, and rebuild it as in the days of old; that they may possess the remnant of Edom and all the nations who are called by my name," says the LORD who does this.

"Behold, the days are coming," says the LORD, "when the plowman shall overtake the reaper and the treader of grapes him who sows the seed; the mountains shall drip sweet wine, and all the hills shall flow with it. I will restore the fortunes of my people Israel, and they shall rebuild the ruined cities and inhabit them; they shall plant vineyards and drink their wine, and they shall make gardens and eat their fruit. I will plant them upon their land, and they shall never again be plucked up out of the land which I have given them," says the LORD your God.

OBADIAH

This is the shortest book of the Old Testament. The prophet, about whose life nothing is known, warns the land of Edom that, for its refusal to fight against the foreigners who conquered Jerusalem, divine judgment will fall on it. He also assures the exiled Israelites that they will be restored to the Promised Land, and then will rule over Edom as well. The disaster to Jerusalem described by Obadiah is probably the sack of the city by the Babylonians in 586 B.C. Since Edom fell to the Nabataeans in 312 B.C., Obadiah's prophecy may be placed between those two dates.

———

THE VISION OF Obadiah.

Thus says the Lord GOD concerning Edom: We have heard tidings from the

LORD, and a messenger has been sent among the nations: "Rise up! let us rise against her for battle!" Behold, I will make you small among the nations; you shall be utterly despised. The pride of your heart has deceived you, you who live in the clefts of the rock, whose dwelling is high, who say in your heart, "Who will bring me down to the ground?" Though you soar like the eagle, though your nest is among the stars, I will bring you down, says the LORD.

If thieves came to you by night, would they not steal only enough for themselves? If grape gatherers came to you, would they not leave gleanings? But how Esau will be pillaged, his treasures sought out! Your allies will drive you to the border; your trusted friends will set a trap under you— there will be no understanding of it. Will I not on that day, says the LORD, destroy the wise men of Edom? Your mighty men shall be dismayed, so that every man from Mount Esau will be cut off by slaughter. For the violence done to your brother Jacob, you shall be cut off for ever. On the day that you stood aloof, on the day that

strangers carried off his wealth, and foreigners entered his gates and cast lots for
Jerusalem, you were like one of them. But
you should not have gloated over the day
of your brother in the day of his misfor-
tune. You should not have stood at the
parting of the ways to cut off his fugitives.
You should not have delivered up his survivors in the day of distress.

For the day of the LORD is near upon all
the nations. As you have done, it shall be
done to you; your deeds shall return on
your own head. All the nations round
about shall drink of my wrath, and they
shall stagger. It shall be as though they had
not been. But on Mount Zion there shall
be those that escape, and it shall be holy.
The house of Jacob shall possess their own
possessions. The house of Jacob shall be a
fire, and the house of Joseph a flame; they
shall burn and consume the house of Esau.
There shall be no survivor, for the LORD
has spoken. The exiles of the Negeb shall
possess Mount Esau, and those of the Shephelah the land of the Philistines; they
shall possess Ephraim and Samaria, and
Benjamin shall possess Gilead. The exiles

in Halah shall possess Phoenicia as far as Zarephath; and the exiles of Jerusalem who are in Sepharad shall possess the cities of the Negeb. Saviors shall go up to Mount Zion to rule Mount Esau; and the kingdom shall be the LORD's.

JONAH

Unlike the other prophetic books of the Old Testament, Jonah is almost entirely the story of the man himself as he answers God's call and preaches against the wickedness of Nineveh. When the Ninevites respond to his message and repent, however, he sulks with displeasure! The book teaches that God's loving care and tender mercy extend even to the inhabitants of a foreign city hated by Israel, and that the Lord is the universal God of Jew and Gentile alike. Clearly it implies that Israel's mission is to proclaim this truth to other nations. The book was probably written after the Babylonian Exile (sixth century B.C.), but Jonah himself lived and prophesied about two hundred years earlier. In the Gospels, Jesus refers more than once to the "sign of Jonah," which in Matthew is interpreted as a prophecy of his resurrection.

THE WORD OF the LORD came to Jonah the son of Amittai, saying, "Arise, go to Nineveh, that great city, and cry against it; for their wickedness has come up before me." But Jonah rose to flee from the presence of the LORD. He went to Joppa, where he found a ship going to Tarshish. Paying the fare, he went on board.

But the LORD hurled a great wind upon the sea, and there was a mighty tempest that threatened to break up the ship. The mariners were afraid, and each cried to his god; to lighten the ship they threw the cargo overboard. Now Jonah had lain down below deck, and was fast asleep. Finding him, the captain cried, "What do you mean, you sleeper! Arise, call upon your god! Perhaps he will save us."

Then the mariners said to one another, "Let us cast lots, that we may know on whose account this evil has come upon us." So they cast lots, and the lot fell on Jonah.

"Tell us," they asked him, "what is your occupation? Whence do you come? Of what people are you?"

"I am a Hebrew," Jonah answered, "and I fear the LORD, the God of heaven, who made the sea and the dry land." And he told them that he was fleeing from the presence of the LORD.

The men were exceedingly afraid. "What have you done!" they asked. "What shall we do to you, that the sea may quiet down?"

"Take me up and throw me into the sea," he replied. "I know it is because of me that this great tempest has come upon you."

Nevertheless the men rowed hard to bring the ship back to land, but they could not, for the sea grew more and more tempestuous. "We beseech thee, O LORD," they cried, "let us not perish for taking this man's life, and lay not on us innocent blood; for thou, O LORD, hast done as it pleased thee." Then they threw Jonah into the sea, and the sea ceased from its raging. The men, fearing the LORD exceedingly, offered a sacrifice to him and made vows.

The LORD appointed a great fish to swallow up Jonah, and for three days and three nights he was in the belly of the fish. Then he prayed to the LORD his God from the belly of the fish, saying, "I called to the LORD, out of my distress; I cried, and thou didst hear my voice. For thou didst cast me into the heart of the seas; all thy waves and thy billows passed over me. The deep was round about me; weeds were wrapped about my head. I went down to the land whose bars closed upon me for ever; yet thou didst bring up my life from the Pit, O LORD my God. When my soul fainted within me, I remembered the LORD; and my prayer came to thee. With the voice of thanksgiving I will sacrifice to thee; what I have vowed I will pay. Deliverance belongs to the LORD!"

The LORD spoke to the fish, and it vomited out Jonah upon the dry land.

THE WORD OF the LORD came to Jonah the second time, saying, "Arise, go to Nineveh, that great city, and proclaim to it the message that I tell you." Jonah went to Nineveh, and entering the city, he cried, "In forty days Nineveh shall be overthrown!" The people of Nineveh believed God; they proclaimed a fast, and put on sackcloth, from the greatest of them to the least.

When tidings reached the king, he arose from his throne, removed his robe, covered himself with sackcloth, and sat in ashes. Then he published a proclamation throughout Nineveh: "Let neither man nor beast feed or drink water, but let man and beast be covered with sackcloth, and let them cry mightily to God; yea, let every one turn from his evil way and from the violence which is in his hands. Who knows, God may yet repent and turn from his fierce anger, so that we perish not."

When God saw how they turned from their wicked ways, he repented of the evil which he had said he would do to them; and he did not do it. This displeased Jonah exceedingly, and he prayed, "LORD, is not this what I said when I was yet in my country? That is why I made haste to flee to Tarshish; for I knew that thou art a gracious God and merciful, slow to anger, and abounding in steadfast love, and repentest of evil. Therefore now, O LORD, take my life from me, I beseech thee, for it is better for me to die than to live."

The LORD said, "Do you do well to be angry?"

Jonah went out to the east of the city, made a booth for himself, and sat under it till he should see what would become of Nineveh. God caused a plant to come up over the booth, for a shade, and Jonah was exceedingly glad. But at dawn the next day God caused a worm to attack the plant, so that it withered. When the sun rose, God sent a sultry east wind, and the sun beat upon Jonah so that he was faint; and he asked that he might die. "It is better for me to die than to live," he said.

"Do you do well to be angry for the plant?" God asked.

"Yes," Jonah answered, "angry enough to die."

"You pity the plant," the LORD said,

"for which you did not labor, nor did you make it grow, which came into being in a night, and perished in a night. And should not I pity Nineveh, that great city, in which there are more than a hundred and twenty thousand persons who do not know their right hand from their left, and also much cattle?"

MICAH

A Judean prophet, Micah was a contemporary of Isaiah (eighth century B.C.). His book comprises numerous short oracles, uttered at different times, and later brought together, but without much effort to smooth the transitions. While Micah denounces Samaria and Jerusalem for religious hypocrisy and oppression of the poor, he also prophesies a glorious future for Israel, and the restoration of the Davidic kingdom. Noteworthy in the latter passage is Micah's prediction of the coming of a messianic ruler who is to be born at Bethlehem (quoted by Matthew in connection with the birth of Jesus). The remainder of the book contains miscellaneous oracles, including a summation of true religion as justice, kindness, and humble communion with God.

THE WORD OF the LORD that came to Micah of Moresheth in the days of Jotham, Ahaz, and Hezekiah, kings of Judah, which he saw concerning Samaria and Jerusalem.

HEAR, YOU PEOPLES, all of you; hearken, O earth, and all that is in it; and let the Lord GOD be a witness against you. For behold, the LORD is coming down from his holy temple, and will tread upon the high places of the earth. And the mountains will melt under him and the valleys will be cleft, like wax before the fire, like waters poured down a steep place. All this is for the transgression of Jacob and for the sins of the house of Israel.

What is the transgression of Jacob? Is it not Samaria? And what is the sin of the house of Judah? Is it not Jerusalem? Therefore I will make Samaria a heap in the open country, a place for planting vineyards; I will pour down her stones into the valley, and uncover her foundations.

FOR THIS I will wail and go naked. I will make lamentation like the jackals. For her wound is incurable, and it has come to

Judah; it has reached to the gate of my people, to Jerusalem.

HEAR, YOU HEADS of Jacob and rulers of the house of Israel! Is it not for you to know justice?—you who hate the good and love the evil, who tear the skin from off my people, break their bones in pieces, and chop them up like meat in a kettle.

They will cry to the LORD, but he will not answer them; he will hide his face from them, because they have made their deeds evil.

Thus says the LORD concerning the prophets who lead my people astray, who cry "Peace" when they have something to eat, but declare war against him who puts nothing into their mouths: Therefore it shall be night to you, without vision. The sun shall go down upon the prophets; the seers shall be disgraced, for there is no answer from God. As for me, I am filled with power, with the Spirit of the LORD, to declare to Jacob his transgression and to Israel his sin.

Hear this, you heads of the house of Jacob and rulers of the house of Israel, who pervert all equity, who build Zion with blood and Jerusalem with wrong. Its heads give judgment for a bribe, its priests teach for hire, its prophets divine for money. Yet they lean upon the LORD and say, "Is not the LORD in the midst of us? No evil shall come upon us." Therefore because of you Zion shall be plowed as a field; Jerusalem shall become a heap of ruins, and the mountain of the house a wooded height.

IT SHALL COME to pass in the latter days that the mountain of the house of the LORD shall be established as the highest of the mountains, and peoples shall flow to it. Many nations shall come, and say: "Come, let us go up to the mountain of the LORD, that he may teach us his ways and we may walk in his paths." For out of Zion shall go forth the law, and the word of the LORD from Jerusalem. He shall judge between many peoples, and shall decide for strong nations afar off; they shall beat their swords into plowshares, and their spears into pruning hooks; nation shall not lift up sword against nation, neither shall they learn war any more; but they shall sit every man under his fig tree, and none shall make them afraid. For all the peoples walk each in the name of its god, but we will walk in the name of the LORD our God for ever and ever.

In that day, says the LORD, I will assemble the lame and gather those who have been driven away. Those whom I have afflicted I will make the remnant; and those who were cast off, a strong nation; the LORD will reign over them in Mount Zion from this time forth and for evermore. And you, O tower of the flock, hill of the daughter of Zion, to you the former dominion shall come, the kingdom of the daughter of Jerusalem.

Now WHY DO you cry aloud? Is there no king among you? Has your counselor perished, that pangs have seized you like a woman in labor? Writhe and groan, O daughter of Zion, for you shall go forth from the city and dwell in the open country. There the LORD will rescue you from the hand of your enemies.

Now many nations are assembled

against you, saying, "Let Zion be profaned." But they do not know the thoughts
of the LORD, they do not understand his
plan, that he has gathered them as sheaves
to the threshing floor. Arise and thresh, O
daughter of Zion, for I will make your
horn iron and your hoofs bronze. You
shall beat in pieces many peoples, and
shall devote their wealth to the Lord of the
whole earth.

Now you are walled about; with a rod
they strike upon the cheek the ruler
of Israel. But you, O Bethlehem Eph-
rathah, who are little among the clans
of Judah, from you shall come forth for
me one who is to be ruler in Israel,
whose origin is from ancient days. Therefore he shall give them up until the time
when she who is in labor has brought
forth a child. Then the rest of his brethren shall return, and he shall stand and
feed his flock in the strength of the LORD,
in the majesty of the name of the LORD
his God. The people of Israel shall dwell
secure, for now he shall be great to the
ends of the earth. And this shall be
peace.

HEAR WHAT THE LORD says: Arise, plead your case before the mountains. Hear, you enduring foundations of the earth, for the LORD has a controversy with his people, and he will contend with Israel.

"O MY PEOPLE, what have I done to you? In what have I wearied you? Answer me! For I brought you up from the land of Egypt, and redeemed you from the house of bondage. O my people, remember what Balak king of Moab devised, and what Balaam the son of Beor answered him, that you may know the saving acts of the LORD."

WITH WHAT SHALL I come before the LORD, and bow myself before God on high? Shall I come before him with burnt offerings, with calves a year old? Will the LORD be pleased with thousands of rams, with ten thousands of rivers of oil? Shall I give my first-born for my transgression, the fruit of my body for the sin of my soul?
He has showed you, O man, what is good; and what does the LORD require of

you but to do justice, and to love kindness, and to walk humbly with your God?

THE VOICE OF the LORD cries to the city—and it is sound wisdom to fear his name: "Hear, O tribe and assembly of the city! Can I forget the treasures of wickedness in the house of the wicked? Shall I acquit the man with deceitful scales? Your rich men are full of violence; your inhabitants speak lies. Therefore I have begun to smite you, making you desolate because of your sins. You shall eat, but not be satisfied; you shall put away, but what you save I will give to the sword. For you have kept the statutes of Omri, and all the works of the house of Ahab; that I may make you a desolation, and your inhabitants a hissing."

WOE IS ME! For I have become as when the summer fruit has been gathered: there is no first-ripe fig which my soul desires. The godly man has perished from the earth, and there is none upright among men. Each hunts his brother with a net. Put no trust in a neighbor; guard the doors of your mouth from her who lies in your bosom; for the son treats the father with contempt, the daughter rises up against her mother; a man's enemies are the men of his own house. But as for me, I will look to the LORD, I will wait for the God of my salvation; my God will hear me.

Rejoice not over me, O my enemy; when I fall, I shall rise; when I sit in darkness, the LORD will be a light to me. I will bear the indignation of the LORD because I have sinned against him, until he pleads my cause. He will bring me forth to the light; I shall behold his deliverance. Then my enemy will see, and shame will cover her who said to me, "Where is the LORD your God?" Now she will be trodden down like the mire of the streets.

A day for the building of your walls! In that day the boundary shall be far extended. In that day they will come to you, from Assyria to Egypt, and from Egypt to the Euphrates, from sea to sea and from mountain to mountain. But the earth will be desolate because of its inhabitants, for the fruit of their doings.

Shepherd thy people with thy staff, the flock of thy inheritance, who dwell alone in a forest in the midst of a garden land; let them feed in Bashan and Gilead as in the days of old.

"As in the days when you came out of Egypt," says the Lord, "I will show them marvelous things." The nations shall see and be ashamed of all their might. They shall lick the dust like a serpent, like the crawling things of the earth. They shall come trembling out of their strongholds. They shall turn in dread to the Lord our God, and they shall fear because of thee.

Who is a God like thee, pardoning iniquity and passing over transgression for the remnant of his inheritance? He does not retain his anger for ever because he delights in steadfast love. He will again have compassion upon us, and cast all our sins into the depths of the sea. Thou wilt show faithfulness to Jacob and steadfast love to Abraham, as thou hast sworn to our fathers from the days of old.

NAHUM

In a rapid, excited style that reveals his strong feelings and his great sense of God's power, Nahum predicts the coming destruction of Nineveh, capital of the Assyrian Empire. For centuries Assyria had been like a lion preying on and dominating other nations of the Near East. Now, declares the prophet, the wrath of the Lord, which none can resist, will be poured out upon it. Nahum was a native of a small village in Galilee. He prophesied some years before the fall of Nineveh in 612 B.C.

———

AN ORACLE CONCERNING Nineveh. The book of the vision of Nahum of Elkosh.

The LORD is a jealous God and avenging; the LORD takes vengeance on his adversaries and keeps wrath for his enemies.

The LORD is slow to anger and of great might; the LORD will by no means clear the guilty. His way is in whirlwind and storm; the clouds are the dust of his feet. The earth is laid waste before him, the world and all that dwell therein. Who can endure the heat of his anger? His wrath is poured out like fire, and the rocks are broken asunder by him. The LORD is good, a stronghold in the day of trouble. But with an overflowing flood he will make an end of his adversaries. "Though they be strong and many," says the LORD, "they will pass away. Though I have afflicted you, O Judah, I will afflict you no more. I will break his yoke from off you and will burst your bonds asunder."

The LORD has given commandment about you, O Nineveh. "No more shall your name be perpetuated; from the house of your gods I will cut off the graven image. I will make your grave, for you are vile." The shatterer has come against you, O Nineveh. Man the ramparts; watch the road; gird your loins; collect your strength. The shield of his mighty men is red, his soldiers are clothed in scarlet. The chariots flash like flame, the chargers prance. The river gates are opened, the palace is in dismay; its mistress is stripped, she is carried off, her maidens moaning like doves, and beating their breasts. Nineveh is like a pool whose waters flow away. "Halt! Halt!" they cry; but none turns back. Plunder the silver, plunder the gold! There is no end of treasure.

Desolation and ruin! Hearts faint and knees tremble. Where is the lions' den, where the lion brought his prey, where his cubs were, with none to disturb? The lion filled his caves with prey and his dens with torn flesh. Behold, I am against you, says the LORD, and the sword shall devour your young lions. I will cut off your prey from the earth, and the voice of your messengers shall no more be heard.

Woe to the bloody city, all full of lies and booty. The crack of whip, and rumble of wheel, galloping horse and bounding chariot! Horsemen charging, flashing sword and glittering spear, heaps of corpses, dead bodies without end! And all for the countless harlotries of the harlot, who betrays nations and peoples with her charms. I will throw filth at you and treat you with contempt. All who look on you will shrink from you and say, Wasted is Nineveh; whence shall I seek comforters for her?

Are you better than Thebes that sat by the Nile, her rampart a sea, and water her wall? Yet she was carried into captivity; her little ones were dashed in pieces, and her great men were bound in chains. You also will be drunken; you will seek refuge from the enemy. Your princes are like grasshoppers, your scribes like clouds of locusts settling on the fences in a day of cold—when the sun rises, they fly away; no one knows where they are. Your shepherds are asleep, your nobles slumber. There is no assuaging your hurt, your wound is grievous. All who hear the news of you clap their hands over you. For upon whom has not come your unceasing evil?

HABAKKUK

This book frankly confronts the age-old problem of God's justice: Why is God *"silent when the wicked swallows up the man more righteous"*? To this perennial cry the prophet receives an answer eternally valid: God is still sovereign, and in his own way and at the proper time will deal with the wicked. The Lord assures Habakkuk that *"the righteous shall live by his faith."* Because of its use by Paul, that sentence became important in Christian thought as the starting point of the theological concept of faith. Habakkuk wrote probably near the end of the sixth century B.C., when the Chaldeans (that is, the Babylonians) had conquered Assyria and were threatening Judah.

_____

THE ORACLE OF God which Habakkuk the prophet saw.

O LORD, how long shall I cry for help, and thou wilt not hear? Or cry to thee "Violence!" and thou wilt not save? Why dost thou make me see wrongs and look upon trouble? Destruction and violence are before me; strife and contention arise. The law is slacked, for the wicked surround the righteous, so justice goes forth perverted.

Look among the nations, and see; wonder and be astounded. For I am doing a work in your days that you would not believe if told. I am rousing the Chaldeans, that bitter and impatient nation, who march through the breadth of the earth, to seize habitations not their own. Dread and terrible are they; their justice and judgment are of their own making. Their horses are swifter than leopards, more fierce than the evening wolves. Their horsemen come from afar, and fly like an eagle swift to devour. Terror of them goes before them, and they gather captives like sand. At kings they scoff, and of rulers they make sport. They take every fortress, then sweep by like the wind and go on, guilty men, whose own might is their god!

O LORD, thou hast ordained them as a judgment, and established them for chastisement. Thou who art of purer eyes than to behold evil and canst not look on wrong, why dost thou look on faithless men, and art silent when the wicked swallows up the man more righteous than he? Thou makest men like the fish of the sea. The wicked foe brings all of them up with a hook, and drags them out with his net. Then, rejoicing, he sacrifices to his net, for by it he lives in luxury, and his food is rich. Is he then to keep on emptying his net, and mercilessly slaying nations for ever?

I will take my stand to watch, and station myself on the tower, and look forth to see what he will say to me, and what I will answer concerning my complaint. And the LORD answered me: "Write the vision; make it plain upon tablets, so he may run who reads it. For still the vision awaits its time; it hastens to the end—it will not lie. If it seem slow, wait for it; it will surely come, it will not delay. Behold, he whose soul is not upright in him shall fail, but the righteous shall live by his faith. Moreover, the arrogant man shall not abide. His greed is as wide as the grave; like death he has never enough. He gathers for himself all nations, and collects as his own all peoples."

SHALL NOT ALL these take up their taunt against him, in scoffing derision, and say, "Woe to him who heaps up what is not his own and loads himself with pledges!" Will not your debtors suddenly arise and make you tremble? Then you will be booty for them. Because you have plundered many nations, all the remnant of the peoples shall plunder you.

Woe to him who gets evil gain for his house, to set his nest on high, safe from the reach of harm! You have shamed your house by cutting off many peoples; you have forfeited your life.

Woe to him who builds a town with blood, and founds a city on iniquity! Is it not from the LORD that nations weary themselves for nought?

Woe to him who makes his neighbors drink of the cup of his wrath, and makes them drunk, to gaze on their shame! You will be sated with contempt instead of glory. Drink, yourself, and stagger! The cup in the LORD's right hand will come around to you, and shame will come upon your glory!

What profit is an idol when its maker has shaped it, a metal image, a teacher of lies? Woe to him who says to a wooden thing, Awake; to a dumb stone, Arise! Can this give revelation? Behold, it is overlaid with gold and silver, and there is no breath at all in it. But the LORD is in his holy temple; let all the earth keep silence before him.

A PRAYER OF Habakkuk the prophet.

O LORD, I have heard the report of thee, and thy work do I fear. In the midst of the years renew it; in the midst of the years make it known; in wrath remember mercy.

God came from Teman, and the Holy One from Mount Paran. His glory covered the heavens, and the earth was full of his praise. His brightness was like the light, rays flashed from his hand. Before him went pestilence, and plague followed close behind. He stood and measured the earth; he looked and shook the nations; then the eternal mountains were scattered, the everlasting hills sank low.

I saw the tents of Cushan in affliction; the curtains of the land of Midian did tremble. Was thy wrath against the rivers, O LORD, or thy indignation against the sea, when thou didst ride upon thy horses, upon thy chariot of victory? Thou didst strip the sheath from thy bow, and put the arrows to the string. Thou didst cleave the earth with rivers. The mountains saw thee, and writhed; the raging waters swept on; the deep gave forth its voice. The sun and moon stood still in their habitation at the light of thine arrows as they sped. Thou didst bestride the earth in fury, trampling the nations in anger. Thou wentest forth for the salvation of thy people, and thou didst crush the head of the wicked, laying him bare from thigh to neck.

I hear, and my body trembles, my lips quiver at the sound; rottenness enters into my bones, my steps totter beneath me. I will quietly wait for the day of trouble to come upon people who invade us.

Though the fig tree do not blossom, nor fruit be on the vines, the produce of the olive fail and the fields yield no food, the flock be cut off from the fold and there be no herd in the stalls, yet I will rejoice in the LORD, I will joy in the God of my salvation. GOD, the Lord, is my strength; he makes my feet like hinds' feet, he makes me tread upon my high places.

ZEPHANIAH

A man of deep moral sensitivity, Zephaniah prophesied early in the reign of Josiah, king of Judah (640–609 B.C.). With vivid power he announces the coming day of the Lord, which is to be a day of catastrophic judgment upon all nations. Judah itself is condemned for its religious and moral corruption, springing from pride and rebelliousness. Hope is held out for the survival of a faithful remnant, but only those who repent and turn to the Lord, the prophet warns, will be spared from divine wrath. Profoundly Zephaniah lays bare the true essence of sin: it is an offense against the majesty of the living God.

———

THE WORD OF the LORD which came to
Zephaniah the son of Cushi, son of Gedaliah, son of Amariah, son of Hezekiah, in
the days of Josiah the son of Amon, king of
Judah.

"I will utterly sweep away everything
from the face of the earth," says the LORD,
"man and beast, the birds of the air, and
the fish of the sea. I will overthrow the
wicked. I will stretch out my hand against
Judah and Jerusalem, and cut off from this
place the remnant of Baal and the idolatrous priests; those who bow down on the
roofs to the stars, those who bow down to
the LORD and yet swear by a foreign god,
and those who have turned back from following the LORD."

Be silent before the Lord GOD! For his
day is at hand. He has prepared a sacrifice
and consecrated his guests. "On that day,"
says the LORD, "I will punish the officials
and the king's sons, those who walk in
foreign ways, and those who fill their master's house with violence and fraud. A cry
will be heard from the Fish Gate in Jerusalem, a wail from the Second Quarter, a
loud crash from the hills. Wail, O inhabit-

ants of the city! For the traders are no more; all who weigh silver are cut off. I will search Jerusalem with lamps, and punish the men who are thickening upon their lees, who say in their hearts, 'The LORD will not do good, nor will he do ill.' "

The great day of the LORD is near, near and hastening fast; the sound of the day of the LORD is bitter, the mighty man cries aloud there. A day of wrath is that day, a day of distress and anguish, a day of ruin and devastation, a day of darkness and gloom, a day of clouds and thick darkness, a day of trumpet blast and battle cry against the fortified cities and against the lofty battlements. I will bring distress on men, so that they shall walk like the blind, because they have sinned against the LORD; their blood shall be poured out like dust, and their flesh like dung. Neither their silver nor their gold shall be able to deliver them on the day of the wrath of the LORD. In the fire of his jealous wrath, all the earth shall be consumed; for a full, yea, sudden end he will make of all the inhabitants of the earth.

Come together, O shameless nation, be-

fore the fierce anger of the LORD comes
upon you. Seek the LORD, all you humble of
the land, who do his commands; seek righteousness and humility; perhaps you may be
hidden on the day of the wrath of the LORD.

Woe to you inhabitants of the seacoast,
you nation of the Philistines! The word of
the LORD is against you, and you will be
destroyed till no inhabitant is left. The seacoast shall become meadows, where the
remnant of the house of Judah shall pasture its flocks. In the houses of the Philistines they shall lie down at evening, for the
LORD their God will be mindful of them.

"I have heard the taunts of Moab," says
the LORD of hosts, the God of Israel, "and
the revilings of the Ammonites against my
people. Therefore, as I live, Moab shall
become like Sodom, and the Ammonites
like Gomorrah, a land possessed by nettles
and salt pits, and a waste for ever. The
survivors of my nation shall plunder and
possess them." This shall be their lot, because they scoffed and boasted against the
people of the LORD.

You also, O Ethiopians, shall be slain by
the sword of the LORD. And he will de-

stroy Assyria, and make Nineveh a dry waste like the desert. Herds shall lie down in the midst of her, and the vulture and the hedgehog shall lodge in her capitals. This is the exultant city that dwelt secure and said to herself, "I am and there is none else." What a desolation she has become, a lair for wild beasts! Every one who passes by her hisses and shakes his fist.

Woe to the rebellious Jerusalem! She does not trust in the LORD, or draw near to her God. Her officials are roaring lions, her judges evening wolves that leave nothing till the morning. Her prophets are wanton, faithless men; her priests profane what is sacred; they do violence to the law. Every morning the LORD shows forth his justice, but the unjust knows no shame.

"I have cut off nations," says the LORD, "so that none walks in their streets. I said, 'Surely she will fear me, she will accept correction.' But all the more they were corrupt. Therefore wait for me, for the day when I arise as a witness. For my decision is to gather nations, to pour out upon them all the heat of my anger.

"At that time I will change the speech of

the peoples to a pure speech, that all may call on the name of the LORD and serve him with one accord. On that day you shall not be put to shame because you have rebelled against me, for I will remove from your midst your proudly exultant ones and leave a people humble and lowly. Those who are left in Israel shall seek refuge in the name of the LORD. They shall do no wrong, nor shall there be found in their mouth a deceitful tongue. They shall pasture and lie down, and none shall make them afraid."

Sing aloud, O daughter of Zion; shout, O Israel! Rejoice and exult with all your heart. The LORD has taken away the judgments against you and cast out your enemies. The LORD, your God, is in your midst, a warrior who gives victory; he will rejoice over you with gladness and renew you in his love. "I will remove disaster from you," says the LORD, "so that you will not bear reproach for it. I will deal with your oppressors, and I will save the lame and gather the outcast, and change their shame into praise. At that time I will bring you home; yea, I will make you renowned and praised among all the peoples of the earth."

HAGGAI

The purpose of Haggai's vigorous preaching was to awaken popular enthusiasm for the completion of the second temple, the first having been destroyed about seventy years before by Nebuchadnezzar. Since the return of the Jews to Jerusalem from the Babylonian Exile, about 538 B.C., nearly two decades had passed, but as yet only the temple's foundations had been laid down. Haggai urges the leaders of the Judean community to take personal charge, in order to hasten its completion. He also calls for the priests to purify the cultic worship, and he links earlier Israelite traditions with the promise of a coming messianic age. The book, which was probably put together by another hand, offers a summary of his teaching.

———

IN THE SECOND year of Darius the king, in the sixth month, on the first day of the month, the word of the LORD came by Haggai the prophet to Zerubbabel son of Shealtiel, governor of Judah, and to Joshua son of Jehozadak, the high priest, "Thus says the LORD of hosts: This people say the time has not yet come to rebuild the house of the LORD. Is it a time for you to dwell in your paneled houses, while this house lies in ruins? Now therefore consider how you have fared. You have sown much, and harvested little; you eat, but you never have enough; you clothe yourselves, but no one is warm; and he who earns wages puts them into a bag with holes. You looked for much, and it came to little; and when you brought it home, I blew it away. Why? Because my house lies in ruins, while you busy yourselves with your own. Therefore the heavens above you have withheld the dew, and the earth has withheld its produce. I have called for a drought upon the land, upon what the ground brings forth, upon men and cattle, and upon all their labors."

Then Zerubbabel, Joshua, and all the

remnant of the people feared before the LORD. Haggai spoke to them with the LORD's message, "Go up to the hills and bring wood and build the house, that I may take pleasure in it and appear in my glory. I am with you." The LORD stirred up the spirit of the people, and they came and worked on the house of the LORD their God.

On the twenty-first day of the seventh month, the word of the LORD came by Haggai, "Say to Zerubbabel, Joshua, and all the people, 'Who among you saw this house in its former glory? How do you see it now? Is it not as nothing? Yet take courage; work, for my Spirit abides among you. In a little while I will shake all nations, so that their treasures shall come in; the silver and gold is mine, and I will fill this house with greater splendor than the former. In this place I will give prosperity.' "

On the twenty-fourth day of the ninth month, the word of the LORD came by Haggai, "Thus says the LORD: Ask the priests to decide this question, 'If one carries holy flesh in the skirt of his garment, and the skirt touches bread, or wine, or any kind of food, does the food become holy?' " The priests answered, "No." Then said Haggai, "If one who is unclean by contact with a dead body touches food, does it become unclean?" The priests answered, "It does." Haggai said, "So is it with this nation before me, says the LORD. What the people offer is unclean. Consider now what will come to pass. Before a stone was placed upon a stone in the temple of the LORD, how did you fare? When one came to a heap of twenty measures, there were but ten; when one came to the winevat to draw fifty measures, there were but twenty. I smote you and the products of your toil with blight and mildew, yet you did not return to me, says the LORD. But since the day that the foundation of the LORD'S temple was laid, consider: From this day on I will bless you."

Then the word of the LORD came a second time to Haggai on the same day, "Say to Zerubbabel, governor of Judah, I am about to shake the heavens and the earth, and to overthrow the throne of kingdoms; I am about to destroy the strength of the nations, and overthrow the chariots and their riders; the horses and their riders shall go down, every one by the sword of his fellow. On that day I will take you, O Zerubbabel my servant, and make you like a signet ring; for I have chosen you, says the LORD of hosts."

ZECHARIAH

In the first section of this book, Zechariah encourages the returned exiles, especially their leaders Joshua and Zerubbabel, to proceed with the rebuilding of the temple at Jerusalem. His prophecies, which may be dated about 519 B.C., are notably different from those of his contemporaries, among whom was the prophet Haggai. They consist of symbolic visions, and dialogues between God, seer, and an interpreting angel. There follows a sermon on the observance of the commandments and the rewards for so doing. In the second section the tone is different, and the circumstances reflect an age subsequent to Zechariah. This later writer, who remains unknown, foresees battles and distress for Israel, followed by eventual redemption. The description of the triumphant coming of the humble king was taken by New Testament writers as prefiguring Christ's entry into Jerusalem on Palm Sunday.

———

In the eighth month, in the second year of Darius, the word of the Lord came to Zechariah the son of Berechiah, son of Iddo, the prophet, saying, "The Lord was very angry with your fathers. Therefore say to the people, Thus says the Lord of hosts: Return to me, and I will return to you. Be not like your fathers, to whom the former prophets cried out, 'Return from your evil ways and from your evil deeds.' They did not heed me, says the Lord. Your fathers, where are they? And the prophets, do they live for ever? But my words and my statutes, which I commanded my servants the prophets, did they not overtake your fathers? So they repented and said, As the Lord of hosts purposed to deal with us for our ways and deeds, so has he dealt with us."

On the twenty-fourth day of the eleventh month, in the second year of Darius, the word of the LORD came to Zechariah; and Zechariah said, "I saw in the night a man riding upon a red horse among the myrtle trees in the glen; and behind him were other men on red, sorrel, and white horses. 'Who are these?' I asked. 'These are they whom the LORD has sent to patrol the earth,' the man among the myrtle trees answered. And the horsemen said, 'We have patrolled the earth, and behold, it remains at rest.' Then the angel of the LORD said, 'O LORD of hosts, how long wilt thou have no mercy on Jerusalem and Judah, against which thou hast had indignation these seventy years?' And the LORD answered with gracious and comforting words. So the angel who talked with me said, 'Cry out, Thus says the LORD of hosts: I am exceedingly jealous for Jerusalem and for Zion. And I am very angry with the nations that are at ease; for while I was angry but a little, they furthered the disaster. Therefore I have returned to Jerusalem with compassion; and my house shall be built in it. My cities shall again overflow with prosperity, and I will again comfort Zion.' "

I lifted my eyes, and behold, I saw four horns! "What are these?" I asked the angel. "These are the horns which have scattered Judah, Israel, and Jerusalem," he answered. Then the LORD showed me four smiths. "What are these men coming to do?" I asked the angel. "They have come to terrify the nations," he answered, "and cast down the horns that were lifted up against Judah to scatter it."

I lifted my eyes again, and behold, I saw a man with a measuring line in his hand! "Where are you going?" I asked him. "To measure Jerusalem," he replied, "to see what is its breadth and length." And behold, the angel who talked with me came forward, and another angel came to meet him, saying, "Run, say to that young man, 'Jerusalem shall be inhabited as villages without walls, because of the multitude of men and cattle in it. For I will be to her a wall of fire, says the LORD, and I will be the glory within her.'"

Flee from the land of the north, says the LORD; for I have spread you abroad as the four winds of the heavens. Escape to Zion, you who dwell with the daughter of Babylon. For thus said the LORD of hosts, after he sent me to the nations who plundered you, for he who touches you touches the apple of his eye: "Behold, I will shake my hand over them, and they shall become plunder for those who served them. Sing and rejoice, O daughter of Zion; for lo, I come and I will dwell in the midst of you. Many nations shall join themselves to the LORD in that day, and shall be my people. The LORD will inherit Judah as his portion in the holy land, and will again choose Jerusalem."

Then the angel who talked with me showed me Joshua the high priest standing before the angel of the LORD, and Satan standing at his right hand to accuse Joshua. And the LORD said to Satan, "The LORD who has chosen Jerusalem rebukes you, O Satan! Is not this a brand plucked from the fire?" Joshua was clothed with filthy garments, and the angel said to those who were standing before him, "Remove the filthy garments from him." To Joshua he said, "Behold, I have taken your iniquity away from you, and I will clothe you with rich apparel, and put a clean turban on your head."

Then the angel of the LORD enjoined Joshua, "Thus says the LORD of hosts: If you will walk in my ways and keep my charge, you shall rule my house, and I will give you the right of access among the angels standing here. Hear now, O Joshua the high priest, you and your friends who sit before you, all men of good omen: behold, I will bring my servant the Branch, and I will remove the guilt of this land in a single day. In that day every one of you will invite his neighbor under his vine and under his fig tree."

The angel who talked with me came again, and waked me, like a man that is wakened out of his sleep. "What do you see?" he asked. "A lampstand of gold," I said, "with a bowl on the top of it, and seven lamps on it, with seven lips on each of the lamps. There are two olive trees by it, one on the right of the bowl and the other on its left." And I asked the angel, "What are these, my lord?" The angel answered, "These seven are the eyes of the LORD, which range through the whole earth, and the olive trees are the two anointed ones who stand by him."

Then the angel said, "This is the word of the LORD to Zerubbabel: Not by might, nor by power, but by my Spirit, says the LORD. What are you, O great mountain? Before Zerubbabel you shall become a plain." Moreover the word of the LORD came to me, saying, "The hands of Zerubbabel have laid the foundation of my house; his hands shall also complete it. Whoever has despised the day of small things shall rejoice when he sees the plumb line in the hand of Zerubbabel."

Again I lifted my eyes, and behold, I saw a flying scroll! "What do you see?" the angel asked. "A flying scroll," I answered. "Its length is thirty feet, and its breadth fifteen." He said, "This is the curse that goes out over the face of the whole land; for every one who steals, and every one who swears falsely shall be cut off henceforth according to it. I will send it forth, says the LORD of hosts, and it shall enter the house of the thief, and the house of him who swears falsely by my name, and it shall abide there and consume it, both timber and stones."

Then the angel came forward and said to me, "Lift your eyes, and see the large basket that goes forth." So I lifted my eyes, and behold, the leaden cover of the basket was raised, and there was a woman sitting inside! "This is Wickedness," the angel said. And he pushed her back into the basket, and thrust down the leaden cover. Then I saw two women coming forward! They had wings like a stork's, and they lifted up the basket between earth and heaven. "Where are they taking it?" I asked the angel. "To the land of Shinar," he answered, "to build a house for it. When the house is prepared, they will set the basket down there on its own base."

Again I lifted my eyes, and behold, I saw four chariots come out from between two mountains of bronze. The first chariot had red horses, the second black, the third white, and the fourth dappled gray. "What are these, my lord?" I asked the angel. "They are going forth to the four winds of heaven," he answered, "after presenting themselves before the LORD of all the earth." The steeds were impatient to get off, so the angel said to them, "Go, patrol the earth." Then he cried to me, "Behold, those who go toward the north country have set my Spirit at rest."

Now the word of the LORD came to me: "Go to the exiles Heldai, Tobijah, and Jedaiah, who have arrived from Babylon, and to the house of Josiah the son of Zephaniah. Take from them silver and gold, and make a crown. Set it upon the head of Joshua the high priest, and say to him, 'Thus says the LORD of hosts: "Behold, the man whose name is the Branch, for he shall build the temple of the LORD. He shall bear royal honor, and shall sit and rule upon his throne. And there shall be a priest by his throne, and peaceful understanding shall be between them both." ' And the crown shall be in the temple of the LORD as a reminder to Heldai, Tobijah, Jedaiah, and Josiah the son of Zephaniah. Those who are far off shall come and help to build the temple, and then you shall know that the LORD of hosts has sent me to you. This shall come to pass, if you will diligently obey the voice of the LORD your God."

The word of the LORD came to me

again, saying, "Thus says the LORD of hosts: I will return to Zion, and will dwell in the midst of Jerusalem, and it shall be called the faithful city. Old men and old women shall again sit in the streets, each with staff in hand, and the city shall be full of boys and girls playing. If this seems marvelous to you in these days, should it also be marvelous in my sight? I will bring my people from the east country and from the west country to dwell in the midst of Jerusalem; and I will be their God, in faithfulness and in righteousness."

Therefore says the LORD of hosts: "Let your hands be strong, that the temple might be built. For before the days that its foundation was laid there was no wage for man or beast, neither was there any safety from the foe; for I set every man against his fellow. But I will not deal with the remnant of this people as in the former days. There shall be a sowing of peace; the ground shall give its increase, and the heavens shall give their dew. As you have been a byword of cursing among the nations, O house of Judah and house of Israel, so you shall be a blessing. Fear not, but let your hands be strong. Speak the truth to one another, render judgments that are true and make for peace. Do not devise evil in your hearts against one another, and love no false oath, for all these things I hate. Many peoples and strong nations shall come to Jerusalem to entreat the favor of the LORD. In those days ten men of every tongue shall take hold of the robe of a Jew, saying, 'Let us go with you, for we have heard that God is with you.' "

THE WORD OF the LORD is against the land of Hadrach and will rest upon Damascus. For to the LORD belong the cities of Aram, even as all the tribes of Israel; Hamath also, which borders thereon, and Tyre and Sidon. And the king shall perish from Gaza; Ashkelon shall be uninhabited; and I will make an end of the pride of Philistia. I will take away its blood from its mouth, and its abominations from between its teeth; it shall be like a clan in Judah. Then I will encamp at my house as a guard, so that none shall march to and fro; no oppressor shall again overrun them, for now I see with my own eyes.

Rejoice greatly, O daughter of Zion! Shout aloud, O daughter of Jerusalem! Lo, your king comes to you; triumphant and victorious is he, humble and riding on an ass, on a colt the foal of an ass. I will cut off the war horse from Jerusalem, and he shall command peace to the nations; his dominion shall be from sea to sea, and from the River to the ends of the earth.

As for you, because of the blood of my covenant with you, I will set your captives free from the waterless pit. Return to your stronghold, O prisoners of hope; today I declare that I will restore to you double.

On that day the LORD their God will save them, for they are the flock of his people; like the jewels of a crown they shall shine on his land. Yea, how good and how fair it shall be! Grain shall make the young men flourish, and new wine the maidens.

THE LORD MY God said to me: "Become shepherd of the flock doomed to slaughter. Those who buy them slay them and go unpunished; and those who sell them say, 'Blessed be the LORD, I have become rich.'

Their own shepherds have no pity on them. For I will no longer have pity on the inhabitants of this land. I will cause men to fall each into the hand of his shepherd, and each into the hand of his king; and they shall crush the earth; I will deliver none from their hand." So I became the shepherd of the flock doomed to be slain for those who trafficked in the sheep. I took two staffs; one I named Grace, the other I named Union. But I became impatient with the sheep, and they also detested me. "I will not be your shepherd," I said. "What is to die, let it die; and let those that are left devour the flesh of one another." And I took my staff Grace, and I broke it, annulling the covenant which I had made with the peoples. And the traffickers in the sheep, who were watching me, knew that it was the word of the LORD. "If it seems right to you," I said to them, "give me my wages; but if not, keep them." And they weighed out as my wages thirty shekels of silver. Then the LORD said to me, "Cast it into the treasury"—the lordly price at which I was paid off by them. So I took the thirty shekels of silver and cast them into the treasury in the house of the LORD. Then I broke my second staff, Union, annulling the brotherhood between Judah and Israel.

Then the LORD said to me, "Take the implements of a worthless shepherd. For lo, I am raising up in the land a shepherd who does not care for the perishing, or seek the wandering, or heal the maimed, or nourish the hungry, but devours the flesh of the fat ones, tearing off even their hoofs. Woe to my worthless shepherd, who deserts the flock! May the sword smite his arm and his right eye! Let his arm be wholly withered, his right eye utterly blinded!"

THE WORD OF the LORD concerning Israel: Thus says the LORD, who stretched out the heavens and founded the earth and formed the spirit of man within him: "Lo, I am about to make Jerusalem a cup to send the peoples reeling. On that day I will make Jerusalem a heavy stone; all who lift it shall grievously hurt themselves. And all the nations of the earth will come together against it. I will strike every horse of the nations with panic, and its rider with madness. But upon the house of Judah I will open my eyes. Then the clans of Judah shall say to themselves, 'The inhabitants of Jerusalem have strength through the LORD of hosts, their God.' I will make Judah like a flaming torch among sheaves; they shall devour to the right and to the left all the peoples round about, while Jerusalem shall still be inhabited in its place. I will give victory to the tents of Judah first, that the glory of Jerusalem may not be exalted over that of Judah. But I will put a shield about the inhabitants of Jerusalem, so that the feeblest among them shall be like David, and the house of David shall be like God, like the angel of the LORD at their head.

"I will pour out on the house of David and the inhabitants of Jerusalem a spirit of compassion, so that when they look on him whom they have pierced, they shall mourn for him, as one mourns for an only child, and weep bitterly over him, as one weeps over a first-born. On that day the mourning in Jerusalem will be as great as the mourning in the plain of Megiddo. The land shall mourn, each family by itself; the family of the house of David by itself, and their wives by themselves; and all the other families, each by itself, and their wives by themselves.

"On that day there shall be a fountain opened for the house of David and the inhabitants of Jerusalem to cleanse them from sin. I will cut off the names of the idols from the land, and I will remove the prophets and the unclean spirit. If any one again appears as a prophet, his father and mother will say to him, 'You shall not live, for you speak lies in the name of the LORD'; and they shall pierce him through when he prophesies. Every prophet will be ashamed of his vision when he prophesies; he will not put on a hairy mantle in order to deceive, but he will say, 'I am no prophet, I am a tiller of the soil; for the land has been my possession since my youth.' "

"AWAKE, O SWORD, against my shepherd, against the man who stands next to me," says the LORD of hosts. "Strike the shepherd, that the sheep may be scattered; I will turn my hand against the little ones. In the whole land, two thirds shall be cut off and perish, and one third shall be left alive. I will put this third into the fire, and refine them as one refines silver, and test them as gold is tested. They will call on my name, and I will answer them. I will say, 'They are my people'; and they will say, 'The LORD is my God.' "

BEHOLD, A DAY of the LORD is coming when the spoil taken from you will be divided in the midst of you. For I will gather all the nations against Jerusalem to battle, and the city shall be plundered and the women ravished. Half of the people shall go into exile, but the rest shall not be cut off from the city. Then the LORD will go forth and fight against those nations as on a day of battle. His feet shall stand on the Mount of Olives which lies before Jerusalem on the east; and the mount shall be split in two from east to west by a very wide valley, so that one half shall withdraw northward, and the other half southward. And the valley of my mountains shall be stopped up, and you shall flee as you fled from the earthquake in the days of Uzziah king of Judah. Then the LORD your

God will come, and all the holy ones with him. On that day there shall be neither cold nor frost. There shall be continuous day (it is known to the LORD), not day and not night. Living waters shall flow out from Jerusalem, half of them to the eastern sea and half of them to the western sea; it shall continue in summer as in winter. And the LORD will become king over all the earth; the LORD will be one and his name one. The whole land shall be turned into a plain from Geba to Rimmon south of Jerusalem. But Jerusalem shall remain aloft upon its site, and it shall dwell in security, for there shall be no more curse on it.

And this shall be the plague with which the LORD will smite all the peoples that wage war against Jerusalem: their flesh shall rot while they are still on their feet, their eyes shall rot in their sockets, their tongues in their mouths. Then every one that survives of all the nations that have come against Jerusalem shall go up year after year to worship the King, the LORD of hosts, and to keep the feast of booths. If any of the families of the earth do not go up to worship the LORD, there will be no rain upon them. And if the family of Egypt do not present themselves, the LORD will afflict them with the plague. This shall be the punishment to all the nations that do not go up to keep the feast of booths.

On that day there shall be inscribed on the bells of the horses, "Holy to the LORD." And the pots in the house of the LORD shall be as the bowls before the altar; every pot in Jerusalem and Judah shall be sacred to the LORD of hosts, so that all who come may boil the flesh of the sacrifice in them. And there shall no longer be a trader in the house of the LORD of hosts.

MALACHI

The Hebrew name Malachi means "my messenger," and the word may not be the actual name of the prophet. Whoever the writer was, he addresses his fellow Jews in the fifth century B.C., some decades after their return from the Babylonian Exile and after the rebuilding of the temple. For their slackness and faithlessness, he rebukes not only the people but also the priests. Like Zechariah, he speaks of the day of the Lord, when the Lord will come in blessing and in judgment. A new feature regarding that day is the promise of a messenger to be sent as a herald. In the New Testament this prophecy is taken by the Gospels as fulfilled in John the Baptist.

———

THE ORACLE OF the word of the LORD to
Israel by Malachi.

"I have loved you," says the LORD. But
you say, "How hast thou loved us?" "Is
not Esau Jacob's brother?" says the LORD.
"Yet I have loved Jacob and hated Esau; I
have laid waste his hill country and left his
heritage to jackals of the desert." If Edom
says, "We are shattered but we will rebuild
the ruins," the LORD of hosts says, "They
may build, but I will tear down, till they
are called the wicked country, the people
with whom the LORD is angry for ever."
Your own eyes shall see this, and you shall
say, "Great is the LORD, beyond the border
of Israel!"

Have we not all one father? Has not one
God created us? Why then are we faithless
to one another, profaning the covenant of
our fathers? Judah has been faithless, and
abomination has been committed in Jerusalem; for Judah has profaned the sanctuary of the LORD and has married the
daughters of a foreign god. May the LORD
cut off from the tents of Jacob any man
who does this, even though he brings an
offering to the LORD of hosts!

And this again you do. You cover the LORD's altar with tears, with weeping and groaning because he no longer regards your offering with favor. You ask, "Why does he not?" Because the LORD was witness to the covenant between you and the wife of your youth, to whom you have been faithless. Has not the one God made and sustained for us the spirit of life? And what does he desire? Godly offspring. So take heed to yourselves, and let none be faithless to the wife of his youth. "For I hate divorce," says the LORD the God of Israel, "and covering one's garment with violence."

"BEHOLD, I SEND my messenger to prepare the way before me, and the Lord whom you seek will suddenly come to his temple; the messenger of the covenant, behold, he is coming," says the LORD of hosts.

"But who can endure the day of his coming, and who can stand when he appears? For he is like a refiner's fire and like fullers' soap; he will sit and purify the sons of Levi and refine them like gold and silver, till they present right offerings to the LORD.

"Then I will draw near to you for judgment. I will be a swift witness against the sorcerers, against the adulterers, against those who oppress the hireling in his wages, the widow and the orphan, and those who thrust aside the sojourner, and do not fear me," says the LORD of hosts.

"For I the LORD do not change; therefore you, O sons of Jacob, are not consumed. From the days of your fathers you have turned aside from my statutes and have not kept them. Return to me, and I will return to you," says the LORD of hosts. "But you say, 'How shall we return?' Will man rob God? Yet you are robbing me. But you say, 'How are we robbing thee?' In your tithes and offerings. Bring the full tithes into the storehouse, that there may be food in my house. Thereby put me to the test," says the LORD of hosts, "and I will pour down for you an overflowing blessing. I will rebuke the locust, so that it will not destroy the fruits of your soil; and your vine in the field shall not fail to bear," says the LORD of hosts. "Then all nations will call you blessed, for you will be a land of delight."

Then those who feared the LORD spoke with one another; the LORD heeded and heard them, and a book of remembrance was written before him of those who feared the LORD and thought on his name. "They shall be mine," says the LORD of hosts, "my special possession on the day when I act, and I will spare them as a man spares his son. Then once more you shall distinguish between the righteous and the wicked, between one who serves God and one who does not serve him.

"For behold, the day comes, burning like an oven, when all the arrogant and all evildoers will be stubble; the day that comes shall burn them up," says the LORD of hosts, "so that it will leave them neither root nor branch. But for you who fear my name the sun of righteousness shall rise with healing in its wings. You shall go forth leaping like calves from the stall. And you shall tread down the wicked, for they will be ashes under the soles of your feet on the day when I act," says the LORD of hosts. "Remember the law of my servant Moses, the ordinances that I commanded him at Sinai for all Israel.

"Behold, I will send you Elijah the prophet before the great and terrible day of the LORD comes. And he will turn the hearts of fathers to their children and the hearts of children to their fathers, lest I smite the land with a curse."

NUMBERS ∂ GENESIS ∂ JOSHU
DANIEL ∂ LAMENTATIONS ∂ Z
LUKE ∂ ROMANS ∂ REVELATIO
MATTHEW ∂ TITUS ∂ HOSEA ∂ G
CORINTHIANS ∂ JONAH ∂ RUT
MARK ∂ THESSALONIANS ∂ NE
SAMUEL ∂ COLOSSIANS ∂ JOH
MICAH ∂ HABAKKUK ∂ PETER
ISAIAH ∂ ZECHARIAH ∂ JUDGE
EZRA ∂ THESSALONIANS ∂ HAG
ECCLESIASTES ∂ CHRONICLE
PHILEMON ∂ AMOS ∂ DANIEL
RUTH ∂ CORINTHIANS ∂ JONA
LAMENTATIONS ∂ DANIEL ∂ H
GENESIS ∂ JOSHUA ∂ LUKE ∂ RO
CHRONICLES ∂ ECCLESIASTE
HOSEA ∂ GALATIANS ∂ CORINT
HAGGAI ∂ MARK ∂ LEVITICUS
NEHEMIAH ∂ EZEKIEL ∂ ESTHE
PHILIPPIANS ∂ JAMES ∂ MICAH
HABAKKUK ∂ PETER ∂ ISAIAH
GALATIANS ∂ ACTS ∂ JEREMIAH
HAGGAI ∂ ECCLESIASTES ∂ CH
ROMANS ∂ REVELATION ∂ PHIL
DANIEL ∂ MALACHI ∂ RUTH ∂